GAME
RETAILER
GUIDE

LLOYD BROWN III

Skirmisher Publishing LLC

GAME RETAILER GUIDE

LLOYD BROWN III

Skirmisher Publishing LLC
499 Mystic Parkway
Spring Branch, TX 78070

http://d-infinity.net/GRG
http://skirmisher.com
sales@skirmisher.com

Editing, Layout, and Design: Michael O. Varhola

Cover Design and Dice Logos: William Thrasher

First Electronic Publication: August 2013; SKP E 1320; ISBN 978-1-935050-18-6.

GAME RETAILER GUIDE

LLOYD BROWN III

THANKS & DEDICATION

Many people have been helpful in providing information, advice, or otherwise increasing my knowedge of this industry. Some of them are (in no particular order): Joe Rapoza, Mike Webb, Michael Cox, Marcus King, Sito Sanchez, David Wallace, Heather Barnhorst, John Nephew, Ed Pugh, Devin & Kathy Barber, Emil Palisoc, Chip Parker, John Kaufeld, Mick Galuski, Chris Schorb, Brian Guenther, David Glenn, Steve and Vida Grohowski, Jim Crocker, Jeremy Mueller, D.P. "Vern" Vernnazarro, Bill Corrie III, Jeff Abramson, Dirk Remmecke, Mike and Michelle Krause, Joe Serafini, Rich Peterson, James Green, Brad Daeda, Chad Erway, and Ali Samiian — one crazy Persian.

TABLE OF CONTENTS

INTRODUCTION

Many people say their job is fun, but how much fun can you have plumbing or filing? Standing knee-deep in sewage sounds unpleasant. Mindless office duty, while more sanitary, might not be better for your sanity. Some jobs have no fun element to them at all.

Other people feel a great emotional satisfaction from their careers. Volunteer work at a homeless shelter can coat your insides with warm fuzzies. The medical profession or law enforcement fields offer emotional fulfillment.

But *fun*? None of those jobs sounds like fun. If you wish to make your living in a field you can enjoy every day, the *Game Retailer Guide* is the want ad you hope to find.

As a game retailer, one of your best methods of selling games is *playing games with people*. This career provides plenty of opportunity for sitting down with friends and family over a table of colorful pieces with a couple of hours of friendly play. The whole business model depends partially on teaching others that the social element of games is superior to other forms of entertainment. This element of game store ownership can be a blast.

Of course, you're still a business owner. You have to pay bills, clean toilets, and work the shifts nobody else will. This book doesn't discuss those elements. If you're not sure the entrepreneur lifestyle is for you, this book won't help you make that decision. All that material has been published many times, including online. The *GRG*'s topics start from the thought, "I'd like to sell games for a living."

WHAT IS A GAME STORE?

Is a store that sells sports cards and two CCG lines a game store? How about a comic book store that stocks a few miniatures behind the counter? A children's toy store that sells a few copies of Apples to Apples and Blokus? Does a school supply store that promotes games as educational tools count?

For the purposes of the advice in this book, a game store is any retail location that wants to increase its game sales. Whether games are your sole source of income or a sideline you'd like to expand, you can use this material to increase game sales. Most of the discussion in the *GRG* assumes that the majority of your sales come from games.

Estimates place the number of retail business that rely on games for a significant portion of their volume between 1,500 and 2,500. Estimates of dedicated game stores that stock games deeply range as low as 700. The remainder of the stores carry other product lines that contribute a significant portion of the store's sales volume.

INDUSTRY GENERALITIES

The adventure hobby industry caters to about 7,500,000 Americans that play either role-playing games, collectible card games or miniature wargames at least twice monthly, plus an equal number that play less often or have played before. These customers spend an estimated $500,000,000 to $1,000,000,000 on their hobby annually.

Of that amount, about 37%, or nearly $300 million, sells through independent game stores. Nearly half sells through big-box retailers such as Wal-Mart and Target or the book trade. The rest reaches the customer's hands through conventions and other direct sales, including manufacturer websites.

About 85% of these customers are male. That number varies by specific game genre within the overall category. *Magic: the Gathering* players top the testosterone meter with a 97% male customer base. At the other extreme, "only" 81% of role-players are male. That's doubly good for you: it concentrates your demographic, making marketing easier, and males are likely to spend more money on their hobby than are females.

The age of these players varies. A large number of players begin playing in high school or junior high school. Many leave the hobby briefly, when responsibilities and other interests start to grow; the 16-18 age group, which you might think has the highest representation, has the lowest. Fully 60% of gamers are at least 19 years old.

Conventional wisdom says that gamers are more intelligent than the average person. I have yet to find reliable documentation for this claim, however persistent it may be. Given the advanced planning required to assess the value of one move relative to another, the judgment required for threat assessment, the weighing of play options, and the strategic decision-making required for deck/army/character construction, an argument could be made that gaming demands a certain minimum of intelligence.

Among role-players, conventional wisdom and sales histories show that game masters spend about five times as much as players. However, I believe that the largest manufacturers, armed with this knowledge, have changed their marketing strategies to spread the wealth around more, and that the disparity between game masters and players has fallen. With board games, CCGs and miniatures games, where each player has the same role within the game, no such disparity occurs.

The industry conforms relatively closely to "specialty retail" generalities in terms of COGS, labor costs, net profit, and other key indicators. For more information about industry demographics, refer to Appendix I.

SUMMARY: KEY DEMOGRAPHICS
- 85% male
- 60% over 18
- Game Masters spend more than RPG players

PERFORMANCE METRICS

You can measure your progress in multiple ways. One is by sales. Others take a bit more calculation. Knowing your contribution margin is helpful. Your turn rate is another useful method of looking your inventory and sales. Understanding cash flow is critical in any business, especially a small cash-based one. Lastly, a square-foot analysis is helpful in determining the best use for the limited space you have.

CONTRIBUTION MARGIN

Contribution margin is one way to compare different product lines. The definition of a contribution margin is the amount left over for your fixed expenses after deducting your variable expenses from each sales dollar.

For example, on $100 in sales, if you spend $55 on the product, $2.00 in shipping that product to you, and $3.00 on the credit card transaction for that sale, your total variable cost is $60. Thus, your contribution margin is $40, or 40% in the case of this convenient example.

In the gaming industry, products do not generally differ in terms of their shipping costs or the percentage of sales by credit card. The significant variable among product lines is their discount off retail. One hundred percent minus this discount effectively gives us the product's gross profit margin, which is the margin this book typically implies.

TURN RATE

Your turn rate is the number of times a product or a product line sells annually. Divide your sales by your average inventory amount for any time period to find the turn rate. Use consistent measurements: if you compare retail prices in sales, use retail prices in your inventory value.

Example: Your *Dungeons & Dragons* line averages $1,000 in inventory at retail over the cost of a year. If your annual sales report says that the D&D line sold $15,000 worth of product, your turn rate is 15.

In general, you want a high turn rate — the higher the better. You could generate a turn rate of 50 easily if you sold four different CCGs out of a mall kiosk. In that case, however, you are probably not maximizing your revenues. It's easy to make $30,000 that way, but it is not feasible to make $200,000. You are not selling sleeves and counters, you are not convincing those customers to buy other games, and you are not providing a unique service that separates you from your competitors.

Going in the other direction, you could continue to add to your inventory until your store became the destination place for everybody. You could add product lines until no customer ever leaves empty-handed. You might have a full store that reaches $1,500,000 a year in annual sales, but your average inventory cost reaches $750,000 because you restock everything, all the time. A turn rate of 2 is sluggish and does not maximize your capital use.

As a guideline, if you can reach an annual turn rate of 3-4 for your store, you are managing your inventory well. This number assumes that your sales are divided among several product lines and no single category dominates your sales. It further assumes that the store has been open a couple of years. Stores in their first two years of operation are still growing their inventory and using an average inventory yields misleading numbers.

Why Does It Matter?

If your annual sales carry a COGS of $100,000 on $50,000 in inventory, you have a turn rate of 2. Many successful store owners will tell you that an annual turn rate of 2 is not bad.

But what happens if, over the course of a year, through careful selection of your product lines and aggressive liquidation of unproductive lines, you can increase that turn rate to 2.5, reaching the same sales with only $40,000 in average inventory? Where did the other $10,000 in inventory go?

It went into your bank account.

Turn rate is only one meter of success out of many, however. Do not let the pursuit of a higher turn rate cause you to miss out on lost sales.

How High Is Too High?

With a selection of inventory, some items undoubtedly sell more quickly than others do. Certain items sell very quickly while others languish. It is not unusual for one item in your store to sell 30 times in a year, while some items sell only once per year.

An item's individual inventory level is too low when frequent stockouts cause you to miss sales.

One way to determine if your inventory level is currently too low for your sales velocity is to divide how many you sell in a year into 365 days to get your average sales cycle. If you sell 36 copies of something in a year, you average about one every 10 days. If your order cycle — the average time it takes to restock — is a significant portion of your sales cycle, then you spend too much time without product on the shelf. If you carry only one of these items, you could afford to add one or more.

In reality, few items reach that sales level. Unfortunately, they also do not sell in easily predictable patterns. If items sold at a measured pace of once every ten days, stocking would be a breeze. Instead, they sell in clumps. A person starts running a role-playing game, and then four customers walk in that weekend in search of the game's core book. Of those four, one might show greater interest and arrive with the intention of buying more of that line's products. Your well-trained sales staff might upsell each player dice and a figure, and one of them will be talked into an additional book. Without the core books in stock, you could lose all of those sales to a competitor.

Thus, keeping some items in stock has a value that exceeds the ability of business math to predict. Keeping multiple copies of your most popular products in stock will — once or twice per year — prevent you from losing a customer. The loss of that customer could mean far more in lost sales than the cost of maintaining one or two additional products on the shelf.

CASH FLOW

You have seen a bank statement before. It does not have the same balance every day. It shows a sequence of credits and debits. With a personal checking account, you usually see a small number of positive spikes — your paychecks — while you see a large number of negative dips — your ATM withdrawals, automatic payments, and the debit card transactions you incur daily.

In a retail business, the spikes and dips reverse in frequency and size. You receive money every day, and you deposit it every day the bank is open. If you don't deposit your cash for some reason, your credit card payments deposit automatically. Your rent, your distributor accounts, and your utilities all create moderate to large downward spikes.

What happens if you get several bills due all at once? Your bank account suddenly and drastically drops. If you have unexpected bills in close succession, you could end up bouncing checks, even if you are making a tremendous percentage of gross profit on each of your sales.

Cash flow is all about managing the crests and dips on that bank statement.

Cash flow is positive when your deposits exceed the value of your debits and negative when you spend faster than you deposit. Managing cash flow requires attention to detail and careful timing.

General books on business and retail might tell you to quicken your accounts receivable. The problem with that advice is that game retailers do not extend customers credit. We do have credit/debit card transactions, but they are a tiny factor in cash flow. They fall one to three business days behind — a minor time frame — and, unlike the customers of service-based industries, they never get any further behind.

You can manipulate this number a small amount. You can designate certain events or promotions as "cash only". Overusing that technique is a dangerous idea for the very reason that you accept credit cards in the first place. That is, taking credit cards increases your available customer base and increases your average ticket price.

The second general point of advice is to time your expenses. If your distributor allows 30 days for payment, take the full 30 — but no more. That distributor relationship is valuable, and you don't want to risk it for a fractional gain in precision on your cash flow management. Pay your utilities, your rent, and your other bills at the last possible date for them to arrive on time. If possible, arrange for automatic transactions so that you never forget and so that you will always know the date of the debit.

Sales tax, if your state collects it, is a great aid to positive cash flow. You collect hundreds of dollars that does not belong to you, only to hand it off up to 3 months after you receive it. In return, some states let you keep a portion of the sales tax. It is like a free loan that they pay you to take out! The danger, of course, is in forgetting that the money is not yours and over-spending based on that "false bottom" in your checking account.

One potential crisis point in game retailing is the "big release." Each new Magic: the Gathering expansion, a hot new D&D book, or whatever is popular in your store requires considerably more initial product than a typical new RPG book from a small-press publisher. In the case of Magic, you might find yourself spending $1,000 or more. Add that amount to your normal weekly restock, and your checking account is in for a heavy dip.

If you are on terms with your distributors, you should be in good shape. If you buy your WotC products with a 45% discount, you only need to sell 45% of your Magic within that 30 days to pay your bill on time. Keep this period in mind when you place your initial order, and make it a rule:

Initial orders should pay for themselves in the time frame in which you pay for them.

A few qualifiers apply to this rule. One, if you expect product shortages later because you believe the product will be more popular than the rest of the industry expects, you might wish to buy more than you normally would. Two, the company has a history of failing to meet demand, order more. Next, if the product is a limited release and this is your only opportunity to get the product, you must order a lifetime supply at once. Lastly, if you are receiving an exceptional discount on the initial order as an incentive or promotion, you might wish to order more heavily. Some advisers urge businesses to look to a loan to manage cash-flow situations. They are not talking to game retailers. This option is not feasible if your problem is that your sales do not cover your orders. That is a sales problem, not a cash-flow problem. These loans apply to service industries, in which the company pays its employees and contractors at the time of a job but bills its clients for later payment. A loan can be an answer to making costly repairs, financing new equipment, etc, but it does not apply to end-user sales in which you typically receive money before you spend it.

Square Foot Analysis

A square foot analysis is one way to measure the effectiveness of the different areas of your store. You measure the area devoted to a product line or a display of similar product lines and compare the annual dollars that space generates to the square feet necessary to display that product. The number this formula generates allows you to determine if a particular product line earns its space. If not, you can attempt to trim back the product line, reconfigure your display, or drop the product line altogether.

Before you start figuring any single product line, figure out your target number for the store. First, measure your usable square footage. If you are in an 1800 sf location, minus bathrooms and storage at 200 sf, 650 sf of gaming space, 100 sf for your nearly-worthless decompression zone, and roughly 50 sf of wasted space from support columns or odd corners, you have an effective 800 sf of sales floor. If your break-even analysis indicates that you need to generate $120,000 per year in sales, each sf of that sales area must earn ($120,000 divided by 800) at least $150/year.

Naturally, you see averages. You know ahead of time, for example, that your RPGs typically have a lower turn rate than CCGs. You might set your expectation for this area lower than your expectation for other areas.

Consider the addition of a freestanding slat wall display known as an H fixture. This fixture is a 2' by 4' display that holds product inside the H and on both ends. You currently don't carry any pewter miniatures and want to put Reaper Miniatures' Dark Heaven product line on it. You estimate the fixture holds 120 blisters, and the average blister retails for $6. That's $720 worth of product at retail. Accounting for some walking space around the display, the display takes up a total of 48 square feet. That display needs to generate $7,200 per year to justify itself. A 10.0 turn rate ($7,200/$720) is higher than your store average, but the goal is possible for tightly-managed Reaper miniatures.

This formula explains something you will quickly realize intuitively: wall space is more valuable than floor space. First, you do not need space to walk all the way around the wall. If the H-fixture could be reconfigured so that it displayed the same amount of product against a wall, you could halve the space required by not needing that extra walking space. Your turn rate would only need to be an easy-to-attain five turns per year.

Similarly, you can fit a "tall" amount of product against a wall. You have roughly six feet vertical feet of effective display space along a wall, as opposed to only three to four feet on a freestanding display. Naturally, the middle regions are most effective, but you can position your products along the wall according to expected sales or customer ability and willingness to reach it. Typically, children are the first to grab the lowest product, while women are reluctant to reach for things up high, where heavy product might fall on them. The elderly avoid either too high or too low product. Overall, each linear foot of wall space yields six square feet of display space.

Given that advantage, a 2,000 sf store that is 40 feet wide and 50 feet deep is less valuable than one that is only 20 feet wide but 100 feet deep. In the latter store, you have an additional 60 feet of wall space, or 360 square feet of useable shelf or peg display space.

Some companies prefer a square foot analysis based on actual square footage rather than usable square footage. Thus, two similar businesses could show substantially different figures. Make sure you specify which method you use when you compare your numbers with other store owners.

Chapter 1:
Administration & Planning

Your planning period could be up to a year in length. Finding a location, negotiating a lease, ordering your product, building out your store, and all the other physical work can eat up the days. Developing a business plan takes an average of 100 hours. You have to decide how you will run your business before you start running it.

What Type of Store

You have some kind of image of the kind of store you want in your head when you say you want to open "a game store." If you are not clear on the details, you probably know whether you want a high-visibility mall location, or a busy commercial street, or a laid-back club atmosphere. Most people entering the industry have already decided whether or not they want to have a game space, before reading the pros and cons later in this book.

Develop Your Idea

Decide on these factors not now, before you know anything about the industry, but as you read these chapters. Some cost more, which might require compromises to your company vision. Keep in mind branding, merchandising, events, and watch how these factors work together and oppose each other.

Test the Market

Test the local market before you open your store. Perhaps your perception of customer needs is inaccurate and the market will not support an additional game store. With a little experimentation, you can test the local gaming market without spending your life savings and gain an opportunity to practice basic skills such as customer service at the same time.

Conventions

Check out area conventions. How are the vendor booths set up? How many retailers are there? Where are they from? What products are they selling? How well are they doing? How many vendors are there compared to the number of attendees? Are the vendors happy? Talk to some of the gamers at these conventions. Find out their perception of the game stores nearby. If you are in the opening stages already, hand out flyers. After attending one or more conventions, you might want to get a table for yourself.

FLEA MARKETS

Experiment at a flea market. A booth at a flea market costs almost nothing, and the experience gives you a chance to practice your display skills, make some customer contacts, and advertise your store. Once you are open, or on the path to opening, you can also use the flea market stand as a way to distribute some flyers or otherwise promote your "real" location. The experience is also very relevant to how you handle your convention sales, because the operation and physical presentation is very similar — only the market is different.

DEMO GAMES

Run demo games or tournaments. Contact other stores, preferably those far enough away that they will not consider you a competitor. Arrange to demo some games you know. This practice gives you the opportunity to practice closing a sale after a demo and make contacts with a manufacturer whose products you'll probably sell in your store. Read the section on running demos on page [pp].

TALK TO MANUFACTURERS

Most of the time, manufacturers would rather have a retail store service a market than do it themselves. Manufacturers started their business so that they can create games, not sell them to customers. You are in a much better position to promote their games directly to the customers than they are. Tell a manufacturer your plans and ask about their sales record to the area. If they share this information with you, be thankful, because they're not required to. Be aware that some of them simply do not collect this information because they outsource their direct sales.

SHOP THE COMPETITION

Visit as many game stores as you can. Spend some time there and try to estimate the traffic that walks through the door. Track the store's conversion rate. Watch the customer reaction as they leave. Do they appear satisfied or unsatisfied with customer service? If they asked for a product, was the clerk able to help them to the customer's satisfaction?

Look at the inventory, too. How much is there? Which product lines? Which are busy and which are covered with dust? How does the store display them? How deep are they stocked?

How big is the store? Does it have a game room? How many tables are there? How busy is it? How is the store's image?

One very inefficient way to gauge sales at a business is to enter the store and make a purchase, then go back after a day or a week at the same time of day and make another purchase. Comparing the difference in receipt number can give you an estimate of the business's traffic count. Estimating the average ticket price and multiplying that number by the traffic count can give you an estimate of sales for that time period.

If you are on good terms with the owner, you could always ask.

SUMMARY: TEST THE MARKET
- Conventions
- Flea Markets
- Demo Games
- Talk to Manufacturers
- Shop the Competition

BUSINESS FORMAT

Choosing your business format is a major decision. These descriptions are generalities only and do not address every detail. Consult your attorney or tax professional before you make your final decision.

SOLE PROPRIETORSHIP

In a sole proprietorship, you are the business. You obtain a DBA (doing business as) or fictitious name, and open up your shop. You have no legal separation from the business, so if somebody sues you, they sue you, not the company. The advantage is that it's quick, easy, and cheap.

You can always "upgrade" to a more professional business

format from a sole proprietorship. Typically, a business owner chooses a sole proprietorship to save as much money as possible at start-up and then incorporates or creates a LLC when sales start to grow. If you choose to start this way, establish the conditions under which you would abandon this format — if ever — and follow through with the change once you reach those goals.

You might wish to operate under this format while you're testing the market. That way, you secure your trade name, and you have a business license already. It reduces the steps you need to take when you incorporate later.

PARTNERSHIP

A partnership includes more than one business owner without the shell of a corporation. A good partnership agreement discusses the share of duties, disbursement of profits and exit strategies for all partners involved. Partnerships have the advantage of multiple owners willing to work long shifts at a salary, greater financial contribution than a single individual can provide, and a wider range of skills brought to the business.

The down side to a partnership is that even good friendships can fall apart in the harsh world of business ownership. Many partnerships fail because the partners' vision of the company changes as the market changes, and the two visions diverge. As each owner tries to make the business fit his image of where the company should be heading, conflict arises.

CORPORATION

A corporation is the standard business format. Because a corporation is legally treated as an individual, the corporation is theoretically the one entering contracts and obtaining credit or debt. If the corporation fails, the officers' personal property should be safe.

This illusion fades from sight, however, once you realize that nearly every vendor of services to small businesses insists on the president of the corporation signing all documents as personal guarantor, thereby obligating you to all debts the company incurs anyway. The corporation does shield you from certain liabilities, however.

An S-corporation is a special designation that gives the officers some tax benefits in that their income is only taxed once instead of twice. In a C-corporation, company income is taxed first as sales revenues and then the officers pay their personal income tax.

LLC

A Limited Liability Company is a relatively new business structure that offers more protection than a proprietorship yet more flexibility than a corporation does. Each state's laws vary in their treatment of a LLC, so check your state's laws before you make your decision.

SELECTING A LOCATION

Selecting your location is probably the most important decision you make before you open. If you do not like your corporate structure, you can change it in a few days for a couple of hundred dollars. If you dislike your logo, you can change it. If your inventory mix is wrong, enough sales bring it into line over time. Changing locations is a difficult, time-consuming, costly, physically demanding chore.

Most of the time, when somebody says he wants to open a game store, he does not want to open a game store. That person fails to state the clause "in or near my home town" because he assumes that it goes without saying.

If you are open to relocation to open your business, you have more options. Your hometown might not be the ideal location for a game store. Or it might be an ideal location, but it already has one and it can't support two.

You need customers. To have customers, you have to have a population. A town of 2,500 cannot support a full-service game store. Depending on what part of the United States you open your business in, you typically need a minimum general population of 25,000 to 75,000.

Often, I see prospective store owners in a rural area who wish to open a store in their hometown of 10,000 because they know a city of 75,000 is a few miles away. They think they'll save money because the rent is cheaper in the small town than it is in the city. Unfortunately, traffic doesn't flow that way. No matter how cool your store is, you won't be able to take advantage of the nearby city's population. If you're in the big city, then you can draw on the numerous small towns around you. One good way to check is to look at your city or town's description at www.city-data.com. If the daytime population is less than the listed population, you're looking in the wrong place.

Identify More Than One

Search the area for the place you want. Write down addresses and keep notes for future reference. Of all of the possible business locations, a couple of criteria will quickly knock out most of the ones that are not right.

First, your location must be zoned correctly. If not, and it appears to be a perfect location for you after all other considerations, you might be able to have it rezoned or receive an exception. However, as a rule, the right zoning is a must.

Second, it must be the right size. "The right size" is not a singular measure. Depending on your goals and budget, it could be 600 square feet, or it could be 4,000 sf. New stores rarely open above 2,000 sf, however, except in rural locations where rent can be very cheap. It is still a good idea to keep in mind some of the larger spaces for comparison, however.

Thirdly, consider the local market. Your primary draw radius, or the map circle from which more than half of your customer base commutes, is 4-5 miles. That number is less in congested urban markets and might be considerably higher in accessible rural markets. If you are too close to a body of water or a mountain, you eat into your customer base. If you are too close to a competitor, you reduce your ability to draw customers.

Compare Your Choices

Once you've assembled a collection of possible locations, prepare to compare them on several points.

▷ How much work does each need?
▷ What are the total costs at each location?
▷ Can the space be expanded upon?
▷ What are the neighbors?
▷ If in a shopping center, are there solid anchors?
▷ Does the location have space for a sign?
▷ Is the space visible from the road?
▷ Can you give simple directions?

Do Your Homework

Find out about planned construction through your city planning department. While construction on your road can reduce traffic, it can improve the traffic count in the long run. Be especially careful if you rely on an Interstate exit that might be closed. Ask about bridges that might greatly increase the ease with which your distant customers reach you.

Reviewing and Negotiating a Commercial Lease

Reading a lease can be a time-consuming headache, but an investment of 10 or 20 hours on this chore can save you liability risk, save you a huge amount of money, and save you more time and headaches later on. Although it's typically referred to as a "lease", you will see that it normally says "lease agreement" at the top when you get it. Never forget that. An agreement is anything two parties agree to. Do not be shy about proposing a change.

If a statement is not on paper, it does not exist. No promises, no assurances, no guarantees that come out of a leasing agent mean a thing. All that matters is the ink on the page.

In most commercial locations, you do not talk directly to the landlord. You want to if you can, but properties are often bought by larger companies as investments. They have as little to do with the property as possible. They use local property managers to handle all of the business of leasing. At one of these locations, you will be talking to a property manager instead of the actual owner.

That's an important distinction. For one thing, it's not the property manager's money that's being negotiated. The property manager might be more inclined to negotiate in that respect, but he'll also negotiate from a prearranged "bottom line". He's under orders not to lease below a certain price. He will not refer back to the landlord and say, "I have an offer for ..." The landlord might be willing to change his mind about that bottom line, but the property manager will not. Also, the property manager's priorities are different from the landlord's. A higher percentage of tenancy is a resume point for them, so they want your business as long as you can work out a deal within the landlord's guidelines.

A Commercial Lease, Clause by Clause

Handling a 30-page behemoth lease agreement can be intimidating when you first look at it. Familiarity with the points makes it seem much shorter. Knowing how to navigate it allows you to turn straight to the trouble spots and identify right away anything you are not willing to sign. These descriptions help speed you through the legalese.

Identification

Leases begin by identifying both parties. The only potential trouble here is very rare but very dangerous: make sure the person you are leasing from has the right to lease to you! Although it sounds ludicrous, con-men have taken money for leasing space in buildings they do not own or represent.

You should note who the landlord considers you to be. Are you Frank Smith, D/B/A Frank's Friendly Game Store? Or are you Frank's Friendly Game Store, a legal person? Whenever possible, obligate your company rather than yourself.

Property Identification

This clause includes the legal description of the property. It might include a diagram as an attachment. This clause should include the square footage and the method for counting the square footage.

Term

The term identifies when the lease begins and ends.

Rent

This key clause identifies how much you pay, how it is computed, and when it is due.

Escalation

The escalation clause often goes hand-in-hand with rent and might appear as part of that clause. It states the increases in rent over the course of the lease. The increase might be expressed as a dollar amount or as a percentage. The increase might arise after each full year of the lease or at the beginning of the calendar year.

Security deposit

This clause identifies how much the security deposit the landlord expects. It should also identify how it will be held and whether it collects interest. The deposit is usually expressed in multiples of rent months, as in "two months' rent".

Renewal

If the landlord offers an option to renew the lease, those details appear in this section. It should include the rate, escalation and all other relevant details.

Use

The use clause specifies any restrictions on the use. None of these restrictions should affect game retail. They might relate to the storage of explosives and other dangers. Cross out anything unreasonable that might restrict your business.

Subletting or Assignment

This option allows you to exit the industry by selling your business to someone who takes over payments on the balance of the lease. By subletting, you allow someone else to come in and make payments in your name. An assignment allows you to transfer the lease to another person. Insist on one or both.

Tenant Improvements

You might or might not be allowed to make any improvements. This clause spells out those rights. Do not expect to be able to make major changes; by the same token question any restriction on your ability to make minor improvements like painting or changing the flooring.

Taxes

This clause identifies whether you or the landlord is responsible for property taxes. It should be the landlord.

Insurance

This clause identifies which party is responsible for which insurance coverages. You might be required to name the landlord as an additional insured for liability coverage.

Utilities

This clause identifies who pays each utility.

Signs

The landlord might require certain standards for signage. He can require or prohibit a certain type of signage. He cannot require that you purchase your sign from a particular merchant. Do not allow any wording that lets the landlord refuse a sign after you have it made. Spending $5,000 on a sign that you are not allowed to use is an enormous waste of money.

Right of Entry

The landlord has the right to enter the property as long as it does not interfere with the normal course of business. You can insist that any visit take place during business hours.

Parking
Some agreements specify rules on parking. These rules might require that you and your employees park in designated spaces or exclude you from using those spaces closest to the building. In large cities, you might be required to pay for your personal and staff parking spaces.

Damage and Destruction
This section identifies the landlord's obligation to rebuild in case of damage or destruction and identifies whether or not you still owe rent on a building that does not exist or that you can not use. Do not agree to pay rent for a destroyed building. Ever. Make every attempt to include a termination clause here. If you must close or move your business for a year or two while the landlord rebuilds, the location will be worthless to you when the space becomes available again.

This article or another article might refer to condemnation, too. The same rules apply.

Compliance with ADA
You and the landlord are both liable for compliance with the Americans with Disabilities Act. In general, the landlord is responsible for property up to the door, and you are responsible for property inside your leased area.

Do not agree to move into a property that is in violation of the ADA unless the landlord offers rent concessions that allow you to bring the property into compliance in excess of any concessions you negotiate elsewhere. Do not accept the landlord's compliance on his say-so. Insist on an audit by an engineer or an architect familiar with the Act.

I advise you not to underestimate the ADA's importance. The Americans with Disabilities Act is an act, not a law. You can't go to jail for its violation. It does allow plaintiffs to sue companies in violation of the act. The act has opened up what has been called "shotgun suits" or "drive-by lawsuits." A person enters your store. He might or might not interact with the staff. He probably asks to use the restroom.

A couple of weeks later, you are served with a lawsuit. It might be that the mirror in your bathroom was too high. One of your aisles was too narrow. You did not have a Braille sign beside the bathroom door (not on the door, because that doesn't meet the Act's requirements). You can either pony up a settlement or face them in court. Because of the cost to fight a lawsuit, only a handful of the hundreds of lawsuits these groups have filed have gone to court. You can be relatively certain that they have a larger bankroll than you do with which to pay their attorneys.

The worst states for this scenario are Hawaii, California, and Florida, but the problem has been spreading. While they primarily target hotels and restaurants, they also target shopping centers exactly like the ones where game retailers place their stores.

One final note about ADA compliance: if you put this expense off on the landlord, review your CAM charges (if any) at the end of the year to make sure he did not sneak it back to you.

Default

This section defines the conditions of default and outlines the landlord's rights in case of default, that is, if you fail to pay the rent.

Quiet Enjoyment

This mysterious phrase is often misunderstood. Many landlords keep it because it was in whatever template they used to create their own agreement. Quiet enjoyment has nothing to do with noise level.

In fact, the covenant of quiet enjoyment is an obligation of the landlord and does not need to be mentioned in the lease. Its presence is implicit in a commercial lease agreement. Quiet enjoyment means that you have the right to conduct your business without interference from the landlord. If you are in a mall and paid for premium spacing next to an entrance that the landlord closes, the landlord is almost certainly in violation of the quiet enjoyment clause because he took an action that hampered your ability to conduct business.

You are best served by striking out any quiet enjoyment paragraph. Its presence in a contract can only limit your rights, never expand them. If you have any questions, consult your attorney.

Competition

If the landlord does not offer this clause, insist. This clause restricts the landlord's right to lease nearby space to your competitors. If possible, extend the non-competition clause to other nearby properties the landlord leases. Point out that a competitor who opens within three miles is likely to cause both businesses to fail, leaving the landlord with two empty locations instead of one.

Warranty
This section states that the property is in compliance with all applicable laws.

Notice
This section identifies how and where either party should send any official notice to the other party.

Successors
This section typically states that the agreement survives either party. If the landlord sells the property, the buyer is obligated to honor the lease. Likewise, if you sell your business and assign your lease, your buyer is obligated to pay the same rent.

Enforcement
This section specifies how the agreement will be enforced and who is obligated to pay the attorney fees. Most landlords require that you resolve any dispute through arbitration.

Final Agreement
This statement states that the lease agreement supersedes all previous verbal or written agreements.

Governing Law
This section identifies which state's law shall apply to the resolution of any disagreements between you and the landlord. An out-of-state landlord wants to use his own state because a) his agreement was written with that state's laws in mind and b) if you have to travel to disagree, it will cost you more and make you less inclined to fight.

POINTS TO ALWAYS INSIST ON
▷ **Non-Competition.** While it's doubtful that another prospective game store owner would be willing to open up in your own shopping center, there's no reason for the landlord to refuse this,

either. If the landlord owns other nearby properties, try to negotiate an agreement that extends to those other properties as well.

▷ **ADA Compliance.** You do not want to have to spend thousands of dollars bringing the landlord's bathroom up to code. It's his responsibility up until the point where you allow him pass that responsibility on to you. Insist that he bring it up to code if it is not already. If he says it is, make sure the lease is clear on that point so that you have it in writing. For more details, visit the official website at *http://www.usdoj.gov/crt/ada/ adahom1.htm*.

▷ **Destruction Clause.** What happens if the building is destroyed? Some landlords try to collect rent from you for your use of a building that doesn't exist. Make sure that it's clear that if the building is destroyed, you do not owe rent until it's rebuilt. If your portion is destroyed, state that you might be convinced to use another suite in the same shopping center if the landlord makes some allowance, such as moving you into a larger suite at the same rent.

▷ **Cap the CAM.** Often, the CAM is stated as $x per square foot, but the fine print might state that this is an estimate only, and the tenant is responsible for the overage. So if the leasing agent states a CAM of $2.50 psf, at the end of the year you get a bill that equates to $5 psf, it's your mistake for not insisting on a cap. A reasonable cap allows a variation of 10-15%.

▷ **Rent Credit.** Similarly, ask for a credit to your rent if they spend less on the CAM. If the annual CAM charges were $5,000 but your portion of the expenditure is only $4,250, insist that you be credited the difference on the next month's rent. For both of these last two reasons, you should insist in the lease that you can inspect the actual statements that contribute to the total CAM amount.

POINTS TO AUTOMATICALLY REFUSE

▷ **Percentage of Receipts.** However the lease phrases it, some agreements include a provision for collecting part of your sales in addition to the flat rent. Never turn over a portion of your sales to a landlord. You should not hear a whimper over this point because they never expect you to sign it. They include it for the people who sign a lease because they do not know that it's negotiable. Malls are the exception. Such clauses are common in malls.

▷ **Responsibility for Fixtures.** If the landlord can convince you to pay for his heating and air conditioning unit, he will. Don't spend $10,000 for a piece of equipment you use for three years. It doesn't belong to you. Don't fix it.

Points to Question

In addition to the automatic dos and do nots are a variety of lease clauses that might pose problems without automatically scratching a location off of your list.

▷ **Required Hours.** While this clause is common in a mall environment, the requirement to be open certain hours appears in strip malls as well. Do not commit to a range of hours you don't need.

▷ **Signage.** Does the lease require a certain type of signage? Upscale shopping centers concerned about their image might require channel can lettering, the most expensive option generally available to game stores. Also, make sure you are allowed to use any signage common to the shopping center, such as a pole sign or a pylon sign visible from the road. Make sure the pylon sign is well-maintained and visible.

▷ **Cancellation Option.** Sales at the location might be terrible, or another place might come open that is better suited for you. Typically, you have to agree to pay a fee, such as 2-3 months' rent. Three months' rent is far better than 24 months' rent. Take it.

▷ **Condition.** Is the place being offered "as-is", or is the landlord offering to vanilla shell it, or is the landlord offering any money for improvement? The standard option is for the landlord to offer to "white box" or vanilla shell the property. That makes it a plain white, empty space for you to start your build-out. Because that can cost from $15,000 to $40,000, depending on condition and the local economics, you can use that to your advantage in negotiation. If you take the location as-is, you are saving the landlord money that he'd have to spend to attract another company. If you take the white box, be prepared to wait 60 to 120 days.

▷ **Traffic Count.** The leasing agent or landlord should know the average daily traffic count (ADTC) for the roadways adjacent to the property. Five thousand is pretty slow. Forty thousand is a busy street. Ask how recently the estimate was obtained. If you don't know the area, ask other business owners on the street when city did any significant construction. If the changes were more recent than the traffic count information, that number might no longer be valid.

A Commercial Lease Glossary

Abatement: A reduction in rent, detailed in amount and time, usually offered as a concession to the tenant as an inducement to lease.

ADA: The Americans with Disabilities Act of 1990. It essentially states that your business must be accessible to disabled people (not just Americans) and includes a long, complicated list of specific requirements. Its website is *http://www.usdoj.gov/crt/ada/adahom1.htm*.

Anchor: In a mall or a strip mall, an anchor is a large store that takes up the central or dominating position. Usually a large department store, the absence of an anchor is a sign of death for a strip mall.

Build Out: Improvements or construction made to a property.

CAM: Common Area Maintenance. This number includes lawn maintenance, shopping center security, signage, parking lot maintenance, and all other factors that apply to the entire shopping center.

CPI: Consumer Price Index. You sometimes see it mentioned in a commercial lease as a reference for your rent increases.
Escalation rate: The rate at which your rent increases. It might be described as a dollar amount or as a percentage of a previous rate.

FFE or FF&E: Furnishings, fixtures and equipment.

HVAC: Heating, ventilation and air-conditioning unit.

Lien: A claim against your property as a defense against default on your part. Everybody wants a lien on your property. For the record, banks only count your inventory as worth 30-60% of your cost. For a specialty market like game retail, expect the low end.

Merchant Association: An association of tenants and sometimes the landlord formed for cooperative marketing to increase traffic to the shopping center.

Personal Guarantor: When you guarantee that you will pay a debt if your business fails, you are signing as a personal guarantor. As a small business owner, especially a new small business owner, you will be required to sign just about everything as personal guarantor.

Triple Net: A lease in which the tenant pays all expenses of maintaining the property in addition to rent, plus utilities, insurance, taxes, and other costs.

Vanilla Shell: Also known as a vanilla box or a white box, vanilla shell refers to an empty commercial suite with plain white walls and no additional interior walls aside from a bathroom and maybe a storage area.

RENT-REDUCING STRATEGIES

Now that you know how much the landlord is prepared to spend to lease that space to you in the form of the vanilla shell spending, you can capitalize on that knowledge. The landlord was willing to give up tens of thousands of dollars to get you there. In all likelihood, if he's not spending $20,000 or more, he might be willing to take less than he expected for the rent.

Because you shopped around and found as many possible locations as you could, you know what the local market looks like. You might, for example, know that you would pay $15-18 psf/yr at some of the brand-new locations on that recently-expanded road, or you could pay $10-12 psf/yr at many not-so-new commercial locations in mixed commercial & residential areas, or you might spend $6-9 psf/yr in the older parts of town closer to the outskirts. Obviously, you are looking at a wide range of locations, one of which is three times the cost of the other.

Let's say you are considering one of the mid-range locations, but the landlord is asking for $12.50 psf/yr. Tell him that you are considering taking it as-is, but you feel the rent is too high. Point out that you could go anywhere for less. He might not know what the going rate is. He might offer you a lower rate — lower than you were thinking.

Do not commit to anything right now, and be guarded in your reaction. Ask for what you think is a reasonable rate according to your research. Do not be afraid to make it 70% of the going rate — or less. In this case, offer maybe $7.25 psf. The offer costs you nothing to make, and the landlord might agree. The worst-case scenario is that he says "no." Fine. Shrug and ask what he can do for you. A single dime in reduction saves you $600 over the course of a 3-year lease in a 2,000 sf location.

Meanwhile, keep talking to other property managers about other locations. You might find one that is not ideal but very willing to negotiate their price. Take that price, and point it out to the landlord at the place you really want. "I can get this shopping center for $8.00 per square foot. Can you match that?" Use the same techniques the landlords do: silence on non-rent issues. Do not mention that the other place has a higher CAM, or that they want three months' deposit instead of two.

Do not necessarily keep closing in until you reach a number you want. Express your gratitude for his time and tell him you will call him back. Make him wait. It's not likely that the place will lease in a week or two. Call back later and say that you are nearing an agreement for another location, but you wanted to see if you could still work something out.

Another tactic in rent negotiation is to step your rent. Figure in a rate you are comfortable with and make it the average of a 3-step increase. If you want to pay $9 psf, offer $7.50 the first year and $10.50 in the third year. If the landlord thinks $7.50 is not high enough, start it out at $8.00 — but cut the second year down to $8.75 and the final year to $10.00. You give him what he wants and save $500.

Negotiating with the landlord sometimes convinces them that they want you in their space. As a new business owner, you will discover that you are a pariah to everyone. No landlord wants the risk of a new business owner. They assume that you are going to fail and stick them with a liability. They expect it. If they can hold on to that place for a moving existing business or a new location for a franchise, they will.

But in the competitive aspect of the negotiation, they forget about that. In an especially hard-fraught negotiation where every topic of their lease is questioned, they feel the rush of victory at coming to terms with you. The effect is much like eBay, where people pay more than they intended to beat out other bidders.

Besides the actual dollar amount of the rent, ask for rent concessions for your expected build-out. Estimate how much you could spend on carpet or tile, lighting, etc. Let's say your estimate comes to $18,000. Ask for that much, plus a little bit of bargaining room. Call our working number now $22,500. The landlord would be reluctant to cut you a check for that much on moving in, but he might be willing to reduce your rent.

Generally, this amount is rounded off to a month's rent in some form. In this case, while you are asking for about 10 months rent, the landlord might agree to no more than 6 months. That's fine. You saved almost $15,000.

One way to leverage this amount is to negotiate over when the concessions take place. It's best for you if this amount comes off the front rent, but that option is least attractive to the landlord. Perhaps instead of 6 months of no rent, you can talk the landlord into 13 months at half rent. He gets the advantage of more money sooner, and you get the advantage of a longer period of easy cash-flow, not to mention a greater net savings.

Another leveraging strategy is to offer to place these free months at the end of the lease if you are reasonably sure you are going to stay there for the duration of the lease. The landlord expects this to be a point in his favor, because he expects your business to fail and for you to leave owing him money anyway. He might be more flexible about rent concessions made on the back end of the lease than the front end.

A word of warning on landlords being too willing to drop their prices is in order. That smacks of desperation. Maybe their tenancy rate is too low, and their cash flow is negative. Maybe they're about to lose an anchor due to an expiring lease. They could be losing money at another location and trying to make up for it here. They could also be preparing to sell and want to inflate their tenancy numbers. Find out as much as you can from the existing tenants.

MALL LOCATIONS

Malls offer a potential for sales that most game retailers dream of. The foot traffic that goes through a mall is enormous. Generating that much traffic to your store through advertisement would cost a fortune. The increase in customer traffic means that a retailer in a mall environment must plan for certain differences from the standard shopping center in operations, finances, and display.

SUMMARY: BENEFITS OF MALLS
🕸 Sales: Much higher sales potential compared to outdoor shopping centers

---

First, customer expectation for image standards in a mall environment is very high. Second-hand furniture won't do unless it is brand new or in excellent repair. The cost of the build-out might be much higher than the cost of similar work in your shopping center. Pegboard fixtures, which might be visually acceptable in an outdoor shopping center, don't pass muster in a mall. Slatwall is the standard.

Second, mall restrictions might mandate certain hours of operation that require unproductive hours for you or prohibit those otherwise reliable late-night sales. Similarly, mall restrictions might not allow you to set up certain demos or other events, use certain types of signage, or use certain types of promotion, such as promoting a second location outside of the mall.

Next, the products that sell differ from the traditional business model. Role-playing games alone won't sustain the sales necessary to pay mall rents because of the low conversion rate. Product that is accessible to a wider range of customers is necessary to convert enough of those customers to pay the bills. Board games, which might be 5% or 10% of the total sales in a suburban strip center, might become your leading seller. Puzzles, action figures, and other mass-market appeal products become more important.

Also, loss due to theft increases. With all of these non-buying browsers, you have more shoplifters in the store, and the crush of bodies can help conceal suspicious behavior or block the actual moment of concealment from your view. Also, the many legitimate customers in the store demand more attention. You can choose to spend money to hire additional staff or lose more merchandise to theft. Unfortunately, additional staff doesn't prevent all shoplifting. Your loss prevention skills need to be top-notch.

Mall property owners and managers tend to hold all the cards when it comes to negotiating the lease. Their lease terms tend to be less flexible than those in an outdoor shopping center, leaving you paying more money for your space.

Lastly, and most importantly, the funds necessary to open and maintain a mall store are enormous compared to any other type of plan discussed in the GRG. Malls might cost up to $100 per square foot per year in some markets. Furthermore, they nearly always expect a percentage of sales in addition to their square-foot rate.

Not only do your monthly expense totals increase in a mall store, your start-up cost is magnified several times because of the impact of the monthly increase on your capital reserve. That $48,000 that might last you a year in an outdoor shopping center might last three months in a mall.

SUMMARY: HIGHER COSTS IN MALLS
- Labor: More eyes to watch the product
- Labor: More bodies to service the customers
- Theft: More shoplifters, less attention
- Fixtures: Better quality fixtures
- Rent: The largest cost increase

BUYING PROPERTY: AN ALTERNATIVE TO LEASING

Purchasing your own building has a strong appeal. Buying can mitigate risk, because if the business fails, you still have real property that has value. On the other hand, buying property greatly increases the capital necessary to start the business.

Two options are available for business owners trying to buy property. In the first and more conventional option, you buy property and a freestanding building. In a variation of this option, you can buy the land and build your store to your specifications on that land. The second and newer option is a business condominium.

In both cases, your monthly cost stays constant, and you can borrow against the equity you build to add on to the building, buy out a competitor, or otherwise finance growth. You do not have to ask a landlord's permission to paint the exterior, add another entrance, or retile the floor. You also gain tax benefits from owning the property, being able to write off expenses for improvements.

The freestanding building has the advantage of being a further means of establishing your brand: you can paint or design the building with a unique identity that the customer learns to associate with your business.

The business condominium involves a conventional shopping center that is owned by the individual business owners and maintained through an association of those owners. You have to agree to the group decision concerning maintenance and upkeep, but the cost of purchase is usually much less than a freestanding building in a comparable market. Unlike with a freestanding property, your design and build-out options might be restricted by group consensus.

SUMMARY: BUYING ADVANTAGES
- Property might appreciate in value
- You can borrow against your equity
- More control over design
- Stable monthly costs

In both cases, you suffer risks. The cost of maintenance might be higher than expected and can raise the total cost higher than a traditional rent rate. Property values might depreciate, placing you in a poor position should you wish to sell the property and move the store. Damage or destruction to the building can leave you without a business, whereas in a shopping center you might move to another suite or to another nearby property with less difficulty.

Some game store owners claim that owning property makes it more difficult to move. Moving your business is difficult either way. With a lease, you might have an option to end the lease early, but if not, you can only move at the end of the lease, which might be years in the future. Your other option is to break the lease, which could cost thousands in debt or litigation with the landlord.

If you own property, you don't need to wait for a lease to end. You can call your real estate agent when you first start looking for another location, list the property, and move. Many property buyers aren't necessarily interested in using the property themselves; they want it for an investment. That means that they don't mind waiting for you to move out, as long as the move takes place within a reasonable period of time. You could stipulate in the sale that you continue paying rent on a month-to-month basis until you find another property. If you're willing to either lease out or sell the property, you have a greater chance of having income from the property sooner.

As the owner of the property, you also face liability for any accidents that occur on the property. If you operate the only business on the property, you at least have full responsibility for who you allow on the property and what kind of activities you allow there, but if you have tenants, almost anything could happen. Creating a separate corporation for your property management needs mitigates the risk to your business in the case of an accident or injury; in fact, the protection extends both ways.

If the business fails, you won't lose the property. If you default on the mortgage or otherwise lose the property, you still own the business and can move it to another location.

SUMMARY: BUYING DISADVANTAGES
- Property occasionally depreciates in value
- Major repairs can be expensive
- Liability for accidents

BUYING INSTEAD OF OPENING

Sometimes you find that you have the opportunity to acquire an existing game store. Maybe the offer to purchase the business is what initially intrigued you about going into this industry. Maybe somebody heard about your goal and made an offer. In any case, buying an existing location is substantially different than starting out on your own.

SUMMARY: BUYING DISADVANTAGES
- No choice of location
- Wasted or unwanted inventory
- Potentially poor image
- Fewer choices
- Unfavorable lease terms
- Potentially negative cash flow

DISADVANTAGES

When you buy an existing business, you do not have the choice of location, you do not choose your initial inventory, and you did not hire the current staff. Your company's image within the community could be poor. You have no choice in any of the initial business decisions. That means that you might have to spend a considerable amount of money to make it the way you want it — or change your business plan accordingly.

The inability to negotiate the lease is a key issue. The climbing rate on the lease could be steep. You probably do not have a cancellation clause, so you are stuck with whatever lease the seller signed. You can renegotiate at the end of the lease, but if that deadline is within six months, you will find your time is running out already.

In the case of buying a store that is going out of business or where the owner is selling because sales are dropping, you have a very serious liability. You have to turn cash flow positive before the business eats up all of your working capital and leaves you in the same position as the previous owner.

BENEFITS

The key benefit to buying an existing game store is that your initial sales are much higher than if you were to start from scratch. Compare the two hypothetical sales records, partially based on actual numbers provided by stores, that appear on the following page. The first chart shows a store with sales below its break-even. Sales climb slowly as the new owner recovers old customers and creates new ones. Sales dip during a traditional slow season for the industry.

SUMMARY: BUYING ADVANTAGES
- Established customer base
- Distributor contacts
- Higher initial sales
- Staff and volunteers in place

For the new store, sales increases are more dramatic, but the year-end total is still lower than in the existing store. Note that no month shows a decrease from the month before, despite seasonal fluctuations, because this new store is more focused toward generating new customers.

The value is still clear here: by purchasing this business, you've managed to put an additional $73,800 in the bank over the course of the year, minus COGs. Based on the new store's sales level, it's still about six months away from catching up in volume, so you will continue to gain an additional $50,000 to $60,000 in higher sales with the purchase of an existing store.

In some ways, buying an existing business seems to offer advantages in simplification, too. You take over the existing store's lease and commercial accounts and move right in.

Not so fast, partner.

For one thing, remember the lack of separation of you and

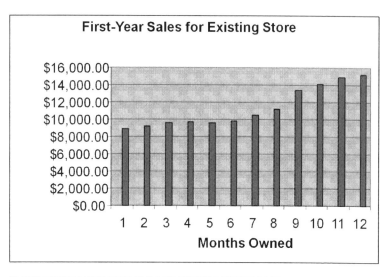

First-Year Sales for Existing Store

First-Year Sales for New Store

the business when you operate a small business. Your distributors will insist that you reapply for credit, even though the company you purchased might have had an account with them for 15 years. Your banker likewise might consider a change of officers similar to opening a new account.

For most of your other service providers, the change of command is less of an issue; you do not generally owe as much for your electric bill as you owe your distributors at any one time. They might want a written statement at most.

Your landlord is an exception. Depending on the lease agreement he signed with the seller, you might have to sign a lease assignment with the seller, or you might have to renegotiate terms completely. If so, your savings in time and energy is drastically reduced, but you have the chance to reduce some costs and risks, too.

Another advantage the existing store has is its human resources. You might have a well-trained staff already in place. Customers might be part of a manufacturer volunteer team. You already have existing customers bringing in new customers through word-of-mouth advertising.

ASSESSING A STORE'S VALUE

If you are going to purchase an existing business, you need to know how much to pay for it. You could pay a business broker to evaluate the business and give you a professional estimate. Such services typically cost $500 to $3,000.

You should definitely review the seller's cash-flow statements, balance sheets and income tax returns for the last two or three years. The seller can talk a good story, but what does his bank account say? Does it groan under the weight of supplier debt, or does it coo contentedly with regular care and feeding? If he is unwilling or unable to provide these documents, then he probably fears that they will not support any claims he makes concerning sales or profits. Be careful.

One rule of thumb method for valuation of a game store is 20% of the store's annual sales, plus the cost of inventory, minus debts. This valuation method depends solely on sales volume. It does not consider the company's image, market share, time in business or anything other than straight sales. This number compares the game industry's numbers to several other retail business that are most similar to us in terms of COGS, rent, and volume. If you mention this method to an accountant, expect a cringe. A rule of thumb valuation is applicable when each item on the company's P&L statement corresponds perfectly with the industry average and the company's sales are not dramatically climbing or falling.

Another method is to add up all of the costs that you would incur by starting your own business with equal inventory and then determine how much you feel saving all of that effort is worth. If you think it's worth $5,000 to save yourself the location scouting, lease negotiation, staff recruiting, and advertising costs, spend it. Remember that you are also gaining a huge jump-start in sales, an advantage that definitely has value.

You could consider the cost of the loans that you are taking out to purchase the business and compare the repayment rate of those loans to the company's cash flow. Look at your principal, APR and term to figure out how much your monthly payment will be, using any standard loan amortization application you can find online. If the company's cash flow is less than that payment, then it can be worth investing that money in the company. Remember not to count a fraction of that money that you will need as a cash reserve for paying bills and remaking the company to suit your needs.

CONDITIONAL AGREEMENT & DUE DILIGENCE

When you begin to negotiate with a seller, you might wish to write up a conditional agreement to prevent another buyer from coming along and buying the business before you have a chance to complete your sale. This conditional agreement should allow you a due diligence period in which to inspect the business.

Due diligence is the process of closely examining a business's financial records and properties so that you do not experience any unpleasant surprises after the purchase. If you rush into a purchase and sign a purchase agreement written by the seller, you might find yourself signing that you have conducted due diligence before you really have. In that case, your ability to take legal action against the seller for any damages suffers.

SUMMARY: DUE DILIGENCE CHECKLIST

- Corporate books and minutes, if any
- Financial statements
- Current service provider statements
- Current supplier statements
- Employment agreements
- Service provider contracts
- Insurance policies
- Corporate tax returns
- Inventory

Don't Buy the Business, Buy the Stuff

In the gaming industry, you can manage to obtain all of the advantages of another store without buying the business itself. Offer to buy out the inventory and fixtures, customer list, vendor accounts, and right to use the trade name. You might negotiate to become an assignee on his commercial lease as well. Because the seller keeps his own corporation (if any), he can pursue other business options without incorporating again.

Using this method, you have the corporate structure of your choice. If the store you're buying is operating as a proprietorship, your LLC can buy the assets and you'll retain your status. You have no fear that a customer will sue you over something that happened months or years before you bought the company. If you purchased the business, you could still be liable for a slip-and-fall that you never knew about. Lastly, you have a bargaining advantage versus buying "a business". You are not buying the owner's equity. You are not asking for "goodwill", or any other intangible that might drive up the price.

SUMMARY: Pros of Buying Assets
- Your choice of business format
- No liability for past incidents
- Lower price

Making a Smooth Transition

Once you and the seller have agreed on a price and a timetable for the transaction to be finalized, prepare the other people you do business with for the change. Contact your suppliers and ask if they want you to reapply.

Review the list of current employees. You might want to keep them, terminate all of them, have them reapply, or change their position. At least review their hiring information to make sure their employment is legal if you are buying the company. If not, then you need to redo it anyway because they are working for a different employer.

Contact the customers as soon as both you and the seller are comfortable with the disclosure. Let them know what strengths you bring to the store without insulting the seller. This continuity break is a perfect opportunity to lose customers. Do not announce any major plans for change right away. Encourage customers to come in and introduce themselves.

If you have not already done so, prioritize all of the changes you want to make. Plan them out at a measured pace instead of trying to do them all at once. Taking some time will also allow the customers to adjust to the changes.

Don't hesitate to make improvements. Painting walls with loose flakes hanging from them, replacing carpet showing wide spaces between the seams, and replacing broken glass are all projects you should accomplish as soon as possible. Changes that can wait are operational procedures like how you handle CCG singles sales, or removing less-productive product lines. An immediate cosmetic improvement can restore customer confidence in the store and generate immediate sales.

CREATING A BUSINESS PLAN

Every detail about how you will run your business, from where you get your product to how you sell it to who buys it, makes up a business plan. A business plan accomplishes two things, and how you write it depends on which of those two things is your primary consideration.

It never hurt to have your ideas on paper. The hard copy will stay objective while you are caught up in the day-to-day operations. It helps you keep an eye on the overall direction of the company. The organization will help keep your thoughts focused when you discuss your company with distributors or manufacturers as well. This plan-for-use is your operational business plan.

A presentation plan is an attractive collection of information and numbers designed to garner financing. Your financing might come from a bank loan, a private investor, or family members. While family members don't always need to see this much detail, having the plan allows you to present the information to the people who do.

If you want to save time in the preparation of your business plan, you can purchase software to guide you through the process. Professional business plan software costs about $100, but you could spend more on higher-end versions. Hiring a professional to walk you through the process costs $400 or more.

PHYSICAL FORMAT

You don't need a physical copy of your operational plan. Any

44

word processing document covers your needs. If you print it for ready use, you can staple it or bind it however you find convenient.

For a plan that you design to attract investor interest, spiral-bind it, use fancier paper, or otherwise dress it up. While lenders say that the content determines their decision, that's not entirely true. If you hand them a stapled copy of your plan with a coffee stain on the cover, they will lay that mental image over whatever picture they develop of your business. If your concept is solid, and your market analysis is promising, but your credit record is less than perfect, and the final decision is up to a loan officer's personal opinion, you don't want to fall short over a trivial reason.

WRITING THE BUSINESS PLAN

Business plan formats vary, but they all contain essentially the same information. They describe the operation of your business, identify who your customers will be, and show how you can repay your lender by providing believable sales figures. The more knowledge you show of the industry, the more confidence you engender in your potential lender.

SUMMARY: BUSINESS PLAN OUTLINE

- ❀ Cover Sheet
- ❀ Executive Summary
- ❀ Table of Contents
- ❀ Company Description
- ❀ Products and Services
- ❀ Market Analysis
- ❀ Operational Plan
- ❀ Management and Organization
- ❀ Financial Projections
- ❀ Supporting Data

Cover Sheet

This mostly blank sheet contains your logo and company name, your title, the business address, the names and titles of any other officers or partners, and any other corporate identity, such as your trade name.

Executive Summary

Write this part last. It's a summary of the rest of the document. You have a better idea of what you are trying to say after you write the rest of the plan.

When you do write it, keep it short — three paragraphs should be plenty. Include the page title at the top, your text, and that's it. Keep in mind that this snapshot of the plan should be enough for the reader to identify who you are and what you want.

Identify the business in general but clear terms. Identify your products, your customers, and your expectations of the industry in the future. The tone here should be positive.

A confidentiality disclaimer should accompany the text. It says that the reader is not to use this information for personal gain or share it with others that might do the same. Non-disclosure agreements are commonplace, and their inclusion in your business plan does not question the reader's integrity.

Table of Contents

Most word processor programs can automatically create a table of contents for you. If yours does not, you can manually create it after you write the text of the document. Include major headers and secondary headers to help the reader find key information.

Company Description

Explain your business to people who do not know the industry. Identify your business format, your long-term plans, your trade name, its location, and where you currently stand in the planning.

Mission Statement

If you have already created a mission statement for your company, include it here. It should be brief, around 25 words or less. A good mission statement embodies the thoughts that inspired you to start the company.

Products and Services

Describe what products you intend to carry in terms that anyone can understand. Avoid industry jargon and acronyms. Identify these products by category and give examples of each category. For example, you might carry board games, European board games like Settlers of Catan and Carcassone, and stand-alone card games like the Toy of the Year Apples to Apples. Describe how much inventory you expect to carry.

If you plan to use an aggressive event schedule to promote games, describe which events you intend to offer and how they'll affect sales. Tools to support this section include manufacturer volunteer programs, statements from other retailers, and numbers provided by the organized play programs from Privateer Press or Konami concerning the number of participants in their programs.

Market Analysis

The market analysis looks at the industry as a whole, your competition and how you intend to stand out from that competition.

When describing the industry as a whole, you can use the national information provided with this book as a starting point. Try to find out from local sources how your own market deviates from the national trend. If you create this information from scratch, identify your target market and how you will reach or create those customers.

For most new stores, your local competition includes other retail stores, big-box stores, book stores, and the Internet. Objectively describe the strengths and weaknesses of each of these competitors and identify how much of the market they currently control. Toys R Us, for example, might sell a relatively large number of D&D Box sets, but that one product is a tiny percentage of your overall sales.

In the final section of the market analysis, point out how you will carve your own pie slice out of the market. If you have a competitive edge, such as a strong marketing background or extensive customer lists provided by manufacturers, note that information in the analysis. Identify your strength, whether it's competitive pricing, superior service, or unique supply channels.

Operational Plan

Your actual operations might seem simple to you. You open the door, let customers in, and ring them up.

Your business plan needs a little more detail than that.

How does your operation help meet your marketing goal? Who places orders? When? How much time does it take? Why will you use those suppliers?

Who receives and merchandises orders? Who hires and trains new people? Who manages the events schedule? Who manages your technology? Which services will you contract out — payroll, accounting, taxes, or none of these, and why?

SUMMARY: STRONG OPERATIONS
◈ Allowances for ongoing training for employees
◈ Contingency plans for emergencies
◈ Accounting for all duties, from cleaning to planning

SUMMARY: WEAK OPERATIONS
◈ The owner does all of the work
◈ Language that trivializes the workload
◈ Necessary duties unassigned or omitted

Management and Organization

While this section can be quite extensive in larger companies, for one person or for a small partnership, it's brief. This section identifies key personnel and what skills each person brings to the company. For most people opening a game store, this section concentrates on one person or the married couple that is going into business.

Think of this section as your resume. Showcase your relevant experience, your education and your strengths. If your spouse will be part of the business, provide the information for both of you and identify how you will share the duties.

You may also include the names of the professionals that support your business, such as your attorney, accountant, and primary banker. This inclusion shows that you are not trying to operate the business without professional advice at some level. The larger the amount you request, the more important this element becomes.

Financial Projections

This chapter requires you to look into the future to find out what your sales will be like. It's also subject to the most critical eye. Investors want to see the potential for return, but they also do not want to be deceived by unrealistically optimistic numbers. Conservative numbers showing a planned sales growth are more useful than fantastically high sales volume and low costs. A dual or triple set of numbers is better: include a worst-case scenario, a best-case scenario, and your best estimate.

Your key documents for this section are your balance sheet, your break-even analysis, your cash-flow statement and your P&L. It's very important at this point to have your numbers consistent as well as conservatively optimistic. Using a figure of $2,400 for rent in one location and $2,800 in another shows that you are either careless or dishonest. Neither trait is one that investors like to see.

Request

The request is simply how much money you are asking for, how long you expect to take to repay it, and how it'll help you reach your business goals. As always, be brief, be clear, and be honest.

Supporting Data

These documents back up the statements you make during the text. It might include statements of intent from other investors, market research, quotes from contractors, and other information that supports the claims you make during the plan. For starting small business, the most vital pieces of information in this section are the full financial data for the principal officers.

PRE-OPENING SALES PROJECTION

Projecting the sales for your business plan or for a major modification to your business plan is the trickiest part of the job. When you calculate costs you can get price sheets from distributors, rate cards from advertising media, and rent figures from commercial leasing agents.

You don't have similar tools when calculating income.

What do you have?

Matrix Projections

If you had access to the sales figures for other game stores like yours, you could compare the size and scope of your store to theirs and estimate your sales based on the comparison. If, for example, a nearby store does $400,000 a year in sales and you plan to carry similar product lines and have similar space, you might be able to count on anywhere from $250,000 to $450,000 in sales, depending on the comparison.

This method faces two major difficulties. First, unless your store is identical in every way to the comparison stores, the comparison will be invalid. You have to adjust your comparison up or down based on the areas in which you are strong or weak. If the stores in your state are doing $200,000 a year, you'd need an exceptional reason for projecting $350,000 annually. With experience and a personal visit or two you can look at a store, gauge its foot traffic, gauge its inventory levels, and estimate its annual sales. Unless you have industry experience, you're not likely to be able to do that.

Secondly, and more importantly, you aren't likely to know how much other game stores do in sales. Most people don't share that information, and some of those are less likely to share it with a potential competitor. On industry-only message boards, discussions of sales are usually relative rather than absolute: "I had a good week", or "Is anybody else way down from last year?"

Inventory Levels and Turn Rates

Add up the value of the product lines you intend to carry. You have your inventory costs from your expenses sheet, so you know about how much you'll spend on your goods. Multiply by a reasonable turn rate (for simple math, I'm suing annual sales divided by an average inventory at cost). What is a "reasonable turn rate"?

It depends. Different products turn at different rates. Collectible card games turn quickly; role-playing games sell more slowly. If you plan to earn most of your dollars from the card-floppers, your overall average turn ate will be higher than that of a store selling principally historical miniatures.

SUMMARY: COMPARATIVE RATES

⊛ CCGs: 6x to 20x
⊛ RPGs: 1x to 6x
⊛ Minis: 2x to 8x
⊛ Board games: 1x to 4x

Stores with a narrow focus — those that see more than half of their sales from a single category — can report higher turn rates than these.

Obviously, these rates vary tremendously. How do you know whether you could use 3x or 8x for your CCG sales? Look at the marketing section of your business plan. To whom are you advertising? CCG players are younger than RPG players or minis players, and they're more likely to be male. Minis players, especially Games Workshop customers, come from higher income groups. If your focus is broad, you'll bring in more board game players than the other groups. How about game tables, if any? If you have enough space to support competitive events, CCG and minis sales go up (RPGs do increase, but not as much). If your tables are the skinny conference tables, they're more comfortable for cards. If they're chest-high and covered with felt, you'll attract miniatures players.

Another factor in calculating an expected turn rate is your inventory level. If your inventory level is too low, your turn rate will be comparatively high but total sales will be small because you're missing out on a number of sales. A 25x turn rate on $1,000 worth of Magic yields $25,000 a year. That's a great turn rate, but you're not putting much money in the bank. You'd be better off if you add a second game for a total category turn rate of 18x on $2,000 in inventory, or 14x on $3,000 by carrying a couple of more games.

On the other hand, having too much inventory gives you greater total sales but a lower turn rate. If you carried $15,000 in CCGs (which would be tough), you're not likely to keep a double-digit turn rate at all.

Things to suggest a higher turn rate:
▷ Good product knowledge
▷ A well-rounded advertising plan
▷ Game space
▷ Good image
▷ Multiple product lines
▷ Frequent activities
▷ A younger population base
▷ Good merchandising skills
▷ A marketing plan that emphasizes competitive prices
▷ Face-out book displays
▷ A focus on high-turn products like CCGs

Things to suggest a lower turn rate:
▷ Low visibility
▷ Low traffic count
▷ Unfamiliarity with the products you carry
▷ High competition
▷ An older population base
▷ Carrying used products
▷ A marketing plan that emphasizes product selection
▷ Spine out book displays
▷ A focus on low-turn products like RPGs

All of this brings us back to "How do I calculate my store's turn rate?" Look at your business plan. Multiply your planned categories by one of the turn rates given within each range. Use a figure closer to the top of the range if you check off items on the "high turn rate" list and a figure closer to the bottom if item of the "low turn rate" list apply to you. Project your sales for each category and add up the totals.

That's a good figure for your second year, once your store begins to "mature."

Your first year will be one of growth, culminating in figures near those. You might want to work backward, counting at month 12 and scaling back a little bit until you get to starting figures half or lower than your final figures. Your first three months should include fairly brisk growth. Monthly growth should slow for a few months and then slow further near the end of the year. Sales growth of 10-20% a year for the next couple of years is normal.

The Wrong Way

Calculate your sales projection based on a realistic expectation of what your business model and resources can generate. If your plan does not work off that level, rewrite your plan to grow sales or reduce costs. Don't keep raising your sales projection to meet your needed capital. That's a recipe for failure.

OTHER ADMINISTRATIVE DECISIONS

A few more touches before you're ready to buy or open. At least make the phone calls even if you aren't ready to sign the documents yet.

BANKING

If you obtain bank financing, the bank expects you to use them for your primary checking account. If not, then you're free to shop around for the best terms. Again, a few phone calls could mean a difference of several hundred dollars per year. Items to compare include basic monthly charges, per-item charges and other fees. The location is important, too. Banking 15 miles away from your store is not a good trade for a $20 reduction in annual fees.

INSURANCE

Insurance is like the bumper on a car. It can minimize damage, but it doesn't prevent a collision. You need liability insurance and coverage for your merchandise for certain. These coverages are also the most costly elements of your policy. You will probably also want to consider business income in case an emergency closes you down, a blanket equipment and media for your POS, employee dishonesty, money and securities, signage, and valuable papers and records. If you see a high seasonal variation in sales, inform your agent how much your inventory might increase during that season.

Shop around for policies. Our industry is not large enough for its own category, but compares with a book store in volume, value of property, and content of merchandise. Your lease might require additional coverage; read it. Watch specifically for glass coverage, flooding, hurricane or tornado coverage, etc.

METHODS OF PAYMENT

Before opening, you need to determine what methods of payment you intend to accept for your sales.

Cash

Cash is your friend. Yes, you will take cash. However, read the section on Safety and Security on page 176.

Checks

With current debit card usage, checks are fading away. In 1999, 20% of all customers paid by check. In some locations, the percentage is now less than one percent. A few years ago, refusing to accept checks meant the loss of a significant portion of your customer base. Refusing to take checks no longer costs customers because the marketplace no longer expects the convenience like they did at one time.

If you live in an area where checks still circulate in the marketplace, you have to plan how you will recover the inevitable worthless checks. You can either do it yourself or pay someone to do it. Collecting on the worthless checks yourself costs less money but more time. You can gain a net profit from it, however, because most states allow you to charge a fee on top of the reimbursement for the worthless check. Essentially, collecting involves sending a firm but polite letter to the person who wrote the check. You can follow it with a second letter, and then a phone call. These simple steps recover nearly all lost funds.

A check collection agency usually requires that once the check is returned, the agency keeps the majority of any fees collected from the customer, although they usually give you a portion. Their professional procedures and knowledge of the law allow them to collect with maximum efficiency, allowing you to spend your time selling your product.

Credit/Debit Cards

Accepting credit/debit cards is so universal that any retail business that does not take them faces a serious competitive disadvantage against his competitors. You can set up a merchant account through your primary financial institution or you can shop around. While the fees vary, banks offer better rates to customers that do their principal banking with them.

In general, you can expect two charges with each transaction. First is the percentage. This percentage is usually 2-4%, with higher rates for the lesser-used cards like American Express and higher-risk transactions, including those in which the card is not physically present. The second fee is a flat rate charged per transaction.

As with any service, shopping around might reveal better rates. If your annual sales are $300,000 and you save a quarter per transaction, those phone calls you make in search of a better price before you sign a contract could save you $750 each year. Do not forget to take into consideration the cost of equipment (purchase or lease) and supplies (which should be provided free in any contract with a major vendor).

One danger of taking credit cards is chargebacks. If a customer disputes a charge, you might have to return the money. One game store owner suffered $60,000 in chargebacks from a foreign customer. The cash loss hurt him severely for a long period of time. His distributor accounts suffered because he couldn't pay them off. His company's growth was set back by years. He only survived because of his exceptional sales. It's an extreme example, but we're all susceptible to that kind of fraud.

Square

At *squareup.com* you can sign up for a credit-card processing payment method that you can operate anywhere, at any time, from your smart phone or Ipad. The device is the size of a stamp and plugs into your AV socket. It's free. You can have multiple phones processing cards into the same account, so everybody in your store can use it. Intuit makes a similar offer, and others are starting to appear on the market. Because of the rate, it's not ideal for a full-volume store, but it's perfect for convention, shoe-string stores, or a temporary fix if you credit card processing isn't arranged by the time you open.

Gift Certificates

Gift certificates sell sporadically throughout the year for birth-day presents. You can use them as payment when you buy used merchandise from your customers. You can reward volunteers with them or use them as promotional items.

The majority of game stores simply print out a gift certifi-cate when needed, either including the specific information concerning amount and identity or printing it up with the cer-tificate. This method is cheap and effective.

The advantage to offering gift certificates is that you pro-vide a gift option for somebody that is not familiar with your product — which is a large percentage of the population. Also, the majority of the people redeeming them spend additional money. The benefits do not stop there: taking money before you give somebody product is a push forward on your cash flow. Check your state laws governing the use of gift certificates. Some states regulate or prohibit issues like expiration dates, fees, or inactivity charges.

Gift Cards

Electronic gifts cards offer the advantages of gift certificates, plus some. They are nearly impossible to counterfeit. They al-low excellent customer tracking.

Gift cards are excellent for purchasing second-hand prod-uct from your customers. When you issue credit in exchange for product, the customer often spends money off of that purchase over the course of several transactions. Taking a paper gift cer-tificate and handing out another gift certificate is more time-consuming than simply swiping a card. Giving back change de-stroys your exchange ratio if you offer more in credit trade than cash trade.

You can purchase gift cards through your credit card pro-cessing or a company that produces nothing but plastic cards, like Able Card Corporation (www.ablecard.com) for prices rang-ing from about a $.25 each to about $.60 each.

Hours of Operation

Because you are paying the same rent to use your location regardless of how many hours you are there, you want it to produce revenue as much of that time as you can. The store should almost certainly be open each day of the week. Friday and Saturday are typically the busiest days of the week in terms of both traffic count and sales. While most of Monday through Thursday is similar, you will have one busier day during the week that varies by your location: new game day. The quicker you receive your new inventory, the closer to the beginning of the week you see an increase in sales.

Most game stores open between 10 a.m. and noon each morning and stay open until at least 7 p.m., and they stay open later on the weekends. A handful of stores find that they do little business during the daytime; these locations typically open by 3 p.m., as they see their business boom when school lets out. If you have a game room, you might want to stay open later. By the time a customer gets out of work at 5 p.m., drives home, picks up something to eat and gathers his friends at the game store, 7 p.m. is looming and there's no time left for a game unless the store stays open late.

Once you establish your schedule, you should adhere to it religiously. Customers do not appreciate yanking on a door at a place that says it's open at 11 a.m to wrench their shoulder out of joint because the door's still locked at 11:10. Neither do they want to pull up at 10 minutes before closing with the expectation of browsing for a bit to find the lights already off.

You can change your schedule; that's different from failing to meet it. Analyze your hourly sales and compare your labor costs to those hours in question. While some hours are always going to be busier than others, look for hours where labor is a very high percentage of sales. In general, it does not take many game sales to justify an employee. Cut hours when you consistently have no customers coming into the store.

Local Laws

Being familiar with the laws in your state and community that affect how you conduct your business is vital. Because theses laws vary and change often, this book does not discuss each individual state's laws. Instead, it concentrates on potential trouble areas you should investigate.

Business License

Most communities require a business license for doing business within their boundaries. The application for this license varies in cost, but it usually falls under $100. You need a picture ID, some sort of proof of the business, and you might need to meet a local requirement such as a zoning certificate. Your fictitious name registration or articles of incorporation suffice for proof of business. In some cases, you are required to have both a city and a county license.

Food Permits

If you sell snacks and drinks, you might need a food permit. Food permits are usually a state function, so you need to contact your state Department of Agriculture or Department of Health, depending on your state.

Sales Tax

Forty-five of the United States collect sales tax, and if you sell products to customers, you must have a license to collect this sales tax. Collecting sales tax is a function of your state's Department of Revenue. Contact them for your application. You most likely need to provide them with your FEIN, your business name, possibly the business address, and describe your type of business, which is "retail".

Shoplifting

Spend a couple of hours reviewing your local laws on shoplifting before you set your company's policies. In some places, the customer has to walk past the last place he could possibly pay for the item before a crime has been committed. In others, concealment is enough to press charges.

Also study your legal options for apprehending the thief. In general, you are allowed to use a certain amount of minimal force, but check to see exactly what your community allows. Some stores place a remote lock on the door that they can operate from behind the counter to keep a thief from getting away. Make sure this method is legal where you operate.

PCG Solutions has a collected list of shoplifting statutes by state to help you in your search. You can find it at *http:// www.pcgsolutions.com/shoplifting_statutues.htm.*

Signage

Before you buy a sign, make sure you are able to use it. Include the cost of any necessary permit with your initial budget. Signage laws are subject to local control. While a good sign maker knows the laws that pertain to his area, take care if you buy a sign in one community for use in a neighboring community.

Zoning

Zoning designations are a local function also. If you are considering a location and the locations around it include retail spaces, it is a good bet that your location is legal for retail, too. The local government will expect to verify that, however.

Obtaining a zoning certificate might be a requirement for a business license in your community.

USEFUL RESOURCES

While I hope this book provides you with plenty of information to plan your business, it's not a Comprehensive Guide To All Things. Fortunately, you have other sources of aid available.

GAMA

The Game Manufacturer's Association (www.gama.org) is an organization mainly for manufacturers. Remember this distinction in dealing with them: retailers are not their main focus. That said, manufacturers are only successful if their retailers are successful, so the constituent members do have your health in mind, even if the focus of the organization as a whole is directed elsewhere.

The main benefit they offer you is that they host the annual GAMA Trade Show. If you are serious about opening a game store or serious about making an existing game store more profitable, then you should attend. You can use the cost of travel and entry as an excuse not to attend if you want, but those expenses will be returned over and over again in the form of a more profitable operation. Recent increases in the attention paid to the seminar track have made this event more significant.

Attending the GTS has its own section on page [pp].

THE SMALL BUSINESS ADMINISTRATION

The SBA's main advantage to small businesses is their loan guarantee program, the famous "7(a)" program. They offer some general business advice on their website and through their educational programs. They offer workshops to help guide a prospective business owner through the basic steps of starting a business.

Find them online at *www.sba.gov*.

Chamber of Commerce

Local Chambers vary from the useless to the extremely useful. In many cases, the principal benefit is the network, while others offer seminars and educational tools that are well worth the membership cost. Contact yours to find out exactly what they offer.

SCORE

Billing themselves as "Counselors to America's Small Businesses," SCORE is dedicated to helping small business get started and succeed. Make sure you visit their website at www.score.org. It has useful workshops, checklists, spreadsheets, links, and more.

The Game Industry Network

The GIN on Delphi's online forums is the most concentrated source of game retail information available online. The membership includes nearly all game manufacturers, all of the largest distributorships, and hundreds of the most successful retailers. It's strictly monitored so that arguments, personal issues, and other distractions do not distract readers from the news. Because the people posting are business people discussing their business, threads stay very topical and very pertinent compared to other message boards you might be familiar with online.

You can find it at *http://forums.delphiforums.com/ titangamesinsid*.

Chapter 2: Building and Equipping the Store

Your business model determines your space and design needs. If you plan to make game room events a fundamental part of your marketing, then you need a game room. If you plan to sell miniatures, you need a place to display miniatures. How you build and fixture your store depends in part on what's available but mostly on how you operate your store.

The Game Space Question

To many people who want to open a game store, the question of whether or not you should have a game room seems odd. Of course you do! Our mental image of a game store often includes the game space as an integral part of the store. However, the issue involves more than your preliminary image. Keep in mind that many of the layman's mental images of the gaming industry are inaccurate. Examine the full impact of the game space on your operations, your profitability, and your image before making a decision.

The Argument Against

Fantasy Shop Comics & Games, a four-store chain in Missouri, does not feature gaming space. The owner, Dave Wallace, contends that because only about 10% of your customers ever use the gaming space, that space is not necessary for sales. Removing that potential customer draw does not mean that those customers will stop buying from you.

It does, however, mean that you stop paying for space you are not using for direct sales. Time for some math.

Our example 2,000 sf game store is divided into 1,000 of retail and 1,000 sf of game space. The rent is $8/sf with a $2.50 CAM. That equals $21,000 in annual rent, of which $10,500 pays for the gaming area. This business does $150,000 in annual sales. Assuming that that the owner does a fair job of inventory management and maintains his COGS at 60%, his game space needs to generate $25,000 in additional game sales to pay for itself. That comparison doesn't count the cost of tables, chairs, and other items associated with the gaming space.

The owner runs several tournaments a week, so he thinks it brings in quite a bit of cash. When he looks at his records, he sees that he generates $4,000 per year in tournament fees. Of his $3,000 in snacks and drinks, half came from the regulars in the gaming area. Does the game space generate over $18,000 in add-on sales? Would those people have come into the store anyway on tournament night and bought something? How much could he generate with another 1,000 square feet of inventory instead?

In addition to the cost, game store owners complain about a long list of issues they have to face with a game room. While none of them is an automatic reason not to have one in your store, the totality might sway your decision.

▷ **Cleaning Up.** Gamers tend to be messy. Besides picking up drinks and food left over at the end of the day, you have to tend to spills and messes during business hours, which can be an operational burden on your staff. The mess also makes your store look less appealing to people browsing your store.

▷ **Language.** When luck turns on a gamer, it can be ugly. Involuntary oaths fly out of a person's mouth before he realizes it. No matter how strict your policies are, somebody will say something wrong when a couple of nuns are leading a group of orphans around in search of a board game. That outburst can make it hard to maintain a family image.

▷ **Noise.** While a certain amount of "buzz" coming from your gaming space adds pleasant white noise to your shopping area, too much noise can be distracting. Background noise that's too loud can cause a store to clear out like a gas leak. Also, the volume in a small store can be so high that you have trouble communicating with customers. That hurts sales.

▷ **Arguments.** An argument between two or more of the gamers can cause one party to have an unpleasant feeling that he will forever associate with your store. It also distracts the gamers around them, and arguments have a way of spreading.

▷ **Cheating.** Nothing gives your store a bad reputation among your regular players faster than a cheat.

▷ **Stealing.** While they're not stealing your product, they are causing you a loss: loss of sales. Customers who have their cards or figures or books stolen while they're in your store stop coming to your store. Worse, they might demand that you reimburse them for it. It's your store, after all, and you are ultimately liable for what happens there.

▷ **Unauthorized Trading/Selling.** Regardless of your store's policy toward trading and selling, it will happen in your back room. You can monitor it closely, but at some point you have to tend to a customer, turn your back to deal with another problem, or leave to go do the rest of your job.

They might not physically hand an item off in your store. They might think that if they go outside and make the transaction at their cars, then you will not mind. You can miss out on hundreds of dollars' worth of sales by allowing your customers to undercut you like this. Worse — your state might declare you liable for collecting and handing over the sales tax on the items they sell.

▷ **Damage.** Accidents happen. Your tables and chairs suffer damage and have to be replaced. People bringing in large armies or boxes of books might knock over shelves on their way to the game room.

▷ **Liability.** No matter how many times you tell kids not to lean back in their chairs, some do. The adults can be worse. The person that falls and injures himself will sue you, of course, not himself. Even if you win the case in court, defending against a lawsuit could easily cost the difference between profit and a loss. Then your insurance premium increases, too — if the company doesn't drop you.

▷ **Babysitting.** Once parents "get" the concept of a game room, some of them try to use your store as a day-care service. They drop off kids and come back at close. You are expected to entertain some kid who might not have any money. At closing time, you might still have kids whose parents had to work late, forgot, or had car trouble.

▷ **Spreading the Discount News.** You work hard to gain or create new customers. You sell them a starter and some accessories and spark their excitement about a new game. Then one of those customers that usually hangs out at another shop comes in and starts telling people about the cool place online where he buys at 40% off, or down the road for 20% off. Store owners who dislike game rooms often cite this reason as their primary reason for not maintaining one.

THE ARGUMENT FOR

The argument in favor of having a game space is simple. Gaming space increases sales. Nobody questions this fact. Retailers disagree on *how much* it increases sales.

One factor is the social element. If you have a group of friendly, likeable people playing a game at a table, and they're having fun, people will be curious about it. A charismatic personality can pull customers to whatever game he plays.

In this way, games grow.

Here is a fact about the gaming industry: games sell when people play them. If you are not already involved with the industry, you might not realize how much of an impact game play has on sales.

A certain percentage of customers buy things for completeness. A gamer might have all of the existing books for an RPG, so when the new one comes out, he wants it, regardless of whether he's going to use it. Some gamers follow their favorite artist, buying whatever book his work appears in, or whichever card game he paints cards for. Many people buy a game with the intention of playing it, but they never make time or never find the right group to play with. All of these customers contribute incrementally to your sales total.

But when a group of people *plays* a game, magic happens.

Among lapsed role-players, 63% cite "too few people to play with" as their main reason for leaving the hobby. If you could provide everybody that wants to play a D&D game with a game, you would increase your role-playing customer retention by an enormous amount right away, greatly increasing the value of each new and existing customer you bring into the door.

I have seen a dead CCG, years out of print, explode onto the shelves. The store owner played it for several hours every day, gave it premier positioning within the store, and taught 15 people how to play. As long as it was in stock, it outsold Magic. Thirty booster boxes sold within a month at a time when the hottest game in the country was selling 6-8 boxes a month in the same store.

While the business owner has a greater impact than most customers have, the anecdote points out a well-known paradigm. Regular play, a willingness to teach, an availability of product, and a network of gamers combine to generate initial sales. Strong game design encourages player longevity, but customer retention is due to your customer service skills, your ability to stock the things the customer needs, and your ability to inform the customer of those products.

Naturally, the hours that you can spend teaching people new games are limited. You have orders to place, shipments to receive, phones to answer, and people to check out at the register. If you have a game room, you have customers that act as a sales staff, teaching new players how to play. Gamers love to introduce new people to their hobby.

Events encourage game play. Events include tournaments, a weekly league game, scheduled demos, painting clinics, contests, in-store auctions, panels, and anything else that you can think of that justifies bringing two or more people face-to-face.

For maximum effect, you want regularity. Urge people to commit to the same day every week. If you have people playing a card game every Saturday, it is easy to encourage them to join a game on that day. If you tell a customer on Tuesday that Saturday a game will be played, you'll lose that customer's trust if that regular Saturday group doesn't meet that day. Obviously, if you can arrange for two groups to play on different days, the impact is stronger. Maybe the curious customer cannot make it on Saturday, but he can swing by with the kids after church on Sunday.

When a game is omnipresent, it reaches that critical mass that provides very strong sales support. If someone is available at any given time to introduce the game to a new customer, your ability to convert customers increases. At this level of popularity, you have enough players for tournaments to go off consistently. Departing players that might force a regular group to collapse because they fail to meet a minimum necessary for play are replaced by new gamers.

DEALING WITH THE PROBLEMS

If you've decided that you like the advantages that maintaining gaming space offers, you have to manage the issues that accompany it. Instead of addressing each item one by one, we'll lump them together so that it's easier to handle. The two major issues are customer behavior and cleanliness.

Customer Behavior

Cheating, cursing, arguing, and otherwise being disruptive creates an undesirable atmosphere at your store. Post your game room policies where people using the space can clearly see them. Besides supporting you and your staff, the sign sends a reinforcing message to customers that your store is a friendly environment for themselves or for their children.

Make sure that you and your staff deal with these issues

consistently and even-handedly. You can't play favorites. If it's important enough for you to make it a rule, then enforce your rules. If it's not important enough to enforce every time, don't make it a rule.

Cleanliness

A "no outside food" policy removes a great deal of the trash. Post this notice with your other rules, and make sure it includes your employees as well, or you will send a contradictory message to your customers. My personal point of view is that whenever you have people, you will have to clean up some trash. Learn to associate this chore with sales. Picking up a mess at the end of the night means the game room was full all day.

In business terms, the labor cost of picking up that trash is no more than $2 per day. You know the game room generated more than two dollars in profit if you have to spend 10 minutes picking up trash.

STORE LAYOUT

Designing a store layout is another job of finding a place for two opposing needs to come together. One need is to pack as much stuff as you can into your store so that you can sell it. The other is the need to have comfortably wide walkways, visibility of product and interesting display areas, so that your store will be attractive and appealing to your customers.

Understanding how to plan your store layout involves knowing how customers react to different situations.

Upon entering your store, they're still slowing down from their brisk outdoor pace, and they do not usually slow down enough to observe anything in their immediate area. It takes about 10 feet for them to adjust. This *decompression zone* is a worthless area in your store for displays because customers blow right past it.

Once inside the decompression zone, they come face to face with your *strike zone*. This area is the first thing they notice, and it's a prime piece of your store's real estate. At this point, the customer is trying to identify what your store is like. It's a good place for small price-point board & family card games or a New Release shelf. Avoid placing high-ticket items like Limited Edition releases here, because customers are very sticker-sensitive about the first thing they see. It sets the tone for your store, and if that tone is "I cannot afford anything here", you probably failed to create the first impression you intended.

Customers tend to veer to the right after entry. How fast they walk depends on what they see. If they see rows and rows of identical items, they speed up. If they see something that makes them stop for a moment, they slow down and read it. They don't look up or down much. Their eyes are fixed at roughly head and chest level. Children look at their eye levels and stuff they can easily reach, which includes things on the ground.

Unfortunately, other considerations often keep game stores from realizing the full potential of this trend. Cost and the desire to keep product visible to the staff at all times (to prevent shoplifting) keep shelves short. If you can solve those problems and use gondolas or shelves that extend up to six feet high instead of four feet high, you will make much more use out of your very finite square-footage. If you can fit 50% more product into the same size store as the competitor down the road, you have a definite advantage.

Shelves don't need to be much higher than that six-foot mark because customers do not like to reach high. They rarely ask for help if they can't reach something, no matter how attentive your sales staff. Plan on somebody 5' tall being able to reach your highest product. Avoid storing heavy product there, like large box sets for miniatures. You don't want it to fall on anybody.

Your aisles need to be wide enough that people can pass by each other freely. They need to be wide enough to accommodate wheelchairs, in accordance with the Americans with Disabilities Act. Beyond that, they should be suitable for the traffic you expect, too. That right-hand aisle next to the wall might be twice as wide as the center aisle where you see the least foot traffic.

In his book *Why We Buy*, author Paco Underhill uses the term "the butt-brush factor" to describe the opposition that people — especially women — have to being bumped by other people while they're shopping. Somebody might ignore it the first time, but that person might become annoyed by a second incident and leave in disgust after a third. Wide aisles increase sales.

Keep this trend in mind when you place your displays and endcaps. If you make a great display that people stop to look at, make sure it doesn't clot up traffic. If it does, move it or rearrange some shelves to give it more room. Avoid placing displays too close together for this reason.

Game Room Design

After your cash wrap, the second major factor in your store design is the game room. Whether it features two tables or twenty, you need to put it where it will do the most good and the least harm. In theory, you want to place your game room where shoppers can see all the activity going on, hear a bit of excitement and become interested in what's going on at those tables.

Contrasting that goal is the need to keep the game room somewhat separate from the merchandise, lest you slowly lose your inventory to book bags and backpacks in the gaming area. You also don't want chairs backing into displays or shoppers, drinks spilling into the same, or customers picking up unattended gamer gear with the intent to buy.

You could separate the game space by having it in a different room. A full wall limits noise to a tolerable level, creates a substantial barrier to product walking off into the game room, and provides more wall space on which to store product. It also keeps you from being able to control what goes on in the game room and retards some of that cross-promoting you hope the game room will accomplish.

A wall about 4 feet high creates a clear border between the game room and the product. It allows customers to see what's going on, although they still have to pass into a clearly different area to reach it. The partial wall also creates a single point in space for staff to watch, so product is still not likely to sneak into the game room.

Glass or Lexan offers a nearly-perfect compromise. You can still monitor activities in the game room, and customers can still see gaming activity. The wall muffles the noise, and product stays on the side it belongs. Naturally, it costs the most of any of these options — although not much more than the price of a full wall.

Any kind of permanent wall has one disadvantage to it. It limits your ability to rearrange the store. If you want to reduce or expand your game space, you have to undertake fairly major construction. This construction might include mandatory electrical outlets, approval from a landlord, or permits.

Cubicle dividers, designed for creating inexpensive office areas, are one option for having privacy without a permanent commitment to a floor plan. They're also fairly effective at reducing sound. The total cost to cover 20 feet of a 24' wide store is about $800.

Clever use of one or more freestanding displays can make a virtual wall. If you have shelves that are flat on one side, as if meant to rest against a wall, you could place several of them side-by-side to create your barrier. Leave your opening in line with one of the aisles created by your shelves and let you customers pass straight through.

You can create the illusion of a separate area with different flooring, wall coverings and possibly lighting. Using a different color of carpet, and a different wallpaper or paint color, you could identify where the retail area stops and the game room starts without having to resort to a physical barrier. In many ways, this option gives all the disadvantages with none of the advantages. Product off the shelves can still wander into your game room, and browsing customers still get the full measure of noise.

A large, relatively open area could separate the two, offering some measure of protection. If you operate a LAN, your bank of PCs or console games could make a perfect barrier that requires nothing else. Your shelves simply end and the LAN bank appears several feet later, allowing room for gamers to move to a seat comfortably. Several feet on the other side, the gaming tables begin. Access to the game room is to the sides of the LAN. The open space above the seated LAN players allows customers to see activity in the gaming room, while the distance diminishes any noise somewhat.

Many stores that have grown over the years wind up with two adjacent suites in their shopping center. They identify one as the game room and the other as the sales area, with a door between the two suites. This option, while expensive, is easy to manage and provides people walking by the store with a very nice view of the activity in the game room. In most cases, the game room exterior door stays locked, allowing the store to control traffic into the game room.

FIXTURES

You can't pile up your entire product selection in a stack on the floor. You have to have some place to put it. This section will help you decide what you need to buy in order to sell your product.

The cost of fixtures is highly variable. Before you spend your money on fixtures, decide roughly what you are going to put where. You do not need to map out every item in the store, but you should know which piece will hold miniatures and which will hold other items. None of these fixtures (except metal gondolas) is designed for great weight. If you intend to put books on them, you need to find a way to support them beyond the suggested methods.

WALL FIXTURES

To get display use out of store walls, you need to add some kind of fixtures for hanging shelves and pegs. The most popular wall shelving options are slatwall, gridwall, and pegboard. Each has its own advantages and different game store owners have their preference.

Slatwall is grooved MDF paneling. It's probably the most attractive shelving option you will have for your store. It's also the most expensive. Slatwall costs $30 to $60 per 4' by 8' sheet.

Gridwall is wire shelving that runs about three-quarters the price of slatwall. It's more versatile than slatwall, being available in frames that you can move into various shapes; you could create interior "walls" within your store with it, while maintaining a level of transparency. On the other hand, many store owners dislike the look.

Pegboard is cheap fiberboard. It's commonly used to hang tools in a garage. It's a few bucks a sheet, making it an attractive option for new stores. You can paint it to improve its appearance. Paint will not add to its durability, however, and you will have a bit of wasted space where you attach it to the wall. It's better than slatwall in that you have more options for adjusting vertical height of your pegs and other fixtures.

When you are opening your store is a good time to consider going with slatwall over pegboard for the bulk of your fixtures. The enhancement to your image is substantial, and it's probably the time in your business when you will have the most funds available to you for this consideration. You could change it over later, or incrementally as cash allows, but with an initial cash layout of $900 to $1,300 difference, why be cheap? That's only a few percentage points of your initial budget, and the difference in your store's image — not to mention improved durability and resale value should you sell — makes the more expensive option far more attractive in this case.

In the case of any of these options, you will also need some form of pegs, shelves and other display accessories on which to place your product. The fixtures cost about the same regardless of which wall covering you use; in many cases, they are the exact same fixtures.

Fixtures	Estimated Cost for a 1,000 sf store*
Slatwall	$1,400-$1,600
Gridwall	$1,000-$1,200
Pegboard	$300-$500

Assuming a total of 80 linear feet of display space.

GONDOLAS

Gondola displays run approximately $100 to $240 per section, depending on height and width, before adding the cost of shelves (shelves tend to cost about $10 each). Thus, two rows running 20' through the center of your store, each with two gondola units back-to-back might cost $3,200 to $5,600, plus shipping.

Gondolas combine some of the best features of wall-mounted pegboard with freestanding displays. They are versatile, capable of holding some books, miniatures, board games, or any type of product. In all likelihood, you'll want to use gondolas as the basis for your interior shelving choice.

71

If you do create aisles in your store with lanes of gondolas, consider placing an end-cap piece at each end of the aisle. Endcaps are high-visibility placement; products on endcaps tend to sell better than products in the middle.

Book Shelves

You can make your own shelves out of bricks and planks of wood for virtually nothing. If that's the kind of image you want in your store, you could make it work. Most likely, you want to build or purchase or build better-quality fixtures.

Bookshelves excel at one thing: displaying books. Depending on design, they might also present your board games favorably. As mentioned above, estimate how many you'll need based on how many role-playing game products you expect to carry.

One thing to consider with making your own bookshelves is *casters*. Having a bookshelf you can wheel around the store makes layout changes a breeze, while the weight of the books keeps the shelves from moving around accidentally. Casters are also safe: instead of toppling over on a baby carriage when two teenagers on the other side of the shelf start playing around, the shelf might slide over a few inches.

Wire Bins

Bins don't see much use in game stores, but they can be useful if you have the right product mix. Bins are great for plushes and other toys that won't be damaged by being thrown on top of each other. If you intend to carry Toy Vault's plush product line, for example, a bin offers a way to display them. It's also very easy to move around: you could leave it with the RPGs for a couple of weeks, move it by the cash-wrap, or place it near the front door, experimenting to find the best place for sales. Most of them also fold up to fit in a closet or other small space when not in use.

Miscellaneous Freestanding Fixtures

Freestanding pieces are available in several shapes: pinwheel displays, H-fixtures, triangle sections, square sections, etc. These pieces are best used as highlight pieces. Use them to bring attention to a product you want to promote or for odd-shaped items that don't fit well on your standard shelves.

These fixtures typically cost $200 to $300, plus up to $100 for shelves and fixtures.

The Cash-Wrap

A cash-wrap is the checkout point of your store; it's the place where the cash register or POS is located, and the place where the customer can often find the sales associate. It's the focal point of the store, and as such, it deserves special mention.

Think of the features of the cash-wrap. Every customer that makes a purchase in your store goes there. It's the only place in the store that has this trait. D&D players might go to the left, while Warhammer 40k players might go to the right, depending on the store's layout. Magic players might skip the front altogether, heading straight for the tournament in the game room.

Customers spend time there. Not that they want to! In fact, one of the best ways to lose customers is to make them spend a long time waiting to check out. But it's a fact of life that the process of scanning or ringing up an item takes at least a few seconds, and making change or swiping a card takes a few moments also.

The cash-wrap might hold unique products hidden behind its walls. If you operate a LAN, you might keep the games you offer on your machines behind the counter so they don't walk off. High-price CCG singles are almost certainly not easy-access items and they stay out of reach. In any case, this close supervision requires that a clerk be available to hand the items out as necessary. That means sometimes frequent visits to the cash-wrap by the same customer, or one long visit by the customer.

These factors combine to make the cash-wrap a prime piece of retail real estate. It's a great place to hang signs and stock impulse items. Small items of a low price point sell well here because of their exposure.

Second-Hand Fixtures

You can save money by buying fixtures second-hand. Retail stores are always closing, and they want to sell their fixtures to help pay their outstanding debts. Check the newspaper, Internet auctions, and watch the roadside as you drive through town for places that are going out of business.

Cities often have auctions hosted by financial institutions that have taken possession of a property in bankruptcy. Check your local papers or financial institution newsletters for these events. The auction terms are usually "cash only", so come prepared.

If you find something useful, figure out how much it would

cost you new using the guidelines above. Ask how much they'd like for some of the fixtures you don't want. The number might be surprisingly low. If so, ask about the items you really want. If the number is not low, you might include an offer for the whole batch, including some items you need. The larger price should have a reduction for taking the whole batch. Then offer a lesser price for the items you want after you get a smaller per-item price. Don't forget to account for transportation, because they probably won't arrange to ship you the items.

One issue with these second-hand fixtures is that you don't have total control of the design of your store. A hodge-podge of gathered second-hand fixtures might work against your efforts to establish your brand. You might want slatwall, but suppose you find $2,000 worth of gridwall for an unbeatable price? Maybe you can compromise. Don't use all of the gridwall. Use it for a section for an odd wall and try to resell the rest. Or use it, but tell yourself that you will replace it in two years. That initial savings at opening might allow you to experiment with 10 different CCGs, or pay for 10 weeks of part-time labor, or buy a week's worth of cable TV ads.

Be aware of brand names when snatching up second-hand fixtures: the shelves you buy cheap at one place might not be compatible with the fixtures you picked up somewhere else.

Don't forget the value of paint in establishing your brand. A consistent color scheme that matches your uniforms and signage can help improve the utility of these less-desirable fixtures. A quick coat of paint also conceals blemishes in second-hand furniture.

Necessary Equipment for Your Store
Besides shelves and games, you need some things to help make your business work. These items are necessary regardless of your product mix, location, or business model.

Computer
Not counting a POS system, you use a computer to make signs, keep track of sales records, read Internet forums, communicate with manufacturers, look up product when your customer only knows part of a name, and so much more.

Fax Machine
You might be able to slide without one for the first year or so,

but the times when they come in handy increase as your volume increases. Increasingly, you can find a fax machine available as part of a single printer/copier/fax unit. You might also use software to duplicate the function of a fax machine.

Telephones

You need at least one phone and probably two or more lines. Your credit card processor might require its own line. Ditto if you have a fax.

OPTIONAL EQUIPMENT FOR YOUR STORE

Consider each of these items and their impact on your operations and customer service when you set your initial budget. Some of these items are relatively expensive, and pursuing the options willy-nilly without looking at the larger picture can bankrupt you. While nicer, cooler stuff can be gratifying, you have to measure their value and pace their purchase out so that acquiring them does not threaten your cash flow.

Security System

While a camera is expensive, it has some minor ability to deter shoplifting and employee theft. More likely, it can help you prosecute thieves that you catch. Digital cameras can hook straight up to your PC. You could set up a camera to your game room and send the feed to your website. Visitors to your website can see activity in the game room from home.

Similarly, you can set it up so that you can monitor your store live from home. You can monitor employee productivity, customer behavior in the game room, and other store activity while you are not there. You can tell if there's a disaster like a robbery or a medical emergency when a lone employee is on staff.

A four-cameras system runs $500 to $1,000 for a usable system. High-tech systems that pan, tilt and zoom, and other pricey options could cost up to $4,000.

You gain more benefit from a security system if:
▷ You have employees run most of your shifts
▷ You see regular unexplained inventory discrepancies
▷ You have blind spots in your store layout

Shrink-Wrap Machine

For $300 or less, you can offer your customers a convenient service that few other stores currently offer. You can allow them to examine a board game or other shrink-wrapped product. The customer appreciation for this service is huge. It increases your ability to close a sale on board games. At an average price of over $40 for a board game, the shrink-wrap machine pays for itself quickly. If the customer turns the game down, wrap it right back up and it is as good as new. You can also use it to re-cover shrink-wrap that was damaged in shipping.

Depending on your policies and product selection, you might also wish to shrink-wrap certain product aimed toward adult audiences.

If you sell used board games, you can also wrap those to prevent further wear or the loss of loose components.

Lastly, you can use the machine to bundle products together for special promotion. One successful example included offering a free adventure with a purchase of the Dungeon Master's Guide. Goodman Games offered a $2 adventure ($1.30 or so at cost) that was perfect for such promotional use by retailers. Because the perceived value of "an adventure" is about $10-12, you could offer an attractive bundle for minimal cost.

A shrink-wrap machine has one use which I recommend you avoid. Certain collectible items sell for higher prices when in their original shrink wrap. Wrapping these products to increase their perceived value is fraudulent, and skilled collectors can detect it. While the extra money might sound nice, the blow to your credibility will be much more costly. Don't do it.

Shopping Baskets

Baskets encourage people to buy more things. People feel awkward if they pick up a basket and then carry around one item in it. They think they look dumb for picking up a basket for such a small purpose. So they add something else to it.

On the other hand, customers refuse to buy more than they can carry in one trip. Give them something that increases how much they can carry, and you increase your sales. You can get a stack of baskets and a sign for about $120. You should be able to make that up in Reaper miniatures sales alone. If you increase your average Reaper sale by one blister pack every two weeks, the shopping baskets earn their keep every 10 months.

Door Chime

If you have a security system, it should come with a door chime. If not, you can buy one at places like Radio Shack for about $30. While you ideally want staff alert enough to realize that a customer is coming in or leaving, the chime is a great reminder.

It also makes everyone in the store look up to see who's coming in. The clerk at the counter perks up automatically due to his training. Your RPG group at the back table wants to know if it's their late player. The card players are hoping it's somebody with a trade binder. Your demo volunteer will look for a new person for his game. All of this attention makes potential robbers and shoplifters uncomfortable.

Price Gun

The price gun should almost be listed under the necessary equipment list. It appears here because if you use a POS system with a bar-code printer, you might not need it. You do need some method of pricing your product, because customers strongly dislike having to look for a price.

Price guns run $60 to $200, although you won't need one of the high-end price guns for a game store. They primarily include more lines of information. The price tags themselves cost about $5 per roll, or a bit higher if you want them personalized with your store name.

Another option, especially if you use commercial shelving like Lozier, is the use of shelf chips. Shelf chips are those plastic things that slide into the edge of the shelves. You stick a price tag directly on them and place it in front of the product on the shelf. This option makes it easier to change an item's price and keeps adhesive off the product's cover.

Interior Signage

Your signage inside your store should always be professionally prepared. Nothing says "low standards" faster than a hand-written sign in an inappropriate place. Using something like a chalkboard to announce daily specials might be great for a restaurant or for announcing what's being played in the game room, but it shouldn't advertise your dice prices.

Your local office supply store carries a selection of plastic sign holders that you can arrange around the store as needed for a few dollars each.

Shelf Talkers

Shelf-talkers are the tags that stick out perpendicular from a shelf, allowing customers to read them as they walk down your aisle. You can use them to separate product lines. For instance, identify the D&D, the Star Wars RPG, the Conan RPG, etc. You can also use them to identify periodic specials, new product, or clearance product.

Department Signs

Department signs help define the areas of your store. You can adhere these to the wall with double-sided stickers or hang them from the ceiling with fishing line or wire. Helping customers locate what they're looking for generates more sales; if a customer can't find what he wants, he's more likely to leave than to ask a clerk.

Corrugated plastic one-color signs are effective and inexpensive. Depending on size and color, you can expect to spend $20 to $50 per sign. You could buy a half-dozen signs individually or you can ask whoever makes your store sign to throw them in at no charge when you negotiate for your outdoor signage. If the purchase is large enough, and the sale is dependent on it, you might get it.

Bulletin Board

If you have a game room or present your store as a place to meet other games some sort of bulletin board is almost a necessity. Your customers can use it to announce their desire to find other gamers. For best professionalism, use a standard form that you keep nearby. You could keep the board under glass and only allow staff to access it; this option gives you the greatest control over what goes on the board.

Odd places: One good place that often goes unused is the counter area. You can cover your sales area with manufacturer advertisements, pre-order sheets, store specials, and other information. Place a cut-to-fit piece of clear plastic over the top to protect it. Customers can see your information, but it's safe from spills and wear. You could do the same with your gaming tables, especially if you have them custom-made that way from the beginning.

POS System

Most successful game retailers rely on their Point-of-Sale system. It's an important tool they use in that most important of skills, inventory management. If it helps you reduce your annual inventory cost by 1% per year, then it pays for itself over and over again.

For full disclosure, at least one highly successful retailer argues that a POS system is not necessary, that it is in fact an unnecessary cost — especially for smaller or newer companies. You can duplicate its functions with good record-keeping, and many retailers that own it fail to utilize it to full extent anyway. Merely having a POS does not improve your inventory control. You must use it and use it properly.

You will find that with a POS system, your orders take longer to receive and shelve. You might spend all day handling a large order, especially one with a large amount of new inventory. You also need to correct your POS periodically, because errors creep in no matter how careful you are.

To be effective, the software needs a bar code scanner, a PC-operated cash drawer, and a thermal or ink-jet bar code printer. These items are usually independent of the software and cost about the same regardless of which system you purchase.

SUMMARY: POS SYSTEMS

- Cash Register Express
- COM-TRAC Plus/POS
- EZPOS
- Microsoft Point of Sale
- Microsoft Retail Management System
- QuickBooks POS
- RegistWARE
- CAM Commerce Solutions RetailICE (Free)
- DynaSCAN The Retail Assistant

CHAPTER 3:
COMPETITIVE ANALYSIS

Your company doesn't exist by itself. Other companies sell the same products you do. Sometimes, their business model is so different, their locations so distant, and their customers so distinct as to have no overlap at all.

At other times, competition opens a mile down the road and specifically targets your customers for their initial growth rate. That makes for very clear, direct competition that you can't ignore. You want to act rather than react.

You can act like you're ignoring it. Refusing to call other game retailers competition is an excellent way to reinforce your image as an industry leader. Games Workshop excels at this: they refer to their customers engaging in "The Games Workshop hobby" instead of the "miniatures hobby" or "the gaming hobby."

BIG-BOX RETAILERS

The big-box stores like Wal-Mart, Target, and Toys R Us operate in an entirely different fashion from independent game stores. They purchase their products by the tens or hundreds of thousands, often months in advance, at prices near production cost. They compete by having enormous selection of products to attract customers to their stores.

The main attractions of big box stores are ease of purchase and price. Because the customer is already there for something else, if he was thinking about buying the D&D box set, he might as well throw it in the basket while he's at Toys R Us. Maybe the customer saw latest Risk variation at his local game store for $45. Because it's here for $22, he can buy it on impulse.

You can't compete against these places on price. Sometimes they sell products cheaper than you can get them through distribution. It's a rare customer that pays twice as much for a game from you when he can get it cheaper than you can.

Your edge against this category lies in your product knowledge and in being the one place to shop to buy everything hobby-related. You must back up the claim. If you want the latest child-targeted CCG sales, you might support your claim with a large selection of back stock, sleeves, binders, and everything else that player might want, all within easy reach. Singles sales, while they might require a great deal of work, are one market in which big-box retailers are not likely to enter.

To reinforce the claim of customer knowledge, invest some time in learning and teaching games to your employees. Once each week or so, break open a game and play it. Better yet, require an employee to learn it ahead of time and teach it to the other employees. You can practice sales and demo techniques on each other at the same time.

GAMES WORKSHOP

Games Workshop places its stores in malls and other high-rent, high-traffic locations to take advantage of the enormous number of customers that come through their doors. Their business model is based around increasing their conversion rate as high as possible and making that initial sale to customers.

The advantage to them is obvious. That average initial sale exceeds $100. At that rate, they need to capture a handful of new sales per day out of all of the teeming thousands of bodies in the mall. Games Workshop benefits by the direct marketing opportunities these new customers open up.

If you don't sell Games Workshop, a nearby store has little impact on you. If you do, it's both a blessing and a curse. It's a curse because the store reaches far more potential customers than you ever could, and a blessing because you can capture some of those customers by running tournaments and other events in your game space — game space that the Games Workshop stores don't generally have. If you offer a wider line of terrain pieces, use that to your advantage.

Variety is again in your court. Perhaps you offer three different paint lines. Veteran painters love paints in the dropper bottles instead of the paint jars that GW uses. As long as you match or almost match Games Workshop's inventory standard, any additional options you offer give customers a reason to shop at your store.

INTERNET SELLERS

The Internet offers customers a long list of advantages that you can't match. The customer is free to shop at any time of the day or night, doesn't need to interact with sales staff, never needs to leave the house and can shop while working in another window. A good website has images of its products and more product information than you could teach even the best sales person.

Your customers and Internet customers represent two groups of gamers. The two groups do overlap. Some customers go to the Internet to make up for deficiencies in your inventory or slow turn-around time on your special orders. Others prefer the real or imagined price advantage of shopping on the Internet.

Very few customers originate through online sales. People simply do not browse Amazon.com or eBay, read a review of the D&D Player's Handbook and start role-playing. They play because of personal contact with a friend or because they were introduced to it at a game store.

That tendency means that very few of those Internet customers started out as Internet customers. They were retail customers that somebody lost along the way. It might have been you, or it might have been a previous owner of the store you bought, or it might have been somebody years ago. You have to re-earn that customer's business.

If you begin to lose a customer to online sales, don't complain to the customer about it. He doesn't owe you anything. He's not obligated to purchase from you. Telling him that game stores will close if all of their customers go to the Internet won't change his buying habits, no matter how true.

Instead, compete on customer service and value. If he connected with his current game group through your store, point that out. If he plays in your game room, point out that you provide that game room at your own expense.

A consistent message as part of your larger marketing plan is the best way to compete against the Internet. Your weekly newsletter might announce a game at a certain price, "plus free shipping (if you pick it up)." This humorous line reminds customers of a hidden cost involved with online sales.

Maintaining a wide product selection is an expensive method of combating Internet sales, but it pays off. One of the main reasons customers cite for making purchases online is that they "can't find it locally."

Another main reason for losing sales to other sources is that the customer doesn't feel appreciated. You can make the customer feel appreciated by:

▷ Simply saying "Thank you" at the point of sale.
▷ Learning the customer's name.
▷ Offering occasional promotions or sales.
▷ Demonstrating over-the-top service when the customer makes a special order.

▷ Offering customers premium or promo items you receive from manufacturers.

▷ Offering the customer a free tournament entry, LAN time, or a small gift for bringing in a friend.

OTHER LOCAL INDEPENDENTS

These businesses operate stores like yours. As such, I prefer to call them "neighboring stores" rather than "competition." They face the same challenges you do and benefit or suffer from the same market changes.

It is true that this other businesses are competing for the exact same market demographic, but that demographic is very local. As long as your stores are a comfortable distance apart, the actual competition for the same customers is slight.

Competitors beyond a certain range are not a threat at all. In an urban area, a store 10 miles away is drawing no more than a handful of your customers. You have no business reason not to cooperate with that store whenever possible.

Other game retailers are a boon: a city of 1 million with 6 game stores is healthier than one with a single store. Think about it this way: if you advertise on cable TV, wouldn't you prefer a market of 7,200 existing gamers to a market of 1,200 existing gamers? Of course you would. Even if the result is that some of those customers go to your competition because of your ad, the sales gain you'll see from that ad is far greater than a sales gain you'd see in a market with fewer existing gamers.

It works the other way, too. If your competitors advertise a new game, your own customers might call or visit to find out if you're carrying it, too. Both locations win.

Preferably, you'll find ways to work with these businesses rather than against them. You might propose a marketing co-op, in which you work to create a general "gaming" commercial, and which identifies each store at the closing tag. You might have rivalry tournaments, with customers fighting for the prestige of their favorite store. Report any gaming theft you hear about to the other stores in case the thief tries to sell the goods there; in turn, you might recover any goods stolen from your store.

Good ways to establish these relationships include referring customers who call from a location near another store, or who ask about a product you don't carry. You might offer to match employee discounts for other stores, or at least offer a token discount to other store employees.

If you find yourself competing with these stores because of an uncomfortable proximity, try to compete on your strengths. If you offer unique product, market that. If you have the largest game space, use that to your advantage. Look for any product or service that you offer that other independent retailers don't have or have in smaller quantity.

Maintain professionalism at all times. Don't allow your employees or customers to trash-talk other stores. Even an otherwise loyal customer might mention the comment to somebody else, and your credibility will suffer.

BRICK & MORTAR DISCOUNTERS

This segment of the competition shares many things in common with the section above, because they are a subset of those businesses. In this case, however, the discounter establishes low price as a major marketing point, and the business is positioned to take advantage of that.

Sometimes.

Often, the discounter simply hasn't done the math and fails to realize the disastrous impact that low across-the-board prices have on his bottom line. A large percentage of these stores close within a year, about the time a healthy business should be reaching a self-sustaining sales level. In the meantime, they have taken some of your customers away and spoiled those customers on paying retail price.

In some cases, the business is run by a trained businessperson who thinks that his marketing strategy can create the number of customers needed to make the business model work. Taking customers from existing businesses might be a part of this company's strategy. Creating new customers through television or radio advertising might also be part of the plan.

Discounters usually thrive on the high-turn products like CCGs and sometimes Games Workshop. They avoid RPGs, board games and other products. If you have a diverse product mix, you can often afford to lose a few of your more price-conscious customers to the discounter. Remember that the overlap between game categories is not great; losing a CCG customer doesn't mean that you'll also lose an RPG customer. That customer might continue to buy his role-playing products from you and buy some or all of his CCGs from the discounter.

Occasionally, you might be near a discounter who has found

a way to make the model work. Perhaps he offers deep discounts on *Magic* booster packs and makes substantial margins on Magic singles, which also provide the majority of his revenues. This competitor will take your intermediate and veteran players away from you. The majority of your *Magic* sales will be from Magic players that you create through demos or that your advertising reaches first.

In any case, the answer is to compete on your strengths. If a discounter relies on Magic, you could sell 10 CCGs that aren't *Magic*. You could display your CCGs prominently, possibly using slanted shelves to display a larger surface for each box, intending to awe customers with your selection. Be content to let CCGs be a smaller percentage of your overall sales and concentrate on the lines that are profitable for you instead.

Also, minimize your losses. You'll lose more box sales to the discounter than you will booster pack sales. Saving $.60 on three packs might not be worth the drive, but saving $40 on a box is worth a trip across town. Instead of reducing your revenues by lowering your ticket prices, you might add more products: anyone ordering a booster box at your normal price receives a fat pack and a box of binder pages at no charge. See the section on Bundled Items for more suggestions along that line.

Chapter 4:
Products and Services

Game stores tend to have a certain core product selection in common. They carry *Dungeons & Dragons*. They carry *Magic: The Gathering*. If they carry miniatures, they carry at least a partial selection of Games Workshop. They carry one or more secondary products in each of the categories that follow those product leaders. They carry a selection of accessory items for those categories. Most stores carry a selection of board or non-collectible card games. You can compete against big-box stores, very specialized stores like "card shops," or bookstores with this generic product selection. However, if you wish to compete against other independent game stores, you need to offer something else. Ask yourself "Why would a customer shop in my store instead of some other place?" The answer to that question is one of your competitive edges.

Product Lines to Carry

Each of these product lines is prevalent in the gaming industry to one degree or another. They are listed in very general order of prevalence, but do not let the order of this list dictate what products you carry. Review each to see if its advantages fit the needs of your store. In some cases, store growth and maturity might be deciding factors in how a product line fits your needs.

After each discussion, you will see a Minimum Level of Investment and a Recommended Level of Investment. These dollar amounts are how much it would cost for (MLI) a barebones selection of the product, such as a new store might carry, or a 2-3 year old store might add as an experiment or (for RLI) how much it might cost to purchase a representative inventory that allows for more substantial growth and fits the needs of a larger store. A well-developed store with full selection might carry triple the RLI or more. Smaller stores might jump straight to the RLI if preliminary market research indicates a strong demand for these products. These numbers will help you determine your initial inventory needed for opening, expanding the selection of a business you intend to purchase, or adding product lines to your store as you grow.

Collectible Card Games

If you open a game store, it's almost certain that you will carry a selection of CCGs, even if it's only *Magic* or the latest hot anime game. CCGs have several advantages that make them very attractive products. If your store does not focus on them, they're an easy way to add volume without much cost.

For starters, CCGs require a small footprint. You can fit a starter and booster of *Magic* in about a single square foot of display space. That alone could easily generate $3,500 per year (see the Square Foot Analysis on page 14 for a comparison).

Secondly, CCGs are excellent generators of add-on sales. For every dollar a customer spends on CCGs, he spends $.10 to $.15 on accessories like sleeves, dice, counters, and card boxes. You can often far exceed your normal CCG margins on these items. Card sleeves can reach 60% margin instead of the normal 47% or so you get from selling most CCGs at SRP. Glass counters can likewise reach pleasing profit margins.

Third, the collectible nature of CCGs means that customers continue to buy them beyond the point where they "need" to. A customer looking to finish off a collection might buy another dozen boosters trying to get that last card. He's more likely to buy that last card, though, if you offer singles for sale.

MLI (*Magic* only): $300
RLI (*Magic* only): $900

MLI (a selection): $600
RLI (a selection): $2,500

CCG Singles

CCG Singles are another product line that many stores are avoiding because of Internet competition. That means it's an opportunity for you to make your store unique. Offering a product that your competitors lack nearly always works to your advantage.

The advantage of CCG singles is in their margin, as with most second-hand merchandise. You will often sell singles at an 80% margin or higher. In the worst-case scenario, these products at least match your average margin across all of your products. Only in the case of very high-priced singles do margins decrease.

That said, you must be prepared to deal with the difficulties of CCG singles to reap the benefits. They take up space. As always, you have to compare the value of the space they take up with alternative products. However, the space they take up is small. Like booster packs, the dollar yield per square foot is very high. CCG singles do require very detailed product knowledge to manage effectively. Good software can help mitigate this and share knowledge among all of your employees. Lone Wolf Development's Card Vault is a great tool for managing your singles sales. It's also a great item to sell in your store, and Lone Wolf offers a free copy for store use. A simple spreadsheet can do the same thing.

Time is an issue because it affects your labor cost. It's possible that a full-time employee can spend nearly all of his time comparing prices to other locations and adjusting your prices. Your very competitive players probably know far more about your prices than you do. Many stores use a standard price from an online retailer and then adjust for their specific market accordingly. In areas where CCGs are popular, the tournament atmosphere competitive, and trade is active, sale prices are higher.

Competing with online stores that offer low prices is an issue. Remind your customers that they do not have to pay shipping when they buy from you, nor do they have to wait a week to receive their product, and that they can inspect the card before they pay for it. You will find that a lack of availability will cost you more sales than you lose due to price.

MLI (*Magic* only): $300
RLI (*Magic* only): $1,000

MLI (a selection): $800
RLI (a selection): $2,500

ROLEPLAYING GAMES

Roleplaying games offer upsell opportunities by requiring dice, being more graphically exciting with the use of miniatures, and being easier to play with the use of a vinyl battlemat. Players tend to buy a bare minimum of product, but game masters buy five times as much as players.

Roleplaying games are part of the image of game stores. And for good reason. They're a stable, if not exciting, part of your industry. Their turn rate will be in the middle of your store's overall rate. While the average customer spends less on RPGs than the average CCG player spends on his hobby, there are many more RPG players in the world. Furthermore, they tend to re-

main in the hobby longer and spend more money as they remain in the hobby.

Roleplaying games require a relatively large amount of space
to sell properly. For best results, you should display game books
face out. Naturally, you can fit far fewer products on your shelves
face out, and you will eventually want to turn many of them
spine out. Once you do, you will see sales decrease. A good
compromise is to leave them face out as long as sales remain at
a certain rate, then turn them spine out after the initial surge
has ended.

MLI: $400
RLI: $1,800

DICE & ACCESSORIES

This category includes dice, dice bags, vinyl battlemats, and
other miscellaneous products designed to sell to RPG customers for use during game play. Dice alone accounts for a huge
slice of this pie. Dice come in a huge variety and could easily
lead to one of the worst cases of inventory creep in your inventory.

For starters, I advise getting sets of dice. Most roleplayers
need a seven-die set, while others need a lot of six-sided dice,
and players of White Wolf's games need d10s. Carry a handful
of each type set until RPG sales increase.

Beyond the basics, dice companies offer an enormous selection of different patterns, colors, and sides. You could spend
hundreds of dollars on your dice selection, and customers will
still come in asking if you have one that matches a set they
bought years ago and has long been discontinued.

Selling individual dice places an operational burden on your
sales staff. If you keep the dice behind the counter, they have to
pull out each individual die or pull out different trays. Why?
Gamers have this strange and irresistible desire to roll dice before they buy them. The roll of the die literally determines their
purchase. If the die rolls well, they buy it. If it does not, they put
it back and select another of the same pattern and color.

Do not attempt to understand it. Do not attempt to explain
basic statistics to them. Allow them their silly superstition and
let them give you money.

MLI: $100
RLI: $600

Used RPGs

Used RPGs offer a strong potential to game store owners. For one thing, they're readily available. Every one of your RPG customer has a game at home. When he's done with it, he can return it to you for store credit or cash.

Used RPGs offer you a chance to increase your average margin. It's not unusual to see a 70% profit margin on a used RPG. The occasional rare, hot item can push margins that approach 100%.

Not all stores carry used RPGs, so this market offers a chance you have to stand out from the crowd and it's another feature that can attract customers looking for such items. Advertising your used selection is a way to bring in customers who might overlap with other game stores nearby or who buy primarily online.

On the other hand, you cannot order to meet demand; you have to wait for a product to come in. If a customer is looking for a true first print first edition D&D Player's Handbook, you cannot call up your distributor and order one. If you attempt to buy one from the Internet or from another retailer, your margin will be small to none.

Another disadvantage is that used RPGs require a great deal of knowledge to maximize your profit. You can mitigate that by setting certain buying and selling standard prices across the board. Maybe you buy at ¼ cover and sell at ½ cover. You can learn while you sell. While you might miss out on some high collectible prices in the meantime, as long as you are making a comfortable margin overall, you are driving interest in your used selection. The customer that finds a H1 in your used bin for $10 will certainly tell all of his friends and half the strangers he meets (Bloodstone Pass currently sells for $100 to $150).

Once you gain that product knowledge, however, the overall margins in your used bin simply climb. If you start out hoping for a 50% margin, that's still better than your overall store average. Many customers sell their products for almost nothing. They don't expect much cash; they want to clear up space in their closet. Cash, or store credit, is a bonus.

You can use store credit to your advantage here, as with all secondary market products. If you offer a current player $50 cash for a box of product but offer $75 in credit, he'll take the credit almost every time. Then he'll spend that $75 to buy product that will cost you about $40 to replace — if you replace it. If he buys clearance items, so much the better.

MLI: $200
RLI: $800

Miniature Games

Miniatures represent one of your key product segments. The industry leader, Games Workshop merits a section of its own, but miniatures in general are relatively easy to order, stock and sell. Pewter miniatures bring in additional sales through paints and hobby supplies, also. Prepainted plastic miniatures allow for immediate play right out of the box.

Miniatures come in blister packs, which typically display on pegs in your pegboard or slatwall, and in boxes, which display on wire shelves or on bookshelves.

MLI: $500
RLI: $2,000

Games Workshop

Games Workshop is the industry leader in hobby miniatures games. They have maintained a dominant market share for many years and are not likely to lose that position any time soon. Their brand strength is exceptional, their reputation for quality is the highest in the industry, their customer loyalty is fanatical, and the profits you can make off of their product are considerable.

One highly successful game retailer who purchases as many as 40 failing stores per year mentions that they nearly all have one thing in common: a large Games Workshop inventory. While other factors were certainly involved in those failures, an inability to manage Games Workshop almost certainly contributed to one degree or another. If you intend to use Games Workshop games as part of your sales strategy, you must be aware of how to manage this product line or you will be crushed beneath its weight.

Games Workshop is not a product that you can simply order from your main distributor. If you use Alliance or ACD you will buy GW at a horrible discount. In this regard, treat "horrible" as "unprofitable." When you cannot order from Games Workshop, you can order through distribution to fill customer special orders only.

Games Workshop implements a policy of planned obsolescence with their products, such that their main lines are revamped about every four years in alternating cycles. That means that about every two years, if you carry both Warhammer Fantasy Battles and Warhammer 40,000, you will have to replace several thousand dollars' worth of outdated product.

Games Workshop products sell a small amount on their own, with no maintenance. You can continue to sell *White Dwarf* magazine, a few copies of each new miniature, and a random selection of back stock. You might sell a couple of hundred dollars' worth a week. It's not hard to do with boxes starting at $30 and sometimes running to more than $200.

Games Workshop products will be your most obvious example of how inventory creep can kill your cash flow. If you sell $900 worth of product a week at retail, but you purchase $500 a week at cost, you end up putting $5,000 worth of profit on your shelves instead of in your pocket. You did almost $47,000 in sales, yet you lost cash on the deal.

It's difficult to think of it as profit when it's plastic on your shelf instead of cash in the bank, but that's exactly what it is. It's not the fault of the IRS if you chose to spend your cash on inventory. It was your ordering decision that made that happen.

Manage your inventory carefully. Take a full inventory several times a year. Conducting weekly spot inventory checks is a great way to train staff on sound procedures and monitor the line for shoplifting at the same time.

If you do decide to pick up this product line, you should plan on some other investments besides the product itself. You will want to establish a demo area. A 2' by 2' portable tabletop with fixed terrain is perfect. Make it yourself or have a contest among your customers, offering a product prize for the winner.

Whenever you have a customer enter the store, offer a demo. If this process is too invasive for your comfort level, do demos on select days of the week, or after 5:00 PM. Insist that your employees follow through with this as well. Learn enough of the game that you can run a demo. GW offers procedures for this demo, including a pre-scripted demo.

The goal here is to create x new GW customers per week, where x is a number you invented. Ideally, you divided your sales increase goal of, say, $500 per week by the number of weeks you are allowing yourself to reach that goal (call it 8) times the average weekly amount those customers spend (count on $20 a week initially). With these sample numbers, you need to create fewer than four GW customers per week to meet your goal.

Resources for Selling Games Workshop

Signage. You can purchase plastic-corrugated signs from online suppliers like *www.buildasign.com.* They're cheap and delivery is quick.

Painting Contests. Your sales rep can sponsor prizes for a GW-only painting contest. If you are willing to special-order some prizes of your own, they're more willing to work with you. Because GW's tournaments hand out prizes for Best Painted Army, painting is important to its players. The nicely-painted miniatures also generate interest in painting among new customers.

Tournaments. GW's branding juggernaut creates loyal gamers that love the official Rogue Trader Tournaments. People will drive for hours to participate in them. Sponsoring one of these tournaments is a great way to increase excitement.

MLI: $5,000
RLI: $12,000

NON-GAME SPECIFIC MINIATURES

By "non-game specific", I mean Reaper Miniatures, the market leader. Their models are well-sculpted, priced attractively to the consumer, widely available, and fully exchangeable through Reaper.

Reaper offers a huge number of SKUs and carrying the entire line can occupy all of a small store's wall space. Fortunately, they offer various size packages for different store needs, all of which are available through distribution. Discuss your goals with your distributor's sales rep to determine which is best for you.

Other manufacturers do produce models in the same category, either because they produce non-game specific products, or because their game does not drive their sales to the same extent as other manufacturers' games. You might have some success with one or more of these product lines if you have a large retail space available to you.

If you carry this line of product, you guarantee yourself a certain amount of paint and hobby supply sales. In fact, in a survey conducted by Reaper Miniatures, well over half of their customers buy their miniatures to paint, not to use in any game.

MLI: $500
RLI: $1,500

Board Games

Board games have the broadest appeal of any of your store's products. While relatively few people play *Dungeons & Dragons* or *Magic: the Gathering*, nearly everyone has sat down to the dining room table with a board game.

Depending on your location, board games could represent a small percentage of your sales or a dominant portion of your sales. The more commercial your location, the more important your board game selection will be.

The good side to board games is their price: a cheap board game is typically $40, and some of them sell reliably at $80. It does not take many tickets at that price to have a good sales day.

The downsides are the space they require and their lack of follow-up sales. A few products, like Settlers of Catan, have expansions and these titles are among your best-selling board games. For the most part, however, if someone likes a game, that's all there is to buy. With *Magic*, you sell a starter one week and then boosters for years to the same person. With RPGs, once you sell a core book, you have multiple additional titles that you might sell to that customer. With board games, once you make a sale, you are probably done with that customer.

You will see exceptions. Some people enjoy learning new games. Some people simply enjoy gaming but do not like the collectible aspect of CCGs and prefer the structure of a board game over RPGs. These people come back over and over for different board games.

Another downside to board games is the low cost available to your mass-market competition. Walmart and other big box stores can afford to sell board games at less than your cost.

Board games should be placed visibly, preferably near the front door. That way, when the customer enters, he can identify with something right away. Many people enter specialty game stores expecting to see video games. By spotting something like a board game, they immediately realize what type of games you sell. You sell things that encourage people to sit at a table and talk to each other.

MLI: $250
RLI: $1,000

Paints and Hobby Supplies

If you sell unpainted miniatures, your customers need these products. You can provide them yourself or allow them to go to other game stores or dedicated art stores. In addition to the wargamers who paint their figures as part of their hobby, many casual painters that do not play any games will buy these materials.

At the minimum, you need a selection of paints, glue, and sealers. Additional supplies include sprue cutters, clamps, pin vices, files, a selection of hobby knives, and some fancier items like painting stations and self-healing cutting mats.

One enormous advantage this area of your store boasts is its profit margin. Because many of these hobby items come without SRPs and have such low prices, it's easy to reach very high margins on these items. In the customer's mind, $1.29 and $1.79 are nearly identical. They're both a dollar and change. You lose almost no sales by pricing an item at far above the SRP indicated through distribution. Item margins of up to 80% allow this product line to easily reach an average 60% profit margin.

Another advantage is the upselling potential. When you ring up a customer that's buying miniatures, ask "What do you use to paint these?" to lead into your store's paint and supply selection. They're priced low enough that you easily upsell an item or two — which demands more purchases later.

MLI: $75
RLI: $400

Snacks & Drinks

A small selection of snacks and soft drinks can be an easy way to add $5,000 to $10,000 in annual sales. If you offer a game room and customers routinely stay in your store for hours at a time, the impact of the snack and drink category is stronger.

Snacks have a couple of minor liabilities. You can occasionally lose product by having it exceed its shelf life on the rack if it's a poor seller. This loss is typically one box of candy at about $10 cost. Obviously, if a product sells that poorly, don't restock it. Toss it, take note, and buy something different next time.

Customers try to leave wrappers, food and cans or bottles all over your store. Ask them to clean up after themselves, and then pick it up stoically when they don't. You will have spills to clean up, also.

The margin can be much smaller than you will make off of

your games. If you don't manage the product aggressively, expect a 30-35% margin on your snacks and drinks. The default assumption is that you contact your local Coca Cola or Pepsi bottling vendor and ask for a free cooler. They usually require that you order your product exclusively through them, but you might be able to reach another arrangement. Rural or small-town markets tend to be much more casual in this regard.

Purchasing a second-hand cooler yourself and stocking it with your own purchases can be more efficient. A small free-standing reach-in cooler or a vending machine might run a couple of hundred dollars, or closer to $800 to $1,000 for the larger sizes. Soft drink prices vary with the local market, but here's a comparison:

If you buy from Coca-Cola and sell 150 drinks a week at $1 each, you spend about $96 and make $150. Your cash flow will be positive after about six days. If you spend $500 for your own cooler and buy cans at your local warehouse club, you can sell them for $0.75 and pay about $0.25. You will increase your profit from $0.36 to $0.50. That's an additional $21 in profit per week, so your cooler pays for itself every six months. Because you bought it used, let's say it has a lifespan of five years on average. Your second-hand cooler pays for itself 10 times over its lifespan in increased margin.

Meanwhile, you have more options with your own cooler. The national chains do not like for you to display other products in their coolers, while you are free to sell anything you like in your own machine. This freedom allows you to respond to customer feedback quickly. For example, Mountain Dew is a favorite among gamers, yet Coke is a better-selling brand nationally.

Fountain drinks might seem an attractive option if you have a background in the food service industry because they offer a very nice profit margin — 75% on average. However, with a 4-spigot fountain at close to $2,000, $500 for an ice-maker, $500 for a purification system, and other costs quickly add up to the point where the extra .10 or so margin would take years to recover. Add in the cost of waste, employee drinks, the operational burden of maintaining the machine, and other considerations, and fountain drinks have no place in all but the most unusual game stores.

Whichever course you choose, remember that you will have to store several cases of product somewhere on site, in addition to possibly empty shells after you fill the cooler. Keeping these near the machine is convenient, but it might occupy useful floor space that could be making more money. Putting them in a non-productive storeroom and restocking on a daily basis makes better use of your space.

> MLI: $200 (assumes a free cooler provided by local soft drink franchise)
> RLI: $1,200 (purchase a drink cooler and stock it yourself)

NOVELS

The book trade works differently than game distribution. The largest difference is returnability; you can return books that do not sell. The margin used to be less, but decreasing discounts in the gaming industry have reduced or bypassed this difference. With equal discounts and returnability, why wouldn't you sell novels?

One reason might be that the large chain bookstores and Internet sites such as Amazon.com have done an amazing job of capturing market share. Independent bookstores have been swept aside almost completely.

However, in all likelihood, you're not trying to compete directly with the big-box stores. You want to add a component to your focus on games and other hobby products. You want a thorough selection of products within limited genres. You don't want to be your city's book store, you want to be the fantasy book store, or science-fiction book store, or some other narrow focus.

Purchasing through the book trade requires an account with a book trade distributor. Certain titles are available through hobby distributors, but if you want a wider selection, contact one of these book distributors:

Book Publishing Distributors
Baker & Taylor
2550 West Tyvola Road, Suite 300
Charlotte, NC 28217
800-775-1800
(704) 998-3100
www.btol.com

Ingram Book Company
One Ingram Boulevard
P.O. Box 3006
La Vergne, TN 37086-1986
800-937-8000
(615) 793-5000
www.ingrambook.com
    Ingram requires an initial order of $500 and $5,000 total annual purchases.

MLI: $250
RLI: $1,500

LAN

A Local Area Network is a potentially high-profit revenue stream that seems to require little maintenance. The ability of players to sit at a computer and play for hours on end gives business owners visions of charging money for hours on end. The reality is a little more, and a little less, than the perception.

"Little maintenance" does not mean "no maintenance." Connection issues, hardware issues, and software issues arise from time to time, and the inability to address them on the spot due to a lack of technical knowledge means lost customers. Having somebody on staff to address theses issues at all times is economically unfeasible, unless that person is also the business owner. One solution is to offer a technical advisor a discount on product or other preferential treatment for his assistance.

The LAN requires space to operate. Different stores use different configurations, but one row of machines is popular for up to eight machines, two rows facing each other is popular for anything from four machines on up. You need to provide comfortable chairs for customers. Unlike role-players, who might dig out a rulebook, get up for a drink, or lean over a table to move a figure, PC gamers might move nothing but their right wrist for six hours at a time.

In addition to the upfront costs of 8+ PCs, you will regularly replace keyboards, mice, and headphones or speakers. You will need at least one copy of each game for each PC.

Revenue varies widely by geography. Some places charge as little as $2.50 per hour, while some charge up to $6 per hour. Discounts for blocks of time are common. Some stores offer monthly rates for a reduced cost.

You need to determine how to keep track of time spent on the machines. A sheet of paper is an easy, low-tech way to track it. Egg-timers work well for low budgets, too. If you are spending the money on a large number of machines, however, you might as well spring for Internet café-style software. Its valuable tracking ability can help you determine more lucrative rates. For example, if you consistently have more players than machines from 6 to 9 p.m., but empty machines during the day, you might lower daytime rates and raise peak-time rates. This variation is easier to judge and manage with software.

Leasing computers could vastly reduce the up-front cost of investing in a LAN, while offering the benefit of being able to let it go with less pain than re-selling a dozen used PCs if the experiment fails. The higher costs would reduce profits in the long run, but leasing for a year or so before choosing what and how much to buy is a good compromise that allows the best benefits of both choices.

A console network is much cheaper.

PCs
MLI: $4,000
RLI: $20,000

Game Consoles
MLI: $2,000
RLI: $10,000

HISTORICAL MINIATURES
Think of all of the vast scope of cultures that have existed across the face of the planet and how much those cultures have changed, moved, fought, and died for the last 5,000 years of warfare. Well, some company has produced miniatures for all of their armies. The diversity is nearly incomprehensible.

This diversity leads to staggering number of available products. You could easily carry 5,000 different SKUs. Stocking all of these products could require several times the square footage available to most game stores.

Historical miniatures are available in different scales. You might feel comfortable with your inventory once you have several thousand bags of miniatures, but the minute you do, somebody will walk in the door asking for something in 20 mm that you only have in 10 mm, 15 mm and 25 mm. That customer goes back home to order it online.

Due to vast closings of stores selling historical miniatures, difficulty obtaining product through local retailers, and other reasons, many existing customers have learned to find their goods on the Internet. They might use your game space, but they have largely moved to warehouses with websites to find their goods. With your inability to stock fully while paying retail rent, the very difficulty of retailing historical miniatures plays into the hands of Internet-based businesses.

Historical miniatures tend to be packaged in a way that the rest of the industry left behind 30 years ago. Plastic bags with poor presentation are the norm. These packages wear quickly and look bad on your shelf. Furthermore, they rarely carry barcodes. If you use a POS and scanner, you must generate these barcodes yourself or enter them manually at each sale.

Turn rates are not as high as the other products you might carry. With a $10,000 inventory, an annual turn rate of 2 would be impressive. The same amount of money invested in a careful selection of RPGs should turn 3-4 times per year. Investing that amount in CCGs would give you a wide selection plus leave you with several thousand dollars left over for promotion and leave 90% of your floor space open.

Many manufacturers are also foreign, making ordering more difficult. Long delivery times, a potential high cost due to the current low strength of the dollar vs. the foreign currency, and difficulty in reaching the manufacturer to correct order errors or other issues make ordering worse.

Historical miniatures manufacturers do not advertise heavily. They rely on word-of-mouth and direct contact at conventions to grow their sales. They are not eager to provide graphics or trademarks for your own advertising of their products. In short, they do little to increase their own sales, much less sales through the retail channel.

One last liability faces would-be historical miniatures re-tailers: distribution. You cannot order all of your products through game distributors. You have to open new accounts, and meet additional order minimums. Discounts typically are not as good as with your other products.

On the other hand, the players tend to be financially stable, have a respectable disposable income, and remain in the hobby for a long period of time. Many of them started as boys and are now teaching their own children to play.

Many of these players have more money than time, and so they tend to buy pre-painted armies. If you are already offering a similar service for sci-fi or fantasy games, moving into historical armies might be an easy way to start. This trend might also mean that new merchandise is not as productive for you.

If you want to carry historicals, talk to your customers or existing game clubs in the area and find out what eras they play. Ask what scale the local gamers play. Offer to host a game day and see what tournaments are run and how many players show up for each game. Stock those lines, instead of trying to carry everything. The most popular periods are Ancients, Napoleonics, American Civil War, and WWII.

You should consider historicals in one of two scenarios. The first is that you have a background as a historical player and are well-connected within that community of players. You may be able to capture the retail market for your area and use it as a base on which to grow. The second case is one in which you already have strong product lines elsewhere and wish to grow your total sales. In either case, you must have the product knowledge, and retail space, and be able to generate a customer base yourself to make historical miniatures successful.

If you do sell historicals, you want to consider Osprey Publishing as an additional line. Osprey makes a fantastic line of books that are available through hobby distribution. Their books are excellent historical guides, although their primary appeal to miniatures players is in their utility as painting guides, thus supporting another product line you sell.

Flames of War has reignited interested in historical gaming in a way that makes them more accessible to new players. Because it's available through distribution, Flames of War solves many problems inherent in selling historicals. Their rules also allow the use of other manufacturers' models, which means you can sell 15 mm figures from anyone to your *Flames of War* players.

MLI: $1,000
RLI: $20,000

Osprey
MLI: $500
RLI: $1,000

Replica Weapons

Swords, axes, spears, and maces. Shields and suits of armor. Replica medieval weapons are always exciting items at conventions. The booth always has a great deal of interest. Can that interest translate into sales for your store?

It can. Weapons are items that might also draw in additional customers, people who do not consider themselves gamers. They're certainly good conversion tools, or at least conversation pieces. Because so few game stores carry them, the addition of replica weapons to your product selection can give you a competitive edge. Margins can be higher than your average, and the average ticket price is on par with the rest of the industry.

Carrying weapons might also bring risk. One lawsuit or local law violation can destroy you. Avoid carrying sharpened knives unless you intend to make this category a significant portion of your sales, and talk to your insurance agent about making sure that you are well-protected.

Weapons require a great deal of your clerk's attention because customers typically want to handle several. You want them visible, but not where children can pick them up and start swinging them around. Keep them underneath a glass case or on a wall display behind a counter. They typically require a minimum of 30-40 sf of display space, and this section of your store should turn at least 3-4 times per year.

Except for certain high-ticket licensed items, replica weapons are not available through game distribution. You need to find an outside source for them, such as BudK Wholesale (*budkwholesale.com*), Knight's Edge Ltd, (*knightsedge.com*) and *CheapJunk.com*. Higher-end products come from Museum Replicas Ltd (*museumreplicas.com*). Orders have a reasonable minimum (usually $100) and a quick turn-around time.

Margins are good because the items do not carry an SRP and customers typically expect a much higher price tag. You can keystone any product and achieve a margin of up to 80% on the higher-end items like spears and pole arms.

With good margins, good turn rate, easy distribution and a reasonable square footage requirement, weapons should seem like an automatic addition. One main factor when considering weapons is the image that it gives your store. If you want to present a family-friendly image, weapons might not enhance that impression in the customer's mind. If you wish to present a high "cool" factor, they are certainly capable of that.

MLI: $450
RLI: $1,000

ART PRINTS & POSTERS

Art prints are high-end items that reach into a very nice price range. As such, they are an item that gives high sales capability in an industry where the average game purchase is less than $50. Prints exceed $200 for an artist like Larry Elmore.

Prints offer a great customer draw, especially for stores that see a high amount of foot traffic. You might find that, if the prints do not sell well themselves, they enhance the sales velocity of nearby products by drawing customer attention to them.

Another advantage prints offer is a good sales record among non-gamers. While gamers might recognize a particular image and recall what book the painting originally appeared it, the general public buys on appearance alone. Thus, prints enhance your sales without cannibalizing any other products in the store.

The difficulty with prints is that they see a low turn rate. Also, art is highly personal. What interests you might not sell to others. You need to display them in a way that both protects them and allows customers to browse them. They need to be clearly visible without being allowed to fade from direct light.

Art prints might require special fixtures for display, and they can occupy a fair amount of space. Prints that are on display sell far better than prints rolled up in a bin. Poster displays run $400 to $3,000, but they display products well and store a significant number of rolled prints. The footprint of the display ranges up to about 24 square feet. Typically, they have a distinct facing, so you place them against a wall or place two of them back to back if you want a freestanding display.

Furthermore, fantasy art tends to run toward adult themes. Gore and naked women are popular subjects. You must consider the image you wish to present to the public along with factors such as footprint and margin.

Fantasy art prints are an excellent addition to a store that already has strong sales or sees a high amount of foot traffic that changes on a regular basis. They carry heavier risk for a new store that has yet to discover which products its customer base demands. If you want to bring them in, bring them in after you've reached a comfortable level of cash flow and you can afford to invest in a lower turn-rate inventory.

MLI: $600
RLI: $2,000

BUMPER STICKERS

Bumper stickers cover topics like gaming, comics, fandom in general, politics, and religion. The discount climbs with the amount of your purchase, so I recommend spending as much as you can afford to risk initially, and then restocking at whatever pace is appropriate for your sales velocity.

You can place them flat on your counter or stack them on a bookshelf, but a custom wire rack is best. The rack itself is 14" x 14", so the rack plus browsing space consumes about 50 square feet of your sales floor. Two or more racks side by side share space well and allow full customer access.

MLI: $175
RLI: $2,000

UNIQUE PRODUCT

Offering something that nobody else has is an excellent way to gain a competitive edge. The trick is identifying what products work for your store and acquiring them. If it is available through your distributor, then it is freely available to all of your competition, as well.

The downside, of course, is that you can not stock your store exclusively with unheard-of items. Your customers expect *D&D*, *Magic*, *Warhammer 40,000*, and other easily-recognizable names. You carry these items. You also offer the unknown or lesser-known items so your company stands out from the crowd.

Unique items offer competitive edge and the opportunity for greater margins. If you are the only store in town with the item, then you can afford to sell it at higher than SRP, or at a margin that makes you comfortable in the case of net items. You fear competition less than if every store in town carried the products.

SMALL PRESS EXCLUSIVES

Selling small press exclusives is another way to leverage your strength. If you can find a gaming product that is not widely available and promote it, these items can do very well for you. As an example, one store encountered a little product called The Everyone Everywhere List, tracked down the manufacturer and ordered a dozen.

It sold about 80 copies in the first year, making it one of the store's best-selling RPG items. It sold for three reasons. One, it was a good product at a fair price. Two, the owner shelved it right next to the D&D Player's Handbook. Three, the store was the only store in town with it, and probably the only store for 300 miles that kept it in stock on a regular basis.

Where do you find this good product? Resources like the Game Industry Network are good. Conventions. The GAMA Trade Show. Message boards online. Solicitations sent to you in the mail by manufacturers. Customer requests.

The competitive edge you gain from these products is as important as the sales. Any time your company is the only source for a product, you give customers a reason to shop with you instead of with a bookstore or another game retailer. A strong competitive edge can make an otherwise marginal product a viable product to carry.

The Internet

If you choose not to sell on the Internet as part of your business model, you should maintain a website so that existing customers can reach you. Within the past few years, use of the phone book to find a local business has gone from 100% to less than 90%, and the current rate of increase in Internet searches guarantees that this number will continue to drop. Ignoring the Internet means ignoring a large number of local customers.

Your Website

The first major decision you need to make concerning your website is whether or not you intend to sell product online. If you do not, then your site is little more than a listing similar to a phone book ad. People already familiar with your store will find you online through their favorite search engine to find out things like your hours or planned events.

For this reason, your website should contain information of general interest to your customers, like:
▷ Hours of operation
▷ The store address and directions to the store
▷ A schedule of upcoming events
▷ New releases
▷ A sampling of products carried

▷ A contact form
▷ Store phone number
▷ A short bit about the store's history or owners

These features make for a standard store website that maintains a presence on the web and answers most of the questions potential customers need to know.

Better than Standard

If you do the same things everyone else does, your business fails to stand out. Additional features you could offer to make your website exceptional include a game room webcam, discussion forums, a regular comic strip, or a podcast.

Website Sales

If you decide that you want to sell products via your website, then you have essentially decided to open an additional business that requires a different business model, its own expenses, and its own operating procedures.

The low-tech way to handle a website is to list tables of product names and prices. You require customers to e-mail, phone, or fax you a list, which you receive and transact at the store, adjusting your inventory manually and processing payment yourself. This system is a huge barrier to reaching a large number of customers.

While some prominent retailers do use such low-budget methods of handling business online, they succeed despite their methods, not because of them. They have unique product, a strong brand name, or years of inventory stockpiling. Unless you, too, have an exceptional draw to your products, avoid such a cumbersome system.

Entry into e-commerce is not as simple as it sounds. You must choose a method of displaying your products, organizing the product on pages, tracking inventory, charging customers, determining shipping costs, transacting funds, and other details. Buying an off-the-rack e-commerce system costs hundreds or thousands of dollars, and integrating it with your brick-and-mortar systems might still require custom work.

Shopping carts range from free (through WordPress) to low-cost options that handle more SKUs to very expensive and flexible options. Find one that suits your volume. Are you just looking to sell industry leaders, like the Pathfinder core book? Then you need low-maintenance small-scale shopping carts. If you want to list your whole inventory, you need to spend more money and invest more time.

Internet sales of retail goods by a retailer virtually demand a discount because of customer expectation and market pressure. Customers can find discounts with ease online, and full-price websites don't interest them. Which creates a conundrum for brick-and-click stores — do you sell for one price online and a different price in the store?

If you do, you engender feelings of low worth in your retail store customers. They feel that you don't deem them worthy of the special discount your online customers receive. The result is lost higher-margin retail sales.

The alternative is to either sell at full price online (which means low sales online), or discount in your physical store (which creates the problem of insufficient profit margins that we've already seen).

The only way to approach or achieve full-price online sales is to have exclusivity or some sense of legitimacy on those products. Manufacturers can achieve both of these goals; retailers can't, by their very nature. You can't offer an exclusive deal on a product you buy from a distributor.

Chapter 5
Marketing & Advertising

We know that the most common reason for small business failure is undercapitalization. Aside from the owners who start without any capital reserve, the culprit is an inability to reach the break-even point before the owner drains his reserves. I believe the blame lies in underplanning or not implementing a sound marketing plan.

Many game stores excel in certain aspects of marketing. They're good at retaining customers. They're good at turning casual customers into gaming experts, increasing how much those players spend. Not knowing how to get more people in the door is a common weakness. A lack of understanding of how all of the elements of marketing work together is another problem; unfortunately, that's not so easy to fix.

Creating a Marketing Plan

People often equate advertising with marketing. Advertising is paid commercials, print advertisements, and other direct to consumer messages usually intended to drive immediate sales. Marketing encompasses advertising, public relations, market research, pricing strategies, and everything else related to encouraging the greatest sales volume at the greatest profits.

Your marketing plan is a combination of the products and services you sell, your pricing, what customer need you fill, and how you promote your store. All of your marketing elements must work together. You cannot effectively promote your store as "family-oriented" if 50% of your products are adult-only anime titles.

Building Your Brand

Creating a brand identity for your company is a challenging task that seeks to associate your company name to a particular feeling or emotion. You apply your logo, associated colors, and other corporate identity to your product. Your advertising helps to create this brand over time with your choice of images that you send to your customers.

Creating a brand as a retailer is difficult, because you do not design the products you sell. You do not package them, you do not control how they're advertised, and you do not create their company slogans or logos. Things you do control include your sign, your website, your uniforms, your store's physical appearance, the plastic bags you hand out with purchases, your business cards, how employees answer the phone, employee attitudes, your service standards — every possible point of contact the customers have with your business aside from the products on the shelf. You can use custom-printed price tags on the products.

The largest retailers have overcome this challenge. Look at Wal-Mart, Target, and K-Mart. They sell many of the same products, yet you have a different mental image and emotion attached to each company.

Let's say the concept you want attached to your business is "the meeting place". You want gamers to meet other games. Well, it sounds like you've already decided to have a game room, but let's go further with that. You won't put up a wall between your sales floor and your game room because that would discourage the free flow of traffic, even though you understand that you have to be extra careful of theft through that route. You might have a small card table that you set up outdoors in the right weather. Rectangular tables are a better fit, but you want round tables for your games. You will almost certainly have the traditional snacks and sodas that go with a game room, but you might do one better: coffee and pastries. These are social foods that encourage people to sit and talk.

Your logo might include silhouettes of two people to encourage the social element. You might offer a "family plan," so that kids that come in with their parents receive a discount on a product or on a tournament entry. This move strengthens the image you wish to project, and brings additional bodies into your store. Speaking of tournaments, make it a point to always offer a non-competition based prize, such as Most Unique Deck or Best Army Theme.

The most important element with creating and managing your brand is consistency. When you break consistency you send confusing signals to your customers and dilute the value of your brand. A small positive reinforcement is better than a conflicting message.

Product Selection and Your Brand

The products you carry must fill a need. If you buy them all based solely on their ability to sell and not on their impact on your image, you will alter your image. Carrying product lines that your customers perceive as unrelated affects your brand.

As an example, you might add some trendy motorized scooters that are currently selling very well. You could bring in a substantial amount of sales, gain the interest of new customers, and open up a whole new product line that you had never considered. On the other hand, what message does this product line send to your existing customers? Did they not mean anything to you? Are you going to abandon them to chase this new fad?

Changing your brand is not necessarily a bad thing. You should expect it to develop over time as you grow your business. However, you should do your best to know how customers perceive you so that you don't send conflicting messages with your marketing package.

Promoting your company requires you to have a good understanding of who you are, who you want to be, and who your customers are. If you want to position yourself as the market leader, for example, you must portray your business in a way that reinforces that image.

If you do present your company as a market leader, and your inventory level or your staffing does not meet your customer's expectation, you send a mixed message to your customer. That customer might lose faith with you and ignore the next message you send.

In other words, your marketing drives your operations. Whenever you consider how many people to have on staff, what kind of uniforms to wear, which products to promote, which shopping center to operate in, what type of font you want for your signage — you must take into consideration the dollar cost of the decision and how it interacts with the image you wish to present to the customer. Are you the Man Place Where Only Boys Hang Out? Then a lacy, frilly decoration in your windows doesn't work. A "No girls allowed" sign in red paint on a wooden plank supports your image better.

Setting Prices

Few beginning entrepreneurs realize the importance of a wise pricing strategy. They assume they will price everything at SRP and concentrate their efforts on selling as much as they can. Sometimes, they have the brilliant idea of using discounting as a method of bringing in new customers and untold wealth. We've already discussed how disastrous that can be.

Books and some CCGs have printed SRPs on the product. Miniatures sometimes carry a printed SRP. Board and non-collectible card games usually have a price printed on them.

For many other products, you are free to price them yourself. You will find that most of these items do have SRPs, but they aren't printed on the product. Your distributors provide these prices on their invoice. You are certainly free to use those prices. This method saves you the most effort and nearly maximizes your profit potential.

Sometimes an item comes in on your invoice with a net cost rather than the traditional percentage discount off of retail. That is, the manufacturer sells it to the distributor at a certain price, and the distributor does the same to you. In this case, you need to price the item yourself.

To match your normal discount of 45 to 50%, choose your margin and divide the cost by one minus that number. Suppose you receive an item with a cost of $9.84 and you want to receive at least your normal discount of 46% that the distributor gives you. Divide 9.84 by .54 and you get $18.23. You could set the price at $17.99, but your actual margin on the item would be 45.3%. If you set it at $18.99, your margin becomes 48.2% — much better. At $19.99, the becomes a more attractive 50.8%

Your immediate concern at this concept is how many sales your business loses by raising the price. The difference is hard to measure in advance. Certain guidelines keep lost sales to a minimum.

One trick is to maximize the pennies by pricing everything to end in .99. The mental difference between a $19.99 and a $20 product creates a definite measurable difference in sales. Two items priced at $19.99 and $19.95 sell in identical quantities. The difference is that one of them nets greater revenues.

Maintaining that first number in the price tag intact is important. The difference between an item's sales at $9.99 and $10.99 is far greater than the difference between $9.00 and $9.99.

Pricing Above a Suggested Retail Price

Many customers fail to notice a discrepancy between the SRP and your price, especially if they purchase multiple items at once. While this works against you if you discount your prices, it works in your favor if you upcharge them. Of course, some customers will complain if you price a product above the manufacturer's suggested retail price, especially if that product is marked with that price.

You hope!

Complaining about the price means that they are comfortable bringing something to your attention. That fortunate circumstance gives you a chance to explain your pricing strategy. Mention that the manufacturer's suggested retail price is just that: a suggestion. One price is not appropriate for all markets in all circumstances. Point out the advantages of buying from you: a clean place to shop, customer knowledge, the community of gamers, diversity of product, etc. Naturally, your store must offer some benefit to the customer if it expects to capitalize on them. Excellent customer service allows this pricing flexibility.

The point is not that you should charge more than SRP for every product in your store. The point is that you should not rule this option out of your business plan for fear of losing customers. A small increase in prices can have a huge impact on your bottom line.

Summary: Products without SRP
- Dice
- Used products
- Some games
- Some CCGs
- Paints
- Hobby supplies

Short-Discount Items

A disturbing trend has been emerging in the industry for the past few years. Manufacturers, unwilling to face angry customers, have been reluctant to raise prices. Instead, they take some of the retailer's margin in the form of reduced discounts to distributors, short-discount items, or net priced items.

"Short" in this case might mean as low as 25%. With a plentitude of products available at 45% margin or higher, customer demand for these short-discount items needs to be intense to justify them. If customer demand is that high, you can trade a number of sales for higher profit per item by raising the price to a more acceptable margin.

A Discounting Strategy

Many startups assume that discounting is the way to go. "If I discount all my games by 20%, I will take all of the business from Frank's Friendly Game Store and make tons of money." This owner's primary motivation seems to be to prove that he can run a game store better than Frank. By "better," he means "have more customers." Thus begins one of our example stores, Dave's Discount Games.

Dave opens his store in much the same manner as Frank. He sets up his distributor accounts, he stocks some product, and he starts selling games. All is well for a month or two. Word of mouth generates traffic. He takes customers from Frank, and he begins to build sales.

But Dave's having trouble keeping his bank account up. He's not sure why. It must be that sales are not high enough. If offering a discount gets him more customers, surely a greater discount will bring in even more customers, right?

Dave increases his discounts on certain products to 25% off, offering some high-ticket prices like Magic booster displays at very deep discounts — 40% off, to retain customer loyalty. A $5 profit is better than making no sale at all.

Well, no. It's not.

If you buy a box of Magic boosters for $74.69, and sell it for $80 to your pre-order customers in anticipation of a big release, you keep $5.31 per box sold.

Spending $75 to make $5 is a very poor return on your investment. That's a 7% gross margin on your sales. With most game stores needing at least a 40% gross margin to pay the bills, you can see where Frank's problem lies.

Comparing Two Stores

Let us explore the discounting strategy a little bit further by comparing the financial statements of the two stores.

Frank's Friendly Games

Revenue:
Net Sales	$180,000.00

Cost of Goods Sold:
Beginning Inventory		$25,000.00
Add:	Purchases	$108,000.00
Less:	Ending Inventory	$25,000.00
	Cost of Goods Sold	$108,000.00

Gross Profit (Loss)	$72,000.00

Expenses:
Advertising	$1,600.00
Bank Charges	$400.00
Credit Card Fees	$2,100.00
Depreciation	$1,000.00
Insurance	$1,300.00
Memberships	$50.00
Office Expenses	$550.00
Payroll	$32,000.00
Payroll Taxes	$4,160.00
Permits and Licenses	$400.00
Professional Fees	$250.00
Rent	$20,000.00
Repairs & Maintenance	$1,200.00
Utilities	$3,300.00
Total Expenses	$68,310.00

Net Income (Loss)	$3,690.00

Then examine the same information on Dave's Discount Games, assuming the same sales on reduced price. For these academic purposes, we are assuming that nothing changes except for the price at which the products sell.

Dave's Discount Games
Revenue:
Net Sales $144,000.00

Cost of Goods Sold:
Beginning Inventory		$25,000.00
Add:	Purchases	$108,000.00
Less:	Ending Inventory	$25,000.00
	Cost of Goods Sold	$108,000.00

Gross Profit (Loss) $36,000.00

Total Expenses $68,310.00

Net Income (Loss) ($32,310.00)

Assuming all non-COGS expenses stay the same, the difference in profitability is $36,000. The operating theory, of course, is that the reduced price brings in more customers. So let us add in an additional 25% to Dave's customer count. Coincidentally, this brings sales back up so that the two stores are at an equal volume.

Dave's Discount Games
Revenue:
Net Sales $180,000.00

Cost of Goods Sold:
Beginning Inventory		$25,000.00
Add:	Purchases	$135,000.00
Less:	Ending Inventory	$25,000.00
	Cost of Goods Sold	$135,000.00

Gross Profit (Loss) $45,000.00

Total Expenses $68,310.00

Net Income (Loss) ($23,310.00)

Dave's is still losing enough money to pay for rent and utilities in double the space! How does Dave recover that money? He has already increased his customer count by 25% without increasing his advertising budget. At what point does this model start to make sense?

With a 50% increase in customer count, Dave's is catching up — the company is $14,000 in the red. Not until he brings in twice as many customers, without spending a single dime to get those customers, does his profitability finally exceed that of the store that sells product at full SRP. In reality, the way to leverage that discount is to advertise the discount, which brings increased costs. Otherwise, Dave would be giving away a discount to people who were willing to shop at his store before they knew about the discount. In addition to greater advertising costs, labor increases, a constant inventory level becomes more difficult to manage, and other costs creep in.

These additional factors push Dave's new break-even goal to over twice Frank's break-even level.

It gets worse. The idea is not to break even, of course. The goal is to make a profit. For each sale that Frank makes beyond his break-even, he makes far more profit than Dave makes because Frank's contribution margin is higher.

Assuming that both companies buy their product at an average discount of 40% off of the suggested retail price, Frank has a contribution margin of 60%, while Dave's contribution margin is 42%. For every $100 in sales over break-even, Frank banks $60, while Dave only makes $42.

How to Fix It

If you have already adapted a discounting policy, you might find it difficult — emotionally and economically — to change your business plan. You know you will lose customers, and losing customers is something that grates at an entrepreneur. Your instinct tells you that losing customers is bad.

Losing unprofitable customers to gain profitable ones is good.

Inform your customers of the change in your business policy. Send out notices and place a brief sign in the store. Enact the change immediately or at a set date in the near future. The sooner you do it, the sooner you start making money again.

If the discount is a benefit of a club you promote, you might wish to continue to allow existing club members to gain the benefits of the discount for the duration of their membership. This move retains goodwill and might encourage the club members to "stock up" by making a large purchase near the end of their membership. Try to find some other benefit for joining the club, such as free or reduced entry into tournaments or the ability to buy certain product earlier than other customers.

Remove the notices after one to two months. Most of your old customers are aware of the change by then, and your new customers might question your prices if they see the sign. If you mention that you used to discount, they might feel cheated.

When to Use Discounts

Discounts are useful sales tools in several situations. One situation is the "loss leader." Advertise an aggressive discount on a price to attract people who will buy that product plus additional product at a higher margin. You might advertise Player's Handbooks at 50% off for a certain period and arrange a display near the front door that combines Player's Handbooks, a small rack of popular Reaper miniatures, large battlemats, and the newest dice cubes.

One common method for clearing out discontinued inventory is to offer a flat discount across the product line. This system is simple, easy to implement, and easy to advertise. Discounts for clearance are painless and do not harm your other product lines.

Running a sale offers another way to make a discount work for you. You might offer a seasonal sale to attract interest in a certain theme or genre of games. Themes such as zombie games around Halloween, anime games around Valentine's Day, or new games on New Year's Day offer a way to clump together diverse product with an otherwise loose connection.

Lastly, if you obtain a large quantity of product at an exceptional price you might offer a percentage discount to increase the velocity at which you move the product. If you get 500 copies of a board game for 70% off, you can advertise it for half the normal price and still make a reasonable 40% margin. The large stack of games and irresistible price point generate enormous interest in the product.

SUMMARY: REASONS TO DISCOUNT
- Loss leader
- Clearance
- Short-term sales
- Pass on a discount to increase sales velocity

IDENTIFY TARGET CUSTOMERS

National demographics are not necessarily your demographics. You need to find out who your customers are. Identifying who your customers are, knowing why they shop with you, understanding what they want, and keeping track of them as they change help you service them better.

The low-tech way to do gather this information is to keep a notepad handy and write down obvious details about the customers as they enter the store. You can at least gather sex and approximate age, and usually marital status. You can also tie that in to what games they buy or play at the same time.

At slightly more cost you can conduct your own unofficial survey. Mail out survey forms and offer some incentive for the return: entry into a drawing, or a one-time discount for a couple of dollars. Have some forms available in the store to enhance your coverage because not everyone is on your mailing list. This method reduces duplication, but it costs a bit more.

Survey Form Information
▷ Age
▷ Sex
▷ Marital status
▷ Address (at least zip code)
▷ Approximate income
▷ Which games do you play?
▷ What other game stores do you visit?
▷ Are you currently involved in a regular game?
▷ What do you like about our company?
▷ What would you like our company to improve?
▷ What other hobbies or interests do you have?

Information you gather from your point-of-sale system:
▷ Average ticket price
▷ Average ticket price by customer
▷ Average ticket price by category
▷ Average frequency of purchases by customer
▷ Frequency of customer visits
▷ Upsell rate

Information to track by observation:
▷ Conversion rate
▷ High-traffic areas of the store
▷ Displays that gather attention
▷ Displays that customers ignore
▷ Traffic chokepoints

ADVERTISING

You have three ways to increase sales.

First, you can increase the number of customers you have. Generally speaking, this method is the most expensive of the three. It involves TV commercials, print advertisement, and your road sign. On the other hand, the potential is huge. While the other methods provide incremental gains, you could multiply your customer count by 10 or more with the right advertising.

Second, you can increase the amount each customer spends per visit. Training employees to upsell, placing attractive impulse items near your register, and raising prices add to this amount. Bundled specials encourage customers to spend more, too.

Lastly, you can increase the number of times a customer visits your store. If you increase a customer's frequency from once a month to once a week, you've quadrupled the number of times he's in the store. While his spending might not quadruple, chances are that he's spending far more than he was when he was in once a month. Bagstuffers, scheduled in-store activities, and e-mail notices of new releases increase the number of customer visits.

ADVERTISING MEDIA

You need to inform potential customers about your business somehow. While you could rely solely on word of mouth and the strident efforts of your best customers, you will prob-

ably want to spend some money to encourage people to spend money in your store.

Some of your advertising choices are obvious, some are less obvious, and some downright strange enough that you would never think of them on your own.

Television

Television offers a range of commercial options that cater to businesses of all sizes and needs. Many of those options do not apply to your business because of the financial commitment they require. Advertising on network channels, for example, can be extremely expensive and does not allow for very precise targeting.

Local cable channels offer the best combination of coverage and targeting. Cartoon Network, the History Channel, the Sci-Fi Channel, and Nickelodeon are likely considerations depending on your exact product mix and customer base. Talk to a sales rep from your local cable company; they have detailed information concerning who watches what.

Advertising on television is a two-part affair. You must first create a commercial. Then you have to air it.

Commercial Production

You could write your own copy, film your commercial yourself and use editing software to clean it up, record your voice-over, and create your taglines. Unless you have professional or extensive amateur experience in this field, you will probably find that the task is beyond your ability or not worth the savings.

You could instead contract the service out to an independent studio. Cost varies greatly in this case according to the demand of the local studio, their experience and equipment, the local market and your commercial's needs. Ads might cost anywhere from $250 to $10,000.

You can leave production in the hands of the television station. They will charge you a competitive rate, but you can often negotiate the production cost down or waive it entirely, depending on how much air time you buy. Naturally, they assume that this is the route you will want to take and the station will spend a minimum of time and effort on your ad.

If you hire somebody to write the ad copy for your commercial, make sure that you have a chance to review it before production starts. Changing it afterward will cost more.

Air Time
You have to pay for each specific ad. Prices run into the millions during the Superbowl. Local rates, however, can be as low as nothing. Because rates are based on viewership, late-night spots on cable channels can cost zero because the viewership rounds to zero. Of course, because television stations generally do not give these spots to anyone who asks for them, you want to negotiate as many as you can with a paid advertising program.

Normal arrangements allow you to buy time slots divided according to the programming and priced by viewership. You will pay for a certain number of spots (commercials) during a time slot. The more people watch a program, the greater the cost of the spot during that program. In general, paid rates go as low as $5 per thousand viewers. So a $20 slot might be seen by 4,000 potential customers. You can usually get discounts for buying packages or for buying a certain number of spots. The sales reps at your local cable company can provide you with an actual rate schedule to help you make your decisions.

Typically, you want to select one or more channels that suit your need for the products you are advertising. If you are advertising your company instead of a genre or product line, a broader range is fine. Choose several, based on your budget, and count how many ads you can afford.

Repetition is essential with advertising. Dozens or hundreds of low-cost commercials on the lowest-rated channels will be far more effective at promoting your company than a single spot on the current prime-time leader. If you estimate each of the free ads as one-quarter of an ad for effectiveness, you are getting an effective 20% discount on your cost per viewer by including one free spot for each paid spot in your agreement.

Another aspect of television watching that you can use to your advantage is that once people see a commercial, they cannot remember when they saw it last. If your ads disappear for a week, people will not notice the absence, except maybe to comment on it when they see the ad again. The television station's sales staff will tell you that you need repetition for maximum effect, but they will not tell you that you can still get strong effect without constant exposure.

Therefore, a cost-effective television ad campaign allows for gaps. You could, for example, run 24 spots per week on a channel for four weeks (insisting on at least an equal number of free ads between 11:00 pm and 6 am), then run no spots for a two weeks. After that, gradually reduce your reduce the "on" time on the on-off cycle. You could run your commercials for three weeks on and 1 week off for three months, then reduce your frequency to two weeks on and two weeks off, for example. Run your ads in cycles rather than constantly for maximum cost efficiency.

The sales staff you are talking to will offer you a 5% or 10% discount if you commit to a year's worth of ads. While that might seem attractive, using this rotating cycle of ads gives you an effective 45% discount. You run fewer ads, but you still achieve nearly the same coverage with a greatly reduced cost.

Curiously, air time is usually cheapest during the gaming industry's slowest months — January and February. Starting your advertising then for the busier spring and summer convention season could pay off and also help shore up sales during a traditional down cycle. If you are looking for a continuity discount, you could buy more spots while the rates are low and buy fewer spots when ad prices increase in the 2nd and 4th quarters.

One final way to get discounted rates is to ask about unsold spots. Time is finite, and the station would rather run your spot at a discounted rate than receive nothing at all. Ask the sales rep about the details on any of these offers. As with all negotiations, the more you spend, they more they're willing to negotiate.

Choosing Your Slots

Before you can choose your slots, you need to identify your market. Are you trying to appeal equally to gamers of all gaming products you sell? If your store's sales are 60% CCGs, you might want to appeal to CCG players for now. In this case, you might be looking for white males age 15-19 with greater than average disposable income.

Ask for breakdowns of the target market for each channel so that you can target your advertising as closely as possible. Use the demographic information in the Appendix to help determine which station and time is best for the products you wish to promote.

Radio

Radio spots break down like television, although the time divisions differ slightly. They divide into dayparts or you can buy ROS (run of station) spots that the station airs in dead time all throughout the day. You never want ROS spots. Don't look at the price. ROS spots give you great "reach," which is the number of different people that hear your message, but they give you no frequency. Getting your message to the same people over and over again is essential, and because ROS spots target different times of day, and therefore different people, they do not reinforce your message with any one group of listeners.

Unlike television, production costs are so low that the radio station doesn't make a point of charging you for the production unless you want to own the ad to use on other stations. If you want to run the same ad on multiple stations and want to maintain your consistency, you can insist that each station use the same gender and same voice (casual, excited, etc.) in their reading.

SUMMARY: RADIO DAYPARTS

⬡ AMD   Morning Drive time, 6:00 AM to 10:00 AM
⬡ DAY Daytime, 10:00 AM to 4:00 PM
⬡ PMD   Afternoon Drive time, 4:00 PM to 7:00 PM
⬡ EVE Evening, 7:00 PM to Midnight
⬡ ROS Not a time, but "run of station" or whenever they have a slot

Radio sponsorships allow the vendor to sponsor a fixed regu-

128

lar feature, usually a weather report, sports or a traffic report. You usually get an intro tag, a closing tag, and an adjacent 15-second spot with your sponsorship. Because these are consistent spots run within a very precise time frame, the odds of reaching the same listeners each time are high. On the other hand, they can be expensive.

Radio is not generally as cost-effective as a cable TV ad, and it should not be your primary advertising medium. It can effectively support a cable TV ad, however, by reinforcing a message your target audience is already receiving. Make sure any ads you run on radio are timed to support your other ad media.

The best use for radio is to announce your opening, possibly with a remote, in which a radio personality airs from your location for several hours. During the remote the personality encourages listeners to visit your location. In small towns, remotes can be very successful for grand openings. In cities, the popularity of the radio personality has tremendous impact and attendance varies accordingly.

Cinema Advertising

Digital technology allows for full motion cinema ads, replacing the old movie stills with a more effective ad experience. The cost-effectiveness compares to television or radio and the segmented customizability allows for relatively low levels of investment. Stores have reported various degrees of success with movie stills, mostly negative. However, a carefully-created ad, with the right price point, and the right location, can be an effective advertising tool. The closer your location to the theater, the better the results.

E-mail

Your e-mail list is a vital tool for increasing sales through increasing customer frequency and increasing customer sales prices. E-mail is essentially free, sends your message directly to your customer base, and it reaches people with low visit frequency who might not be in the store to see a sign or a store display.

Building an e-mail list is easy. Print a sheet where customers can voluntarily list their name and contact information. Leave it on your counter where people can see it. Train your staff to solicit customers for this information. You will get some physical addresses and phone numbers. You will get more e-mails.

This list will build constantly as new customers come in. Ideally, ask customers what type of games they play so that you do not target them with notifications that do not apply to them. Your e-mail list is several lists, sorted by game type: RPG, CCG, board games, etc. Customers may be on more than one list.

This customer list is important. You notify these customers of new releases, events, and specials. They come in and give you money. It costs you nothing to maintain and yields extensive rewards.

You need to pace your e-mail notices. Customers who see it too often ignore it, delete it, or ask to be removed from your list. At the other extreme, if you never use it, you receive no benefit. Unfortunately, this tolerance threshold for e-mail frequency varies from person to person. Create a regular schedule of no more frequently than once a week and no less than once a month. For infrequent important news, deviating from your schedule will not hurt.

Adding some sort of hook to the e-mail increases its utility tremendously. You could include a gaming-related trivia question each week. At the same time, you answer the previous week's trivia question. Make the question appropriate to the list's customers.

Flyers

A flyer is meant to get attention and bring a customer into your store. It should not contain a great deal of text or try to teach a game. It should include your store's name, your logo, and a catchy phrase to get people to want to come visit you. Colored papers work well for flyers, too. You could call yourself the "Coolest Store in Town" (a claim made very effectively by Titan Games of Battle Creek, Michigan).

Distributing flyers costs little more than the labor. You can place them on windshields in parking lots, hand them out at trade shows, have a pizza delivery place them on box tops, trade counter space with nearby businesses, or use a variety of low-cost methods of distributing them nearby.

At a cost of less than $.05 per piece, you can spread flyers to hundreds of people at very low cost.

Brochures

Most current word processors feature a brochure template, allowing you to design a three-fold brochure on your own. You can print and copy them yourself to keep costs at a minimum. In this respect, they're like flyers.

Brochures have a different purpose than flyers. Brochures contain more word space than a flyer, so you can use them to describe your business in greater detail. Because of this trait, brochures work well as an informational guide. As an example, you can explain the concept of hobby gaming to the uninitiated to recruit new customers and showcase your product and service mix for the established gamer to reclaim customers lost to the book trade or mass market outlets.

Brochures are useful for handing out to people with whom you have already made contact. Low-cost versions cost no more than any other flyers, but you could spend a great deal more to make them more professional in appearance. You might want to use this type of brochure for recruiting staff, for example.

Bag Stuffers

Bag stuffers are a hodge-podge of calendars, manufacturer flyers and catalogs, and whatever else you would like. Fill your bags with these when you ring up a customer. These items increase sales by encouraging your customers to come back more often, and are one of the lowest-cost ways of increasing sales. Encourage customers to return by notifying them of an event or promoting a new release.

Newspapers

Newspapers are effective for certain types of advertising. If you are advertising a price-point on a mass-appeal product and want an immediate response, newspapers work. Advertising your price on items found in Wal-Mart is bound to be counter-productive, however, and the general populace will not recognize any of your other products.

In general, game retailers that have advertised in the newspaper have been disappointed. Save your newspaper use for seeking new employees through the Classified Ads.

Smaller newspapers, like college or high school papers, might be an exception. Check into them individually, starting with those closest to you.

Yellow Pages

The market share of the Yellow Pages has fallen below a critical mass, in my opinion. That's simply not how people look for things anymore. I would take the free listing that comes with a phone number, if you use the local phone company for your phone. I would not spend money on an ad.

Signage

Signs are your most cost-effective forms of advertisement. Their longevity is the main reason for this value. You can use a sign for as long as it physically lasts with little additional cost. The right sign might last 20 years. Considering how much to spend on your initial store sign is a weighty consideration.

Exterior Signage

You want the sign to be large enough to be read from the road. To decide the size of the letters you want, measure or estimate the distance to the road from the sign's location. Your landlord should also be able to provide you with that distance in the legal description. Measure to the far side of the road to account for traffic going in both directions.

Letter Visibility Chart

Letter Height	Ideal Distance	Maximum Distance
3"	30'	100'
4"	40'	150'
6"	60'	200'
8"	80'	350'
10"	100'	450'
12"	120'	525'
15"	150'	630'
18"	180'	750'
24"	240'	1,000'
30"	300'	1,250'

SUMMARY: EXTERIOR SIGNAGE

- Wooden sign
- Box sign
- Channel letter sign
- Pylon sign
- Pole sign

One of the cheapest and most common options for new stores or stores that do not intend to draw much on the general public is a wooden sign. A custom sandblasted wooden sign might cost $40 to $90 per square foot. You want to keep your sign brief enough that people can read it as they drive by. Installation is relatively simple because it does not involve electricity.

Box signs are back-lit boxes with your graphic on a Lexan or Plexiglas panel in the front. Thus, you have the benefit of reasonable price on a lit graphic. These overhead signs are usually operated by a timer and/or manual switch found near your breaker or fuse box in most commercial spaces. This type of sign generally runs $15-35 per square foot for the facing, plus the price of the box. One way to save money is to find a used box sign from a business that has closed or is upgrading their signage and simply replace the facing.

Channel letters are the most expensive type of wall signage you will consider. Letters usually cost over $100 each, not counting installation. Shopping centers might require channel letters for signage to maintain consistency of image among tenants.

Pylon signs or pole signs are freestanding units near the road. Usually lit, they are generally beyond the budget of businesses in our industry. They usually start at $10,000 and climb from there. However, if your store is part of a shopping center, you can expect to receive space on a common pylon sign. The center might or might not charge you for the right. Providing the sign is your responsibility.

Vinyl Banners

Vinyl banner signs work well for off-site sale such as conventions and special promotions. They cost $3-$8 per square foot and have a lifespan measured in years. They handle travel and wear well. Because of their low cost, you can affordably make a huge sign that gives you premier visibility at any event you attend.

Vehicle Magnets

Usually available for under $50, vehicle magnets are durable, professional signs that you can take everywhere you go. If you find yourself traveling to conventions often, driving a long distance to the bank or to buy supplies, or commuting between home and the store, you might wish to consider a pair for your car.

One minor liability to vehicle magnets is the ease with which they come off: for some inexplicable reason, people occasionally steal them. Remove them at night to minimize loss to random theft.

Street Signs
In addition to your permanent lit signs, more portable items like a wooden A-frame sign that you set out on the sidewalk are extremely visible and well worth their cost if you have any measure of traffic at all. They are generally available for under $200 and often under $125.

Billboards
Billboards are huge signs placed in high-traffic areas. These two reasons — "huge" and "high-traffic" — translate into costs far too high to be of any value to most game stores. The signage alone costs $2 to $5 per square foot. At a standard 672 sf, that's over $3,000. Paying for the right to use the billboard might cost $500 to $5,000 per month or more in an urban market, typically requiring a year-long contract. Adding in graphic design to make the sign in the first place, you could easily spend $10,000 on a billboard.

Also, given that the only thing you would target with a billboard is location, not gender, interests, or age, billboards are not an ideal medium for advertising the gaming hobby.

My research has turned up one example of billboard usage by a game retailer. The sign was very near the store, the store was an established location with a solid customer base, and the billboard was maintained over a fairly substantial period of time. I have no information on the actual number of customers it drew in, aside from the implied value due to its longevity.

YOUR ADVERTISING PLAN
Advertising is not a matter of calling the local TV station and ordering a certain number of spots. Your advertisement should be budgeted, planned out, and have a purpose. Advertising directed toward existing customers differs from advertising directed toward gaining new customers.

Plan out a total advertising budget and attempt to plan ahead for growth. Perhaps you will spend $5,000 before opening, then $6,000 per year after that. If, after you are open for a couple of years, you realize that you see a Christmas sales spike, maybe you will change your annual advertising budget to $7,500 but spend half of it during the 30 days before Christmas.

Do not plan on every single ad equating to an increase in sales. While we discuss a means to measure the effectiveness of a single ad, the ad has other impacts that you cannot measure. How well did the ad reinforce your brand? How much did it enhance the value of other forms of advertising you do? Did the ads succeed in creating gamers but fail in that they sent those gamers to your competition?

Sector Analysis

A sector analysis is simply a look at where your customers live. The sector analysis is a tool to aid in location-based marketing, such as direct mailouts by ZIP code or choosing a billboard location. It can also be useful if you're considering moving your store.

Before computers, doing a sector analysis meant putting a map of your market on a piece of cardboard and sticking push-pins in it. Now, you can use mapping software to plot out where your customers live if you need a graphic representation. Otherwise, a tabular list of addresses by zip code can provide you with what you need to know.

When using this type of advertising, consider why you're advertising. If you're attempting to gain new customers, direct the advertising toward the sparse areas. You'll have a higher incidence of potential customers in that area, and your potential gain is higher.

If you're advertising to existing customers, you probably have more cost-effective methods than a direct mailout or a billboard.

Measuring an Ad's Effectiveness

Determining whether an ad that you ran was productive involves a bit of math and preparation. First, you must have some method of determining where new customers come from. Coupons excel in this area, because they're a physical thing the customer hands you at the register, so it's very easy to track. Asking for a particular deal or using a catchphrase is another method that's almost as easy to use and track.

Next, determine the total amount of sales brought in by the ad or promotion. This tracking might require the creation of a special sheet kept by the register, or by creating a yes/no field for a POS system. If your ad was timely (such as a coupon with a use-by date, or a seasonal print ad or TV commercial), track through the time allowed and then for about two to three weeks afterward. If not, set a time frame. Most coupons and similar offers see a very high return rate immediately that tapers off within a month or so. People forget ads quickly, which is why companies have to keep spending money on them.

Compare the sales brought in against all of the costs associated with the advertisement, including graphic design, delivery method, the cost of replacing the sold product, and any tracking costs. If the net profit is greater than the cost of the advertisement, the ad or ad campaign was definitely profitable.

If not, it might still have been worthwhile. One source of advertising alone often fails to generate a new customer. A combination of factors support each other in creating new customers — maybe the customer saw the cable TV ad but didn't decide to visit until she saw your store sign. Therein lies the difficulty of determining ad effectiveness.

Thus, in a way, you can measure your advertising effectiveness in the way that astronomers search for new planets: by looking for the absence of something rather than the presence of something. Astronomers find possible planets by observing a dark spot where a known star should be. You might gain feedback on your advertising campaign by the reduction of new customers following the end of a campaign.

Projecting an Ad's Effectiveness

It's more difficult to estimate an ad's value in advance of running it. You need several numbers first. For starters, you need to know how many people will see the ad. Either the salesman offering you the ad can provide this information, or you determine it yourself, such as when planning a direct mail program.

Next, you need to know how many of those people will respond to the ad by entering the store and making a purchase. This part is difficult to measure, but you can use 1/1000 as a base number for untargeted advertisement. That means if the ad is seen by 20,000 people, then approximately 20 will come into the store because of the ad. At the other end of the scale, a mailout to customers who voluntarily added their information to your mailing list will be much more effective — maybe as high as 1/20.

For the last step, you need to know your average sale for that product line. If you are advertising Dungeons & Dragons, check your sales records to calculate your average D&D sale for the past three months. If you are promoting a new product line, this number is more difficult to pin down. Use a couple of numbers: a worst-case scenario and a best-guess scenario. For example, if you want to promote the board game line you added, you could use $20 as a worst-case scenario and $40 as a best-guess. The worst-case scenario figures that customers will pick up a card game like Lunch Money and ignore the larger boxes. The best-guess scenario might assume that the Settlers line will be popular.

Multiply your expected number of customers by your average sale to see the total estimated revenues from the ad. Figure your average profit margin according to what product lines you are advertising. Compare the expected profit to the ad's cost to determine whether or not it's viable.

You might be willing to utilize an ad even if the numbers do not prove favorable. Principally, you can expect that many of those customers will make repeat trips, therefore multiplying their value many times over. Also, you might be able to utilize a manufacturer co-op to soften the cost. If a manufacturer is willing to repay you in product for the cost of the ad, you can add the retail value of that product to the total earned to calculate the actual cost.

Manufacturers that do not have such a program might be willing to work out something on an informal basis. The more you are willing to spend, the more willing they're going to be to help out. After all, you do not care what you sell, as long as it's profitable. If one manufacturer does not want to contribute $200 worth of product to help decide where your $5,000 advertising budget goes, another manufacturer might.

A Sample Ad

Consider a neighborhood magazine that offers ad space for $500. The magazine claims a distribution of 20,000 around the city, of which 3,000 are in your immediate neighborhood. You choose to advertise board games for the broadest appeal and because you recently repositioned board games in your store for better visibility. You figure you will reach 1/1,000 of the overall population, but you hope to bring that number to 1/500 for the local customers, because the ad impression is bolstered by the customers driving by your store and seeing your sign. 1/1,000 times 17,000 is 17; 1/500 times 3,000 is six. Therefore, this ad is likely to bring in 23 customers.

You search your last three months of records and determine that your average board game sale is $24 and your average discount on board games is 47%. You make an average $11.28 profit from each board game sale. Therefore, your expected revenues are 23 customers times $11.48 for a total of $264.08. Unless you manage to reduce the cost of the ad such as by committing to multiple issues, this ad will not be immediately profitable.

If you increase your average ticket price to $47, you barely break even (23 customers times $22.09 profit per ticket for expected revenues of $508.07). You could also make it work if you brought the ad cost down to $300, or if a manufacturer promised to send you $200 worth of games in a co-op deal.

OTHER OFF-SITE PROMOTIONS

Your ability to capitalize on mainstream events depends on your product mix and your marketing strategy. If you sell primarily board games and non-collectible card games, you will be able to capitalize on non-specialized events. If you don't sell many of these products, off-site promotions might still offer a chance to attract new customers. Don't rule them out completely if you cater primarily to hobby gamers.

MOVIE THEATRES

Topical movie releases offer a great opportunity to get out in public at low cost, hit your target demographic, and meet some potential customers.

Specifically, doing a movie theatre release involves setting up a table and a display in a movie theatre during the opening day or weekend of a popular movie that's tied to the products you carry. Any fantasy movie might work for D&D, and comic-book related titles are popular right now. Crossover potential is everywhere.

Arranging this setup involves contacting the theatre manager and explaining what you want to do. Sometimes, larger chains want to charge you a couple of hundred dollars, but this price might be negotiable. Because it has no cost for them, they're flexible on the terms.

When you arrive, set up a sign — the bigger the better. Movie theatre posters, studio-provided signage and the theatre's permanent signage are very large, so you need gigantic signage to stand out. If you have a mascot outfit, or some kind of costume, that's better. One display for the Fellowship of the Rings release featured a volunteer dressed as a Nazgul walking around with a replica sword for the Lord of the Rings release, and the effect was very impressive.

Set your table up beyond the ticket booth. Generally, after the ticket booth comes a large lobby, with theatre entrances to either side and a concession stand dead ahead. You want to set up on one side away from the concession stand and in the direction of the movie you are tying in to your products. Angle your table slightly so that you face the incoming crowd, but be considerate of your host's space and traffic needs.

Your table should be covered with a cloth and with the product you are promoting set out on display. Make sure you have something to give away. Carry plastic miniatures, cards, dice, or some kind of premium item that you physically place in the movie watcher's hand. Develop a short catchphrase that you say as you hand it out, something intended to generate interest. "After the movie, come to Frank's Friendly Games for the sequel."

Whatever you hand out should at least have your store's name attached — and preferably an address, logo, website or phone number. The idea is to get these customers to visit your store. Make it easy for them to find you.

On your table, besides your premium items, you have the product you wish to promote. Have components out where people can put their hands on them. People walk by quickly, but if you are able to catch their attention for a moment, you might be able to show them a few moves of a game. Review your demo skills, and keep your goal in mind: increase traffic flow at the store. You are not going to teach somebody how to play. You want to spark their interest. Be content to express the concept of a game. "They make a game for this?" is a comment you hear often. Keep in mind that early movie watchers have more time to see what you are showing than the people who scurry in right as the movie is starting.

Traffic is sporadic as movies start and finish. Between the rushes, talk up the theatre's employees. The staff will be as interested as anybody else — and they most likely fit your demographic well.

SUMMARY: MOVIE PROMO COST

- Fees: $0-$300
- Equipment: $200 (reusable)
- Premium Items: $50-400
- Payroll: $30-60

TRADE SHOWS

Malls host general-interest events, and you can find similar events through your local Chamber of Commerce. Because the demographic for these events might not be very selective, it's often a better idea to approach the event with a view toward public relations or promotion rather than direct sales. Concentrate on getting people to your booth or table and handing out flyers or brochures. Try to find out what other vendors will be there. If you can, ask those vendors about their experience with previous events. More importantly, ask about vendors who have chosen not to return, contact them, and ask what led to their decision not to attend this time around.

USING MANUFACTURER TOOLS

Manufacturers want you to sell their products. To this end, they offer useful tools for helping you do that. They know that you have limited time available on your hands, so they want to create aids that reduce the time you spend on them, increase their product's visibility in your store and help drive their customers to your location.

SUMMARY: MANUFACTURER TOOLS

- Catalogs
- Sell Sheets
- Product Display Boxes
- Signage
- Retailer Locator Lists
- Co-ops
- Free Product
- Tournament Support
- Volunteer Program

Catalogs

A manufacturer catalog can be a great addition to your sales by encouraging existing customers to spend more per visit. Stocking the catalogs in the same section as the manufacturer's products is a great way to make certain that customers know where to find them. If you do not stock an entire product line, catalogs help to promote special-orders.

Encourage any customer that buys from that product line to take one home. Ask, "Do you have a Fantasy Flight Games catalog at home?" as you ring up the customer's Twilight Imperium. If he says no, place one in the bag. Do not ask if the customer wants it, because asking the question allows the customer the opportunity to say no. By placing the burden of refusal on the customer, you increase the likelihood that he will take it home and use it.

One of the best and most consistent catalogs is Reaper Miniature's Casket Works. It has pictures of all of Reaper's miniatures, enabling you to offer those miniatures without necessarily having to stock them all. If you do stock them all, the catalog can increase sales by encouraging painters to buy a wider range of figures.

Sell Sheets

When you open a package from your distributor you often see piles of strange pieces of paper that are not your product and are not packaging material. Your natural inclination is to throw this garbage away. Resist that urge for a minute.

Most of those items are sell sheets. Sell sheets are an important tool for the manufacturer. A sell sheet is a paper that tries to sell you on the product. The manufacturer is giving up some of his profit by selling through retailers and distribution to achieve greater total sales than if he sold directly to customers. That sell sheet gives you the manufacturer's perspective on how you can sell that product to his customers.

Review these sell sheets. They give you important information about the product. They tell you who the target market is, how much it costs, how much it weighs, and maybe what other products their target customer buys. You might find that these sell sheets describe a product that would be good for your store. You might find one that describes a product you already carry. Sell sheets can be great for discovering that one-line sell that you need to describe a product to a customer.

Naturally, you don't have to wait to open up a box to get these sell sheets by accident. You can contact the manufacturer directly. They might fax them to you. They might make sell sheets available on their website for download.

Once you have these sell sheets, discuss them with your staff. Review them from time to time to cull items that you are not carrying anymore, items that never released, or items that have changed editions, trade dress, or price. Make sure your staff is especially familiar with sell sheets for games they're not familiar with. They have to sell all your products, not just the ones they play.

Sell sheets give you one final advantage. You can use the information contained in it to make a pre-order list for upcoming product. Up to 90% of a product's lifetime sales come within the first 30 days. If a game reaches critical mass quickly, it can become an evergreen product. If not, it will appear, get some interest, and then fade away in favor of the next new thing. Generating excitement over that initial release is extremely important and can generate hundreds or thousands of dollars worth of sales over the lifetime of a product.

PRODUCT DISPLAY BOXES

Another manufacturer tool that you can use is the product display box. Games like Lunch Money are sometimes available individually. You might not want to buy five or six or 12 of something. But if a game has sold a couple of copies for you, and you think it might be successful, you might benefit by ordering in a display quantity to get the cardboard display. The carefully-designed art and signage increase your sales. If, for example, you sell a copy of Lunch Money every month, ordering a display is a good idea. Your turn rate drops, but remember the caveat to turn rates — they're a meter, not the ultimate goal.

To look at the math another way, buying a display increases your cost on that copy of Lunch Money by about $44. To make that money back, you would have to sell an additional five copies. A well-designed display can easily do that.

Signage & Shelving

Some manufacturers provide signage of various types to stores to help promote their products. These signs include:

▷ Danglers
▷ Window stickers
▷ Cardstock wall signs
▷ Posters
▷ Cardboard standees
▷ Header cards

Shelving units are rare and sometimes expensive, but you can often get the fixtures at no cost with a substantial product purchase. Wizards of the Coast, Mongoose Games, Reaper Miniatures, Games Workshop, Osprey Publishing, Upper Deck and White Wolf have offered fixtures of various kinds. Offers like this usually are usually finite. Ask your distributor about similar offers currently available. They include:

▷ Wire racks
▷ Spinner racks
▷ Cardboard display racks
▷ Wooden shelves

Retailer Locator Lists

One of the best things a manufacturer can do for you is to prominently list a retailer locator on his website. These locators form one of your largest sources of new customers. As such, you owe it to yourself to be on the locator listing of every manufacturer whose products you carry. It might be worthwhile to stock a product to earn a place on a listing.

Check the manufacturers whose products you carry and make sure you're on all the lists you should be. Make sure the information on those listings is up to date. It would not hurt to contact the manufacturers individually to see if they have any new programs or products you should be aware of.

Co-ops

Sometimes a manufacturer offers an advertising co-op. In this arrangement, you and other retailers help soften the manufacturer's cost for an advertisement by paying a small fee, which the manufacturer reimburses in product. The manufacturer wins because he is essentially paying for his ad at his product cost. You win because you are getting advertisement that's normally far beyond your budget for a nominal price.

Assess these deals as you would any other advertising plan (see Measuring an Ad's Effectiveness on page 135), although they are usually very useful if you sell any measurable volume of the manufacturer's products.

Free Product

I estimate that I received over $2,000 worth of free product over the course of a year.

The GAMA Trade Show was a big part of this because you receive a large quantity of free product in one fell swoop. The amount of free loot varies each year, and the quality of it varies as well. "Swag hounds" — customers or retailers who attend solely for the free merchandise — are a plague on the convention. You're welcome to it, but take only what legitimately interests you.

Sometimes manufacturers offer a prize based on a display of their products. Winning one of these contests might earn you a bonus for something you regularly do anyway. Create a display, take a picture and win loot. You were going to do it anyway, so you might as well collect a reward for it.

Other companies offer a free copy for ordering a certain amount of product. The Game Industry Network forum is one source for learning about these promotional items. New and existing manufacturers offer demo copies of their games. While they do not want to give them to everyone, a store that sells six-plus copies because it demos a game is a worthwhile investment. Hence, some manufacturers offer free demo versions with the purchase of multiple copies of a game. Investigate those games that seem to fit your needs and ask for those.

Finally, watch the mail. By making your company name available to manufacturers, some companies send you promotional games in the mail. A lot of the product is junk. Either it's poorly produced, poorly packaged, or poorly designed. Some of it simply does not work for your company and your image. Wading through this junk can sometimes reveal a surprise hit.

Use, do not abuse, these products. You could simply take the free product and sell it. Sometimes that works best. Nearly always, it's not the best use. You want to use the product to do what it's intended for: sell the game. First, learn to play it. Play with your crew or with a regular customer who has expressed interest. Then learn to teach it. Identify the key traits of the game and teach those elements in your demos. This might mean ignoring certain elements of the game during your demos; that's fine.

Also, be considerate. Send the manufacturer a thank-you e-mail for the product. Follow up with it and let him know how useful it was — or was not. Let him know what you did with it and how you disposed of it. Most manufacturers don't have any more money to spend on market research than you do, and this feedback is important to them. It also lets them know that you're a good candidate for the next time they offer a free game.

Tournament Kits

An active tournament schedule is an excellent manufacturer program that drives customers to your store. Stay aware of any such programs for games that you support and keep on the look-out for new programs as they arise. Programs frequently change, so check the Game Industry Network, read the manufacturer's website, or ask your volunteers to help you keep track of changes.

Manufacturers often provide kits, either free or at a nominal charge to cover expenses to support their tournaments. These kits usually have special prizes, pairing diagrams, instructions, and reporting forms. Different manufacturers have varying degrees of restriction regarding the use of their tournaments, so make sure to ask how stringent they are with their use before you modify the format to fit your store. Some manufacturers will cut off your direct sales, stop listing your store on their website, or otherwise punish you severely. Others say "Great idea! Do you mind if we share it?"

Managing your Volunteers

Manufacturers understand the value of hands-on promotion of their game. They know that the best way for a game to grow is for an enthusiastic player to teach the game personally to other players. Most successful manufacturers have dedicated programs that utilize their most dedicated fans to spread the word by direct contact in game stores.

You can reach these volunteers by going straight to the manufacturers. Check their websites for information and arrange to have a volunteer get in touch with you. Schedule a meeting with the volunteer to make sure it's somebody that you think will positively reflect on your image as well as the manufacturer's image. If not, you might be better off doing the job yourself or recruiting a new volunteer.

These volunteers receive product from the manufacturer in exchange for their services. In some cases, they receive a very large amount of product for their services. While you might also compensate them out of generosity, you do not need to.

Where many game stores fail is in managing their volunteers. They schedule a demo and then let the volunteer do the rest. Like anything else you do, plan out these events and use them as tools to reinforce your brand, to deliver a service to your customers, and to sell products.

Interview the volunteer like you would any other employee. You would not trust a stranger with your cash drawer, would you? Don't entrust your image to a stranger, either. Have some questions ready for your first meeting with the volunteer. Find out how familiar he is with your company, how well he knows the products he represents, and how he receives compensation. Make absolutely sure he's somebody you want representing you among your customer base.

Require a dress code of your volunteers. They shouldn't need a suit and tie, but they shouldn't come in with shorts and sandals, either. If you have a store shirt, you might want to offer them one. Alternatively, you might make the shirt a prestige item and reserve it for volunteers that run three or four demos first. Make them eager to prove themselves to you before they're allowed to wear your corporate identity. Make sure that the shirt is somehow unique from the staff dress code so as not to confuse customers. It might be a different color or have "volunteer" written across it. While they might be well-informed about the game they promote, they might not be prepared to field questions about other products or store policies.

Follow through on paperwork. If the manufacturer requires you to fill out a form, try to have the volunteer do as much of it as possible. Ideally, the volunteer does most of this work anyway. Manufacturers have learned through feedback that stores do not have time for most of them. Store owners have to pick and choose where they spend their time. Naturally, if a manufacturer requires less time, he becomes more attractive to the store owner as a partner to support.

Train the volunteer. The volunteer might know the product titles; in fact, he might own them all. Does he know their prices and current availability? Keep him informed as to current production status of the products he represents. Suggest cross-promotion opportunities for him to recommend to the customers. Make sure he's comfortable asking customers to buy product from you. Let him practice a sales pitch if he needs reinforcement in that area. Making an actual sale is very important, and volunteers are often weakest in that area.

Monitor the volunteer's activities. Make sure he's not selling his product by trashing a competing product. Volunteers that enjoy their own game too much are often too competitive during events, using draconian adherence to the rules when it gives them an edge in a tournament or a friendly game. Do not allow them to use your store to make their own sales. Do not let them argue with customers, even when the volunteer is right. Encourage volunteers to let new players slide on the rules in the interest of speed and momentum.

Communicate with the manufacturer. Many manufacturers try to keep in touch with stores to find out how well their volunteers are doing. If you are happy with one — or unhappy with one — let the manufacturer know what you do and do not like. If they improve their program, you benefit as well.

Learn from your volunteers, too. The volunteer can probably inform you about upcoming events and current trends. If a volunteer experiments with a new technique, find out how well it works and discuss how it can be improved or leveraged for maximum impact.

If you compensate your volunteers with either cash or product, they're either employees or contractors, not volunteers, and you must fill out a Form 1099 for them and file income tax if the value of that compensation exceeds $600. Review www.irs.org for full details on this procedure.

USING EVENTS TO DRIVE SALES

One key way to add value to your company is to create a busy events schedule. If you "spend" some of your productive retail space on game space, you should do everything you can to make that game space work for you. Simply opening up tables for free play fails to capitalize on one of your best marketing tools.

This discussion refers to an Events Manager. It can be the owner, or it could be an employee hired specifically for this purpose. You might choose to divide these duties between multiple employees, each of whom has slightly different skills.

The Events Manager's duties include:

Managing manufacturer volunteers. In this capacity, the Events Manager keeps in contact with the volunteers, prevents conflicting events, makes maximum use of the volunteers, and tries to recruit new volunteers in accordance with the owner's overall plans for product line promotion.

Maintaining contact with manufacturers. The Events Manager provides feedback to manufacturers concerning volunteer performance, submits required event reports, keeps track of available event options, offers suggestions for improvements to manufacturer plans based on experience, and solicits manufacturers for promotional materials and product, registers events with manufacturers or supervises volunteer registration.

Promoting events. Within a stated budget, the Events Manager advertises events among the customer base and encourages regular customers to increase their rate of visit by participating in these events. Cost-effective ads include e-mail, flyers, and in-store signage. For large events, consider postcards.

Encouraging sales. Increasing sales is the ultimate goal of the program, of course. Specifically, the Events Manager maintains product knowledge relevant to the events he supervises, offers purchase advice to players based on their experience within the events, and communicates with the person in charge of inventory management concerning additional stock for major events.

Recruitment for the position of Events Manager is best from within the ranks of existing volunteers. A person with a proven track record for improving sales along one line of products is a strong candidate for improving sales in other lines as well.

The Events Manager does not necessarily need to be trained in cashier duties, cleaning, or other non-specific applications. The Events Manager needs to be comfortable dealing with the public. The Events Manager should be thorough and knowledgeable about the products he sells.

SUMMARY: STORE EVENTS

⬡ Tournaments
⬡ Leagues
⬡ Demos
⬡ Painting clinics
⬡ Painting contests
⬡ In-store auctions
⬡ Game days
⬡ GM Panels
⬡ Flea Markets
⬡ Costume Contests

Part of the Events Manager's time must be spent in record-keeping, planning, preparation, promotion, and reporting results. The goal is to minimize this time while maximizing the actual events. A goal of 30 hours per week spent on actual event execution is a good place to start.

With 30 hours per week, you might decide to plan for 10 events in three-hour blocks. In reality, some events take much longer, and some require less time. For convenient math, this example uses 10 events.

With a margin goal of 40%, the Events Manager must generate around $1,000 per week to justify the labor expenditure. That rate equates to $100 per event in this example. For this example, consider a company that wishes to increase its sales in miniatures, with some emphasis on new CCGs and moderate emphasis on the existing CCG base. The owner is also willing to experiment with a board game night.

The Events Manager, after discussing the owner's goals, chooses to break his 10 event slots into four miniatures-related events, five CCG events and one board game.

The first event is a Warhammer 40k eight-week campaign game targeted toward the existing customer base. Between league maintenance fees of $5 per week and increased product sales, this activity generates $350 per week.

The second is a *Warhammer Fantasy Battle* league designed to introduce the game to new players. Players start with a low point value and increase their army size each week, requiring them to buy and paint figures on an ongoing basis. These sessions bring in $240 per week. The owner expects this number to decrease slightly once all of the players have built armies suitable for play.

The third miniatures session is a Warmachine league that caters to a mix of veteran and new players. It generates $120 per week due to the lesser buy-in vs. Games Workshop's games and a smaller player base.

The last miniatures event is a painting workshop. The Events Manager helps the new Warhammer Fantasy players assemble and paint their new armies and paints miniatures for the store's demo armies. This event generates a mere $80 per week, but the owner notices that the items are often high-margin add-on sales and contributes to participation in the previous three events; dropping this event might cost more than the $80 it generates.

Of the CCG slots, two apply to Magic. One night the Events Manager organizes a booster draft that draws at least eight players for a minimum of $90 in sales, and the other is a constructed tournament that generates $60 in tournament fees and an average of $75 in sales of singles, booster packs and accessories.

The Events Manager also runs weekly tournaments for a secondary card game in the store, such as Legend of the Five Rings or Pokemon. A regular group of six-eight players contributes an average of $35 in tournament fees and $50 in sales.

The two new CCG slots start out slowly, but the Events Manager and the owner understand that. Each brings in an average of $40 per week, most of which is one-time sales to people interested enough to buy starters but not interested enough to continue play on a regular basis.

The board game night features rotating games voted on by the players present. Because board game players don't need to continue buying products after they have their board game, sales are sporadic. The Events Manager also sneaks in some low price-point card games like Munchkin, which sell well and encourage additional sales through supplements. This event slot generates an average of $40 per week — barely the equivalent of a single board game each week.

This set of events puts $1220 a week in the register, which is enough to justify both the Events Manager's salary and the cost of the prizes for the tournaments he runs. None of the estimated numbers used represents a difficult goal to reach.

Why not all miniatures? You might wonder, with the huge discrepancy in expected results between miniatures and CCGs on one hand, and board games and RPGs on the other hand, "why not support only the most-productive events?"

Some companies do. They base their business model on the market leaders: either Magic or Games Workshop. You could, too.

This model does have advantages: it's easier to train employees to learn one game than it is to learn a dozen. You can focus your advertising efforts more tightly. You need less space for retail, allowing more space for in-store gaming. You can buy or build your gaming tables with a particular game in mind: long, narrow tables for pairs of CCG opponents or tables sized to fit Games Workshop's battlefields.

The risk with this business model is that your company's existence is based on one other single company's success. If you create a Games Workshop-only retail store, and Games Workshop fails, changes focus, loses its position as industry leader, becomes unprofitable due to a change in its retailer terms, or otherwise substantially alters its products' feasibility, your business suffers. If you sell a wide variety of products, you stand a better chance of surviving industry fluctuations.

Running a Great Demo

This Guide frequently refers to running a game demo. Demonstrations are one of your best conversion tools. Once a colorful display or your one-line sell has generated a customer's interest in a game, the demo convinces a customer to jump into a game with both feet.

You can use the demo in two ways: first as an immediate tool to help sell games directly to a single individual who walked in the store. In this case, the demo is a conversion tool to help you turn a potential customer into an actual customer. For this situation, have the game handy at the counter or set up on a permanent demo table that's readily accessible. Place cards in his hand. Move straight into the demo before the customer knows he's playing a game.

The second method caters to existing players. It serves the purpose of generating more sales from a single customer rather than creating new customers. Also, you usually demo to a group instead of an individual or a couple. These scheduled demos seek to introduce a game to gamers that are already familiar with the hobby. With a scheduled demo, you often have much longer to spend with the customers. They might plan to sit down for an hour or more, whereas you have no longer than five or 10 minutes with unscheduled demos.

Before you start doing any demos, plan out your demo strategies. What's your purpose? Will demos be a part of your conversion toolkit or will you use them to increase customer spending? Or both? Knowing your purpose dictates how you will approach the demos. Being the practical person that I am, I'm going to call the short impromptu demo you use at the counter a conversion demo and the scheduled demo you use with your regular customers a scheduled demo. Both have some elements in common.

Create a Script

Have a general outline for how the game's going to develop and what you tell a customer before, after, and during the demo. Your script should call for the customer to win. Make it as subtle as possible, but customers who win are far more likely to buy the game. "Did you see that? I beat the game store owner!" You might hear boasting. I hear a cash register ringing.

Conduct the Demo

Begin your demo by introducing yourself and any other regular customers or employees who will be playing. Take this opportunity to learn the customer's name and use it during the game.

Next, briefly describe the background and the goal as you lay out the game. This summary should be longer than your one-line sell but not very detailed.

> "The name of the game is *Guillotine*, ladies and gentlemen. We're executioners during the French Revolution. We've lopped off thousands of heads and we're getting bored, so we're going to assign points to the heads and have a contest among ourselves. At the end of the game, the person with the most points wins."

> Identify key components briefly. "Purple cards are nobles. Red are soldiers. Gray cards are the good guys; don't kill them if you can help it."

Explain game play as you go. If you have cards in your hand, you can leave them on the table to allow people to see what you are doing. If the game is as simple as *Guillotine*, you play it out as is. In the case of something more complicated, restrict the

152

options available to players and make a "cheat sheet" of options that you keep handy for new players. A laminated sheet on the table is perfect.

In either case, dole the information out in manageable chunks to allow people to digest it. Streaming it out in bits allows you to keep their interest longer, too; they want to know what's next. Explain new card types or game play options as they arise.

During play, be decisive and tell a new player what to do if he asks for a suggestion. Avoid evaluating every single option. By now, the player is already mentally planning his moves. If you help guide him through things, he'll develop his own strategies and goals for next time. When he starts thinking about the next time, you've done your job. He's ready to buy.

Be prepared to adjust your script if necessary. If things go entirely your way due to randomness, accept that you might accidentally win. If you see it coming, do your best to play up the fun aspect of the game rather than any competition. Make funny faces. Voice sound effects. Put on a show.

End the Demo
Ideally, you should spend five minutes or less on a conversion demo. If you can play the game in that time, play it out. If not, your script should not call for a full game. "Normally, *Guillotine* takes place over three 'days' of 12 cards. For this demo, we'll play through one day." Play enough of it that the player can see how different mechanics work, and then wrap up the game in narrative summary.

Close the Sale
Afterward, move to close the sale. "So, will the original Settlers box be enough for you, or do you need the five to six player expansion, too?" Do not be timid about asking a customer to buy something he clearly enjoys. That was the point of the demo.

Remember to plug the network capability of your store. e.g., "You can find people willing to play that with you practically anytime, but especially on the weekends. In fact, we're having a tournament on the 3rd of next month, and I'm sure people will want to practice."

Review
Revise your script as you do the demo a few times. Learn what questions people ask and incorporate the answers to those ques-

tions into your dialogue. Be careful with timing; do not bother to explain something too far in advance, or the player will forget about it by the time he encounters it.

Another method of review involves feedback from the demo participants. Get their contact information when you run the demo. Two to three days after the event, send them an e-mail or a post card asking a few questions about their experience. You want to find out if they had a good time. By asking them that question, you are reminding them that they did have a good time. If they didn't, you are creating an opportunity for them to express any concerns they had. Maybe the person running the demo is not well-suited for working with customers. Follow-up like this might let you know before you start losing customers.

Things to Avoid

One natural tendency when you demo a game is to make it look appealing by comparing it to another game. Be careful. It's very easy to make the other game look bad by comparison.

I've seen many volunteers thinking they're helping the company promote a miniatures game by telling people how overpriced Games Workshop is. They don't think you'd rather sell $80 worth of miniatures than $300 worth of miniatures. They think they're doing the customer a favor by pointing out a better value.

Also, don't oversell. Don't make the game out to be some magical experience that will zap fun straight into a player's brain. Be positive, but be honest.

Scheduled Demos

If the demo is a scheduled event, plan it a couple of weeks ahead of time. Give yourself time to prepare for the demo and time to notify your customers. Make sure it either does not conflict with any other event or is intentionally placed near another event to gather the attention of those players.

Promotion

Scheduled demos need to be promoted; they don't just happen. Send out an e-mail, post cards, or other notices. Make a sign for the game room. If you keep a calendar, note the event there. Scheduled events primarily cater to existing customers, so keep this fact in mind when you plan your promotion.

Provide Exciting Visuals

For a game you demo frequently, consider designing a special oversized or graphically exciting board or graphic. I've seen board games that use a cloth rollup map about eight times the normal size, with hefty wooden game pieces. For a role-playing game, provide painted miniatures for the players and make sure the villain figures are outstanding.

Rio Grande Games runs a demo game of *Ra* that uses an oversized cloth "board" instead of the normal board. The demo setup has custom over-sized pieces. Their demo table is a piñata of visual excitement.

SUMMARY: SUGGESTED DEMO VISUALS
- A framed map of the setting for an RPG
- Painted miniatures (better if the player can keep them)
- Use minis instead of normal board game tokens
- A custom-painted oversized board
- Sleeved cards
- Order-of-play reminder cards

RUNNING LEAGUES

Leagues provide existing players with a regular play environment. The goal is to encourage gamers to commit to a regular day of the week and encourage competitive play without the pressure of a tournament.

A league lasts for several sessions: six to 12 weeks is a good span. Players typically earn points for participation and additional points for winning. Providing partial points for participation encourages players to show up when they're not in the lead. Players typically receive a minor prize for participation and then additional prizes for winning the most points, or a final tournament-style event.

One way to encourage miniatures purchases is to graduate the campaign. For the first two weeks of the campaign, players use an army of 500 points, adding 100 points each week to their army roster. You might encourage terrain sales by allowing certain tactical advantages to players who bring their own terrain.

Leagues are most popular during the summer. Summer allows more to commit to a regular play schedule.

Running Tournaments

The frequency of tournaments varies with the format, but it involves matching players against each other in a structured competition, presumably for a prize of some sort. The fee should at least cover the cost of materials and prizes, and should include some sort of fees to cover time and labor, as well.

A tournament kit provided by the manufacturer usually includes information on how to run the tournament. Otherwise, tournaments follow a fairly standard procedure.

If you haven't run a tournament before, you'll want to arrange for a tournament item code for your POS so that you can track of your results. If you include prizes, then you might have to account for the inventory usage, too. Do not ring up the booster pack as a sale; count it as an item used for promotion/marketing. That way, you keep your inventory records accurate while recording a marketing expense that you can record when you file your taxes. Marketing expenses are tax-deductible. Sales are not.

Promote the tournament in-store for two to four weeks before the actual event. If you're running something very special, you might advertise longer. If you plan too far in advance, though, you risk customers forgetting about the event. Use all the usual media for this: e-mails to the appropriate customer groups, signs on the store bulletin board, fliers in your bag-stuffers, a notice on your calendar, announcements on your online bulletin board, etc.

Decide on a format. You often have to choose from different methods of matching opponents past the first-round random draw, methods of determining advancement and a final winner. If the game doesn't provide such guidelines, you must decide them yourself.

If so, encourage formats in which people play multiple games. Assign points to wins and losses and add point totals rather than using simple single-elimination matches to drop players from the competition. Use methods that encourage elements other than straight competition, like Best Painted Army and Best Sportsman.

Establish floor rules ahead of time. Do you require armies to be painted? How long do players have to start a match once you announce pairings? Are players allowed to leave the building between matches? Do you check army or deck lists for legality ahead of time? Decide on all of these things and whatever else comes to mind. If possible, announce the floor rules in advance so that you don't surprise players on the day of the tournament.

Uniformity forestalls accusations of unfairness and keeps your players happy. Again, the specific game often provides rules like this for you.

Secure a judge. The judge should be competent in the rules, but it's possibly more important that the judge be someone capable of settling disputes fairly, which doesn't always require rules knowledge. Decide whether or not you allow the judge to compete and who judges the judge if you do. Have a backup in case the judge can't make it to the tournament for some reason.

Have a method of determining random seating or match pairing. Writing names on pieces of paper and pulling two at a time out of a jar works fine. From there on, it's all downhill. Your tournament format determines winners and losers, and you hand out prizes.

Afterward, thank all the players for showing up. Some stores post pictures of the winners on their website or on a bulletin board in the store. The younger players love that, and more of the older players than will admit it like it, too.

Social Networking

Social network marketing has become the new fad for businesses. It is a no-cost way to reach a very large number of potential customers. Although we often lump them all together in conversation, each of these networks has its own unique characteristics, user expectations, demographics, and best uses.

Generalities

With no cost involved, time is your only limiting factor. Done right, managing your social media requires investments of both reading and writing. Social media, especially as I envision the gaming industry, relies on interactivity. You can't just send out notices, you have to seek out interesting conversations and reply to them, and make topical posts, not just ads.

Mix up media. Post a link. Post a picture. Make a funny comment. Post something personal. Mention a new release. Repost a video from YouTube.

Address customer service issues quickly. If a customer complains on your Facebook page that his opponent cheated in a Magic tournament, don't delete it — address it. That lets other people know that you care and that you respond positively to feedback.

Facebook

Several pages on Facebook have been created for the purpose of discussing game retailer issues. Search for them and you'll find them. Facebook will also start recommending them for you once you join one. Game Store Retailer is the one I find most useful.

Facebook needs at least one post per day, but not too much. You can post product shots. Be more personal on Facebook than on some others. Share more about yourself and encourage your crew and customers to do the same. Facebook isn't about news, it's about keeping in touch.

LinkedIn

Although it is more appropriate for business-to-business enterprises, LinkedIn can still be a valuable tool. Connect with your distributors, friendly local competitors, manufacturers, and others in the industry. Ask customers for reviews and ask your network for recommendations.

Twitter

Feel free to lean on Twitter a little harder than you do Facebook. You can make multiple — even numerous — posts per day without losing followers. You must keep them short to fit Twitter's capacity, so make them concise and punchy. Post less fluff on Twitter than you do on Facebook.

Use hashtags to make your posts more search-friendly. For example, include #rpg when you announce D&D Encounters night. Keep your hashtags focused and few. Using a half-dozen hashtags buries your message.

Google Plus

Google+ works like Facebook in most ways. It is easier to use and has more tools for organization, but its use for your business is very similar. You can use the customization to your advantage. If there is an issue you want to bring up with distributors and manufacturers, and those people are all in a circle, blast them off a note and don't worry about diluting the message to your customers.

Pinterest

Pinterest focuses on images, and you have plenty of those. Product shots make it easy to announce what's new. Just pin the photo to your page and there's your announcement.

But that's not all there is to it. Pinterest's users are mostly women, and you can use that to determine what you post and what comments you make on your pins. If your store focuses solely on Magic, with its 97% male customer base, Pinterest will do you no good. If you have an anime club with 90 women in it, Pinterest might be very useful to you.

Pin or Repin

▷ Product shots
▷ Pictures of games in progress
▷ Photos of tournament winners
▷ Geek humor
▷ Fan art related to your products (e.g., comics, games, anime)
▷ Movie posters

MEETUP

Check existing Meetups before creating one of your own. Don't look just to gaming. You might find science fiction or fantasy fan clubs, anime clubs, comic book lovers, or the like. Join them. Offer your store as a place to meet. As always, make a useful contribution to the group.

YOUTUBE

YouTube might seem a little more labor-intensive than other types of sites, but you can make it work for you. Even if your YouTube channel does not attract its own following, you can use it to host the occasional videos you make for specific purposes.

YouTube videos you might make include:
▷ Box openings
▷ Short game demos
▷ Store tours
▷ Crew member interviews
▷ Store development clips, like receiving your first merchandise, or painting the walls

Chapter 6: Operations

Operations are similar to other specialty retail stores. Customers see your print advertising, hear about the store through their friends, or see your roadside signage. They enter the store, browse your wares, and listen to your sales pitches. If your merchandising works, they buy something. If your sales staff is doing its job, they'll come back.

Most of your operational effort revolves around inventory control.

Assemble Your Staff & Volunteers

While you might start out with no help, at one point you will need an employee to give you a break. Seven-day work weeks get old after a couple of years. Depending on your expected sales volume, you might want the help right away.

Employee Handbook

Before you hire anyone, it is helpful to know what you expect out of an employee. Take a few minutes to write down your expectations and what you plan to do for the employee as well. These notes will form the basis of your Employee Handbook. Even if the "Handbook" is two pages of job description and pay rate, it's a useful operational tool and legal tool to protect you from lawsuits, unemployment insurance, and other possible loss. If an employee does something in violation of your Employee Handbook's guidelines and you have a signed statement indicating that the employee has read and understood your handbook, you have greater protection against unemployment claims if you terminate that employee as a result of his misconduct.

The employee handbook takes some employee-relevant information from your Operations Manual, so if you already have an Operations Manual, you have already written part of your Employee Handbook. Make sure that if you change one reference, you change the other.

An Employee Handbook outline is included in Appendix II for your reference.

Hiring New Employees

Hiring an employee requires several steps. The first is to advertise that you are looking for an additional employee. This announcement is usually followed by a flurry of offers from people who are willing to work for nothing but the benefits. Few of these people realize how much actual work is involved.

After that, review your applications. Reject outright applications that are incomplete. If someone cannot follow the rules on a single sheet of paper, how much trouble will they be to work with?

Interviewing

The next step, interviewing, weeds out the people who want benefits without work and helps you select the employee with the right attitude. Ideally, you want someone who likes working with people, is willing to learn to play games and is willing to work weekends.

Schedule the interview at a time when you are not working the counter so that you can give the interviewee your full attention. It could take place in the game room before the store opens, in the office during business hours, or at a nearby restaurant. Be on time and re-read the employee's application beforehand so you are familiar with it during the interview.

Once the applicant arrives, introduce yourself and ask a couple of social questions to put him at ease. "How are you?", "Were you able to find the store without any problem?" and other conversation will help bridge the introduction and the actual interview. Show the applicant where to sit, seat yourself and begin. Be clear in your transition: "Let's get started," says it all.

Begin by telling the applicant a little bit about what your business. Consider this part of your branding and remember that this person might not be suited for the job. If you hire him, you establish the importance of branding. If you do not, then this speech reinforces your brand with that potential customer.

Then explain that the purpose of the interview is to find out if the applicant is best suited to help you achieve your goals. Explain that you have high standards for customer service and reliability. If you do not hire this person, this part of the interview reinforces a good public image and maintains that person as a customer and as a potential future employee should circumstances change.

The point of the interview is to find out as much as you can about the applicant's work ethic, honesty, initiative and other useful traits. Ask open-ended questions to force the applicant to expand his responses. Give him every opportunity to trip himself up. One way to get the applicant to keep talking is to be patient and wait. If you are not talking, the applicant often feels like he should be!

SUMMARY: GOOD INTERVIEW QUESTIONS

🌐 "Tell me about the best example you remember where you gave or received excellent customer service."

🌐 "We pride ourselves on always being available for our customers. How do you feel if you have to stay late because your relief isn't in yet?"

🌐 "How do you feel about confronting potential shoplifters?"

🌐 "How would you handle a customer who becomes angry over a lost or mistaken special order?"

Certain questions are illegal to ask during an interview or on a job application. These questions seek to identify a person's national background, religion, or other off-limit areas. Refer to the Equal Employment Opportunity Commission for more details. You can find more information online at *http://www.eeoc.gov/abouteeo/overview_laws.html*.

Example questions include asking the applicant what kind of name he has, or asking a female if her husband minds her working late. The first question could identify race or ethnicity, and the second identifies marital status. Because it is illegal to make hiring decisions based on any of these factors, asking them during an interview opens your company to legal liability.

During the interview, note the applicant's dress and behavior. Does he interrupt you? Is he underdressed for the job? Is he unclean? Remember that people present their best image for an interview. Are you comfortable hiring this person if this is the best he's going to be?

Refer to your company, or your business, when you mean those things, rather than the store. The "store" is a place you lease that makes it easy for you to meet customers. The "store" does not make hiring decisions, have policies, or do much of anything. Your company hires only drug-free personnel. By reinforcing that you operate a business that exists to make money, you impart a professionalism that your employees will remember.

If an applicant thoroughly impresses you all the way through the interview, make no verbal commitments at this stage. Thank the applicant for his or her time and inform him or her that you will inform the chosen candidates of your decision soon. Your work is not done yet.

Follow-Up

Check references for the people you have interviewed and have not rejected yet. Legally, the only things a prior employer can tell you are 1) dates the employee began and ended employment and 2) whether or not the person is eligible for rehire. However, the person you speak to might not know that. You are allowed to ask any question you like. If the applicant can take any legal action over any conversation at this point, his previous employer bears full responsibility.

A professional Human Resources department at a large company is likely to be aware of these laws and tell you only the required information. You can learn more from a smaller company that will answer your questions. If possible, ask why the employee left. Ask if he was punctual when he was there. Ask if he worked well with others. Gather any information you can to help you make a hiring decision.

You may choose to have your prospective employees undergo drug testing. You should provide them with a written notice about this requirement. Have them sign an agreement to perform the drug test, and schedule the test for as quickly as possible to reduce the opportunity for drugs to pass through the applicant's system.

Run a criminal background check on every applicant. Game stores typically have minors in the store at all times. The public relations nightmare that would occur if the press finds out that your Saturday evening clerk is a convicted sexual offender is not something you want to experience. Similarly, if the person you hire steals your weekend deposit and your entire singles inventory, it's your fault if you didn't realize he had multiple burglary convictions.

If the position is managerial or otherwise allows for a large amount of control over your business, you should seriously consider running a full background check. If the employee will be driving for you (such as taking bank deposits or attending conventions), you should run a check of the applicant's driving record as well.

Paperwork

Once you have chosen your new employee, you have to do some paperwork. The I-9 is a federal document that verifies an employee's eligibility to work in the United States. Fill out the I-9, following the instructions on the form. Photocopy the documents used to verify the employment eligibility so that you will have proof in case the government wishes to verify it later.

Have the employee fill out the W-4, fill in your section at the bottom and send that in to the address given.

Both of these documents are available online for free. Some companies will gladly charge you for them if you let them. Don't. Have the employee read and sign the Employment Agreement if you have one. Give him a copy for his own records.

> ### SUMMARY: EMPLOYEE RECORDS CONTAIN
> ❦ A copy of the I-9 and referenced documents
> ❦ A copy of the W-4
> ❦ The original signed application

Employee Agreement
Your employee agreement is a useful tool that helps limit your liability in case you have to terminate an employee and otherwise protects you from the employee after the employee leaves your company. It is a document that you prepare before deciding to hire any employees. It should be uniform for all employees; if you make changes before hiring somebody new, have your employees sign an amendment of the previous version they already signed.

Exact provisions of the employee agreements vary, and if you have a question about what you can include, consult your attorney. These provisions are a good standard to base your employee agreement upon.

Acknowledgement of Company Policy
The employee's signature on this statement indicates that the employee is aware of your company policies. Obviously, you

must provide a written copy of your company's policies before having the employee sign this provision. These policies should include attendance policy, uniform policy, drug policy, and all other expectations.

Non-Compete Agreement
This document prevents your employee from going to work for a competitor or opening up a store of his own after leaving your employ. The degree to which you can enforce this varies, but you can almost always insist on your local market, and if you have multiple locations, you might be able to enforce a greater range. Duration is similarly a question of what your attorney feels a judge will support — up to five years is common.

SUMMARY: OPTIONAL DOCUMENTS
⊛ Original employment application
⊛ Employment agreement
⊛ Non-compete agreement

Rejected Applicants
You don't need to inform rejected applicants that they were not hired. They can figure that out when you do not inform them that you've hired them.

Out of courtesy, many employers send out a letter to rejected applicants. This letter should be brief, clear and objective. A form letter works well. It reduces your workload and reduces any chance of a later claim of discrimination or nepotism. Thank the applicants for considering your company for employment. Your letter should simply inform the applicant that, after reviewing all of the applications, you filled the position with the applicant that seemed to best suit your needs at the time.

The applications of rejected applicants are required to be kept on file. Check your state Department of Labor guidelines for how long you must keep these records.

Training
Training a new hire should begin with an orientation of about five to 15 minutes. Non-gamers might need the full 15 minutes. Give employees a tour of the store showing the breakdown of

products by genre or type of game, where to find paperwork, and other necessities.

A person should never work alone on his first shift. The trainer should work beside him for several shifts before allowing him to work alone. Prioritize the tasks the employee needs to learn and teach them to each employee in a consistent order.

The Teaching Process

1. When you teach a new technique, explain what you are going to show and why you do it that way. Example: "Let's discuss handling credit card transactions."

2. Next, demonstrate the technique. Show the technique all the way through once. Then break it down step by step.

3. Supervise. Allow the trainee to practice under your supervision. Watch the trainee and praise him for doing something right. If he needs help, point out one item that needs work. Make sure you phrase the criticism positively. "You are doing a great job on upselling to the miniatures players. Next, I need you to work on upselling to the role-players, too."

4. Follow up. Once the employee is able to perform the technique on his own, check back periodically to make sure he's following proper procedures. Commend him on practiced techniques and attitudes, preferably publicly.

Sales Techniques

The ability to sell something is the key trait you want your sales staff to learn. Your advertising can be amazing at getting people in the door, but if your sales staff can't sell to them, you're wasting money. Your employees can be the fastest cashiers in the world, but if you don't have any transactions to ring up, they're useless.

Sales staff should be comfortable with the idea of approaching customers. The thought that maybe customers prefer to be left alone when they shop has no place in a salesperson's mind. The salesperson should be able to address customers with confidence, suggest a product that meets that customer's needs and close the sale. The key trait to learning strong sales techniques is consistency. A sales associate who consistently approaches customers gains that confidence. Practicing sales pitches helps develop a smooth, unforced delivery that works well. Consistent upselling yields more sales in total than the occasional spectacular upselling.

Equipment Operation

Nearly all employees operate the cash register, so you must teach this skill. I personally recommend that you teach sales skills first. It sends the message to employees that their primary duty is to make sales. The mechanics of ringing up the transaction are secondary to making the sale in the first place.

Other equipment might include:

▷ Alarm system
▷ Shrink-wrap machine
▷ Fax/copier

Software

As with equipment, your employees might have to learn different applications to perform their duties. Typical requirements include:

▷ E-mail
▷ Tournament/event reporting software
▷ POS system
▷ Daily/weekly reporting

Product Knowledge

An employee involved with sales needs to know how to identify and price CCG singles, how to identify the manufacturer of a product, how to look up unfamiliar product, and how to find product in the store if a customer asks where it is. Employees should be familiar with current promotions, aware of upselling potential, and how to answer the most common customer questions.

Product knowledge is the largest single block of information that your employees will learn. An employee could spend years gaining product knowledge. Possession of this knowledge often trumps other considerations when considering an employee.

Opening Procedures

If an employee is to open the store, the trainer should go over opening procedures with that employee. Outline your store's opening procedures and make a copy of them available for new hires. He or she should know how to turn on the "Open" sign, know where the light switch and thermostat are, and have a way to contact another employee in case an emergency prevents him or her from opening on time. Make sure you identify how early you expect your opening employee to arrive for work.

If you have a safe, your opener might need to know how to open the safe in the morning. This procedure can take a bit of practice, so make sure he can do it before he opens alone. You don't want the new opener calling you at home 20 minutes after the store's supposed to open because he can't get the money out.

Merchandise Handling Procedures

Most employees will be responsible for inventory counting of some kind. They should know your expectations concerning frequency, timeliness and accuracy concerning these reports.

If the employee's job includes receiving orders, the employee needs to understand your company's receiving and stocking guidelines. The employee might be responsible for pricing these items or adding new items to a POS system; if so he or she needs clear guidelines on how you expect these things done.

If the employee's duties include packaging mail-order or Internet orders, the employee should be taught these duties, as well.

Closing Procedures

If an employee is to close the store, the trainer should go over closing procedures with the employee. Make sure the closing procedures are available for employees to review on their own. Closers need extra attention to cash handling policies and safety and security policies because they are at the greatest risk for a robbery.

Thinking Outside the Cash-Wrap

I strongly recommend that you direct your clerks to stay out from behind the counter whenever possible. If there is work they must do there, they should do it there. But if they can do the work from the other side of the counter — the customer's side — then they should.

The benefit is that clerks on the customer's side of the counter are far more approachable. Customers are more likely to ask the clerk for assistance. Idle clerks should get out among the product, straightening shelves where they need it, and replacing items that have been moved by customers. If you have them actively performing partial inventories several times per week, they already have an excuse to get out from behind the counter. Developing the habit is easy.

Getting out from behind the counter has additional benefits as well. By being among the customers, the clerk has a ready excuse to closely monitor potential shoplifters. By showing that he is alert for product out of place, he's letting these would-be criminals know that he will notice something missing. He also will not be behind a physical barrier should they attempt to grab something and run.

A clerk on the customer's side can also more easily make his second approach to a customer. Having once turned down the ubiquitous offer for help when the customer entered, he will be more likely to accept an offer from a nearby clerk who is obviously willing to get out and do something instead of sitting on a stool behind a counter.

For this reason, you — or your principal sales person if it is not you — should always be in this position on your high-volume days. During times when the person working the cash register is tied to that machine and unable to "float", you should be working the floor. Make yourself known to your customers. Learn what games they play. Learn who they like to play games with and who they do not. Look for potential demo volunteers.

This concept has one minor liability: it's not as easy for the customer to identify who works there when you have multiple regulars sitting around talking. The customer might be reluctant to ask for help. Easily identifiable uniforms help fix that problem. Clerks following your rigidly-enforced policy of approaching customers when they enter the door solves nearly all of these issues.

Training the Trainer

If you do not plan to train employees directly, you should discuss training techniques with the person who will. You should make sure that the trainer is proficient with training techniques. Prioritize the skills you want employees to learn.

You might not want an employee handling money right away, for example. By stressing the sales aspect of the job over the trivial task of making change, you demonstrate to the employee where his priorities should lie. Paperwork should always be secondary to customer service. By teaching employees these skills in this order, you reinforce that message with your crew.

For that matter, an employee might not handle cash at all. The register might not be a part of an employee's job descrip-

170

tion. The trainer should be fully aware of the employee's position in the store and the duties that position demands. Having written job descriptions for all employees helps standardize this task.

Job Descriptions

In all likelihood, your staffing needs will be small. You might or might not run the company as the manager. You will probably have fewer than a half-dozen crew members, most of which will be part-time. These four general categories of employee should cover all of your needs.

If not, feel free to create specific descriptions for additional employees you hire. If your crew approaches a dozen or more, for example, you might find it expedient to hire one person primarily for cleaning, repair, and other mundane tasks. If so, you could create an abbreviated list of duties from the part-time crew member and expand it to fit your needs.

Similarly, you might choose to offer a limited position to a highly skilled manufacturer volunteer. Create a new position with duties concentrating on events and sales and identify that position's duties on paper. In this way, you and your employees all know exactly what you expect out of each person.

Part-Time Crew Member

The Part-time Crew Member might see the customer less frequently than other crew members, but his duties are no less important. The Crew Member should know his customers, should know the product well to upsell effectively, and should strive to maintain a positive image. Specific duties include:

▷ Greeting customers briefly but cordially as they enter the door.
▷ Answering questions by customers concerning products, release dates, etc.
▷ Upselling customers by suggesting additional material to help their game.
▷ Keeping customers informed about activities in the store.
▷ Ensuring that the store remains clean at all times.
▷ Promoting games on the current demo schedule.
▷ Recording special orders for customers.
▷ Performing spot inventories according to the weekly schedule.
▷ Preventing shrinkage by watching for shoplifting while customers are in the store.
▷ using down-time profitably by keeping busy (sorting cards,

painting miniatures for displays or demos, checking walls for out-of-place merchandise, folding cardboard CCG boxes).

▷ maintaining cash control within company guidelines.

▷ other duties as assigned.

Full-Time Crew Member
The Full-time Crew Member is the backbone of the store. Customers recognize this crew member, and his attitudes and preferences directly and materially affect the company's sales. Specific duties include:

▷ Knowing the release schedule of different game manufacturers.

▷ Running scheduled game demos in a variety of games systems.

▷ Receiving and merchandising product deliveries.

▷ Handling special orders upon delivery.

▷ Knowing rules to different popular games to field player questions.

▷ Setting up and removing displays as requested and on schedule.

▷ All duties of part-time crew members.

Assistant Manager
The Assistant Manager's primary duty is to learn to handle the tasks of the manager by undergoing training and by applying these lessons in the daily execution of his job. He also assists in ensuring excellent customer service, maintaining accurate paperwork, and promoting game play in the store. Specific duties include:

▷ Preparing inventory orders for the next order.

▷ Purchasing used games from customers at a profitable margin.

▷ Training crew members and manager trainees.

▷ All duties of other crew members.

Store Manager
The store manager is responsible for overseeing the smooth operation of the store, maintaining excellent customer service, increasing sales, and controlling costs for maximum profitability. Specific duties include:

▷ Reviewing the performance of other employees and making suggestions to help employees improve when appropriate.

▷ Ordering product on a consistent and timely basis.

▷ Improving the performance of unproductive stock or liquidating dead stock.

▷ Keeping equipment operational and stocked, including register, credit card machine, light fixtures, copier, and lit display cases.

▷ Merchandising product attractively and profitably.

▷ Maintaining an active schedule of events that caters to different markets.

▷ Encouraging regular game activity in the store.

▷ Rotating displays in the display cases to show attractive and current products.

▷ Planning and implementing regular mailouts to bring existing customers into the store more often.

▷ Setting and adjusting cash on hand to meet the requirements of sales.

▷ All duties of other employees.

Additionally, all team members are encouraged to do the following:

▷ Carry business cards to hand out to prospective customers.

▷ Play or run games at the store in their off-duty hours.

▷ Become official company representatives for game manufacturers.

▷ Support sales by using miniatures, terrain, counters, or other games accessories in games.

▷ Attend gaming conventions.

Evaluation

Employee evaluations are a method of continually training and refocusing the attention of the employees to the duties they're assigned. It lets them know which areas they need to improve and alerts you to potential weaknesses in your training program.

All employees should receive an evaluation within a week of their employment. An immediate evaluation does two things. First, it lets the employee know that this is a standard aspect of their job that should not surprise them or cause them undue stress. Second, it allows you the opportunity to point out things the employee is doing right.

Plan an evaluation schedule ahead of time. Initial evaluations should come frequently. You might insist on one evaluation after two weeks, a second after thirty days, two more evaluations after 30 days each, and then quarterly evaluations after that.

When you are ready to do an evaluation, let the employee know ahead of time. Schedule some time with the employee when you can sit down without interruption for the evaluation. Go over each item, scoring the employee and explaining your reasoning behind each rating. Encourage the employee's responses to these scores. Sometimes their responses will make you change your mind on your score. Be flexible but fair.

The purpose of the evaluation is to elicit improvement. Provide positive steps the employee can take to step up performance in weak areas. Praise the employee for areas in which he excels.

Allow the employee to make written comments about the evaluation afterward. Make a copy for the employee and place the original in the employee's folder.

Scheduling

For most purposes, the store needs one person on duty at a time. Openers should be in place a few minutes ahead of time for preparation, while closers might need up to an hour, depending on their familiarity with paperwork, allowing extra time for late customers and other duties.

Busy traffic in the sales area requires an additional person on duty. Generally, Friday evening and Saturday afternoon are the busiest times for the industry, but special events on regular days might create enough traffic to require a second person. The guideline for what a single person can handle is about $300 per hour. If your records show that on a certain night you have one or more $300 hours, you should schedule a second person for that shift. At $300, a minimum wage employee equals 2% labor. Remember that a busy clerk makes cash register errors, might not be able to monitor potential shoplifters, and will not get any other chores assigned. That extra few dollars of labor costs far less than losing a customer because he could not get any service.

The basic labor goal for most stores will be in the range of 20%, although this number varies wildly. For one thing, game stores might range in volume from under $100,000 per year to over $900,000. Meanwhile, the owner's salary certainly does not increase nine-fold. A small-town salary of $20,000 per year in the low-volume store runs 20% of sales, while a comfortable $45,000 salary in the higher-volume store runs 5% of net sales.

EMPLOYEE COMPENSATION

Employees in a game store do not expect to receive high pay. Most game stores pay them minimum wage or slightly greater. In metropolitan markets, the average pay increases because of the higher cost of living.

If you wanted really cheap employees, you could probably

find that a large number of your customers will be happy to watch the counter for nothing more than the employee discount. You probably hear semi-serious offers from these customers from time to time. You do not want those people behind the counter. These volunteers do not realize how much work the job demands and exactly how much training they need to do the job right. Also, what's cool and fun for a couple of days becomes a chore after a bit of repetition.

Keeping that in mind, offer a fair pay, but pay what you can afford. Your labor is your second-highest controllable cost, so keep it as low as you can while still keeping competent help. Most often, people do not steal from you or leave you because of low pay. These issues arise from poor treatment.

Employee benefits that are important to your employees include:

▷ Discounts on products. Retailer opinions on discounts range from only 10% to cost. Most discounts fall within the 20-35% range and specifically exclude low-margin items. Many stores also disallow buying at a discount within a certain time period of a product's release to avoid being bought out by an employee when you could be selling the product at full price to customers. Once an item's sales start to plateau and keeping it in stock is not an issue, employees are free to buy it up. They could also special-order it so they're not cannibalizing shelf stock.

▷ Free LAN time. If you have a LAN, free time on the LAN is a very popular benefit. Make it clear that paying customers have priority over employees.

▷ Free locker. If you offer something like this, it's a way to encourage your employees to be in the store running or playing games when off duty.

▷ Health Insurance. Most of the young people that work in game stores place a low value on health insurance. If you find a reasonable rate, however, you will find that the number of people you can attract climbs accordingly, giving you more options for your staffing.

PAYROLL

Handling payroll correctly is a hurdle that causes many small businesses to stumble. Sadly, it's not that difficult.

The easiest and safest way to handle payroll is to outsource your payroll to an outside company. A payroll service like Paychex cuts your checks, handles your reporting, and automatically pays your state and federal liabilities. They also add 5-10% to your cost of labor with their fees.

You might find that your accountant will calculate your payroll for a smaller fee. For most game store needs, this solution offers a good compromise between professional oversight and affordable cost.

You can handle payroll yourself with QuickBooks or other accounting software. Once you enter the appropriate information, the software automatically deducts the correct amount from the paycheck and records it so that you can make federal and state payments yourself.

The risk with handling your own payroll is that, in case of an error, you're responsible for paying any fees and fines. If you outsourced the work to a reputable company, the company assumes liability for its errors. You might find that the risk far exceeds the money you save.

SAFETY AND SECURITY

Safety and security is an ongoing concern. The downside is that there's not much potential gain here. You won't get rich merely by running a safe workplace. On the other hand, you can easily go out of business if you handle this area poorly.

PREVENTING ACCIDENTS

Game stores have few accidents. The most common is a slip and fall, usually caused by a wet floor. If you have tile floors, keep a welcome mat inside the front door. Ideally, use two: one outside and one inside. A large welcome mat also keeps your floor clean, making less work for you and your staff.

Mopping should ideally take place after hours. If you must mop when customers are present, use one of the yellow cautionary signs that are generally available wherever you buy your mop. Try to mop with as little water as possible so that the floor dries quickly. Avoid using too much soap, too, because that makes for a slippery floor. Clean up accidental spills right away so you spend less time at risk of an accident. Dry stores can cause problems, too, if they are dusty or cluttered. Pick up anything left in an aisle. Keep both broom and mop handy.

Don't allow reckless behavior by your customers: running, leaning back in chairs, throwing things around the glass display cases, etc.

SHOPLIFTING

Shoplifting costs retailers about ten billion dollars a year. Shoplifting can greatly damage your bottom line. If not controlled tightly, it can bankrupt an otherwise well-managed store.

Identification and Prevention

Shoplifters tend to be two types: opportunists and professionals. Professionals tend to work busy department stores, whose high-priced products they can sell right away. Your industry protects you from that. Barring some mainstream success like *Pokemon*, most of your items have little resale value to the general public.

So this discussion concentrates on opportunists. These shoplifters might steal out of a psychiatric condition that forces them to steal, but more often, they steal out of disrespect for you or for the challenge of getting away with something dangerous. You cannot predict these cases, but you can keep an eye out for tell-tale behavior.

Before you even start looking for shoplifters, review the physical layout of your store. Look at the inventory from the counter, where your employees spend most of their time. Can you see all of the products? If not, can you at least see the high-risk items: CCG singles, CCG boosters, Games Workshop blister packs? Your store should be arranged for maximum product visibility. Customers should shop where you can see them from the side. You can watch their hands, you can watch your product, and you can watch their other hand, one that might be in a pocket or a bookbag.

Convex mirrors ($40-$100) can help monitor this activity, but their main use is as a deterrent. A shoplifter that thinks he might be seen from all angles might be discouraged. Shoplifters can use mirrors against you, however, by watching in the mirror to see if the person on duty is paying attention.

Cameras have some value as a deterrent, although their main use is in helping to get a conviction once you catch somebody. If you want to stress the deterrent value, you can supplement real cameras with a couple of dummy cameras ($20 to $45 each). Modern fake cameras feature a red light that makes them look very realistic.

Installing a door chime is a good method of identifying customer entry and departure. The clerk looks up at the chime. Customers within sight of the door often perk up and look, too.

All that attention makes prospective thieves uncomfortable.

The best line of defense is a well-trained staff. Make sure your sales staff is familiar with your policies and capable of executing them. Knowing what you expect is not enough.

Greeting the customer as he walks in the door is one way of stamping out a problem before it develops. The practice is good customer service, and it shows the person that somebody is paying attention to him. Following up on the greeting later shows a potential shoplifter that he is still being watched.

Merely watching a potential shoplifter will not solve all of the problems. Your staff should know exactly what to watch for. Watch for bookbags and backpacks, especially if they are open or easily opened. Tell-tale behavior includes handling a product for a long time, watching to see if you are watching him, moving product from one place to another, and fidgeting around a lot. Watch out for people who split up when they enter the store, especially if one of them comes straight to the counter and asks you questions. He's distracting you. Move so that your line of sight includes both.

SUMMARY: SHOPLIFTER BEHAVIOR
- Handling a product a long time
- Watching the sales staff
- Looking for cameras or mirrors
- Moving product
- Fidgeting
- Sticking hands in pockets

You can use a partner to catch a shoplifter, too. Make yourself obviously distracted — after you've sent a subtle prearranged signal to your other employee. Make a big show out of digging out something beneath the counter, where you obviously cannot see the potential shoplifter. When your head comes up, a nod or head shake from your partner tells you all you need to know.

Knowing your product is another tool you can use. If you perform spot inventories frequently, you are more likely to notice something out of place. For example, if you did an inventory of the Warhammer line right before somebody came into the store, and you notice a blister pack missing, you have a good idea where it went. Check the area nearby first to see if it got moved. Take the opportunity to follow up contact with the customer by asking what army he plays or whether he wants to participate in a demo.

Unfortunately, paying attention to potential shoplifters only goes so far. The moment you turn to answer a phone or take care of a real customer, the crime is committed. It takes just a few seconds.

If you return to such a customer and notice a behavior change — like he is now eager to leave or seems especially cocky — start to look for missing product while you talk to him. If he insists on leaving, you have to make a decision. You are in the right to confront him, but the potential liability if you make a wrong accusation is very high. He might be in a position to sue you for discrimination. He might at the very least damage your reputation among customers at other stores.

One area at high risk is the transition from your retail area, where you have product on shelves, and the game room, where customers have their own gaming material on tables. It's easy for a book to make its way across that barrier and onto a pile of stuff the thief already owns. Once a product makes its way to the gaming area, it is difficult to establish ownership.

In many cases, you are able to detain a suspected shoplifter based on probable cause; that is, you saw an item on the shelf, you turned away, the item was gone. When you called the police, they found the item on the person. If you have witnessed or have probable cause to belief that a person has shoplifted an item, then you need to approach that person and detain him. If you checked your local laws before opening and setting these policies, you should be in good shape.

The Confrontation

When you confront a possible shoplifter, you should be prepared for violence, even while planning for a safe and professional experience. Alert any other employees in the store. If possible, have them call the police while you make your approach.

Approach the person directly, from the front if possible. Be polite and professional. Try to take the person someplace private. You are protecting his dignity — which makes him less likely to fight or run — and you are removing him to a place where you have greater control. The best method is clear and direct: "Excuse me, sir, I'm Frank, the owner. I'd like you to come with me to the office to discuss that blister pack in your pocket." Listen for spontaneous utterances like "I was going to pay for it." You haven't accused him of not paying for anything. Spontaneous utterance is a specific term in law enforcement, and if you mention it to the police when you call them, they know what you're talking about. Volunteered comments like that indicate a guilty conscience.

At this point, you are probably detaining that person. Detaining has a specific legal meaning. It is not arrest. If your state does not allow a merchant or merchant's employee to detain a suspected shoplifter, then you might have to make a citizen's arrest. Again, check your local law. In either case, call the police as soon as possible.

Once you have detained the shoplifter, you can ask him to return the items. You can — probably — lie to him to encourage his cooperation. "I'm not going to press charges. I just need the information for my paperwork."

Once the police arrive, explain the incident fully. They will be alert for certain key phrases in your description. Make sure that you point out that you 1) saw the suspect approach the merchandise, 2) saw him pick it up, and 3) saw him conceal it. If your state and local laws require it, mention that the person passed by the last place he could pay for the item or he left the store.

Do not lie, of course. If you did not see one of these things, explain what you did and did not see to the police. Regardless of the outcome of the shoplifting charge, take this opportunity to fill out a trespass warrant. If that person comes on your property again, you can have him or her arrested right away.

No Confrontation

You will probably play many games while you own a game store. One game you will never win, no matter how many times you play is "Make Money off a Shoplifter." Spending long hours in pursuit of them is a waste of your time. You can watch some people for hours, day after day, yet they still steal from you as soon as you turn your back.

If you think that a person has been shoplifting and you simply are not able to witness it or even be certain that an incident has occurred, remember your ultimate weapon in any such unwinnable situation: ask the person to leave.

Your business is not a "public space," as the law defines it. A business is a private place, and you own the business. You may freely ask any person to leave at any time. You do not need to state a reason. Here's a sample conversation:

"Hi, I'm Frank, the owner. I'd like you to leave my property now."

"What for?"

"I'm not required to give any reason. Have a nice day."

"What if I don't leave?"

"Then you'll be trespassing, which can be punished by a thousand dollar fine and up to a year in jail." [Or the appropriate penalty for your state.]

If he refuses to leave, call the police. The person has no legal argument. He can whine, complain, cajole, and threaten, but in the end he has to leave. If he does not leave of his own volition, Officer Friendly will be glad to give him a ride.

You are likewise free to ban a person from your store for as long as you wish and to rescind that ban at your whim. If you use this tool, thoroughly document your actions and attempt to gather witness statements when possible to protect yourself against lawsuits for discrimination or other potential liability.

Follow-Up and Record Keeping

At the very least you should write a record of the events immediately afterward so that they will be fresh in your memory if the police or your local district attorney follows up. If possible, take a picture of the shoplifter and post it where employees can become familiar with it. Inform them on the procedures they should follow if this person comes into the store.

How far you push prosecution is up to you. You could actively follow the case and maintain a public display of how many shoplifters you have sent to jail. A sign depicting your success against shoplifters might deter some. It might inspire others to attempt to outsmart you.

You can even pursue civil litigation against the shoplifters in an attempt to recover your lost time, profitability and, of course, the legal fees involved in the litigation itself. Suing a shoplifter that stole from you has a certain satisfaction to it, but it's probably not as profitable as another use of your time. Should you sue a shoplifter over a $40 RPG book, or should you run a dozen board game demos? Time is finite after all, and putting money in your pocket might ultimately be more satisfying than getting a favorable outcome in a lawsuit.

Law vs. Exposure to Liability

Legal considerations are important for prosecution, but you must also take precautions against possible civil litigation. If the shoplifter is of a different sex, try to have an employee of that sex in the office if possible. This safeguard minimizes the chance of any allegations of sexual misconduct later.

Be very careful with any physical contact with the suspect during the entire procedure. Make absolutely certain that you understand your rights to physical means of detaining a suspect in your location. It would be better to let the suspect run away with $20 worth of product than to face a lawsuit for $1,000,000 because you tripped him and he sustained serious injury.

EMPLOYEE THEFT

Estimates place employee theft as responsible for up to 40% of retail theft. Catching the thief can range from ridiculously simple — I've seen embezzlement identified within 20 seconds of an observant manager walking into the building — to very complex.

Employees steal from you in a number of ways. Some of them take cash out of the drawer. Tight cash controls, such as counting the drawer down between each shift, help reduce this problem. Having a second person verify every count helps even more.

SUMMARY: SIGNS OF EMPLOYEE THEFT

- Cash overages
- Cash shortages
- Customer returns with no record of original sale
- Customers asking for a particular employee
- Employees not buying products for games they play
- Excessive "no sales"
- Excessive voids
- Inventory discrepancies on spot checks

Taking product without paying for it is a large problem as well. Many employees come from a gaming background. Your product has value to them. Watch products for the games your employees play, especially second-hand items, because they are often more difficult to track.

Reviewing your cash register tape is the easiest way to discover employee theft at the cash register. Watch out for unusual transactions: overrings, returns, voids and even excessive "no sales." Cash overages sometimes come about when employees create a surplus in the cash through fraud and then lose track of how much they took. In the case of a cash shortage, they take money and want to see your reaction to the missing money. Make employees responsible for shortages over a certain amount. A reasonable goal is $.50 to $1 margin of error for each $1,000 in sales.

Let employees know that you are alert for scams. Ask them about any returns and mention that you intend to follow up with the customer. If you are tracking sales by customer, it should be easy for you to call or e-mail the customer to ask why he returned the item and if he was happy with how the transaction was handled. In this way you simultaneously improve relations with that customer and verify that your employee was not ringing up a fraudulent return.

For many employers, employee theft is emotionally harder to handle than shoplifting. You have spent time and personal effort in finding, interviewing and training this employee. Now he has hurt your business by taking money or product from you, and he has betrayed a trust.

You might be reluctant to monitor employee activities because of an emotional attachment to them. You must overcome this reluctance. Think of it as another part of your job. It's no less desirable than sweeping the floor, placing an order, or paying your electric bill. It's just another job. Check up on them as if they were total strangers, no matter how well you know and trust them. As former president Ronald Reagan said, "Trust, but verify."

One good example of this monitoring is a policy requiring another person to handle all employee purchases. If employees are required to go through a manager for their own sales, they have less opportunity to ring up less than they take home. Removing opportunity is one of the best methods of reducing theft.

I strongly recommend terminating immediately any employee you suspect of theft. If you suspect it, it's probably there, and waiting could cost you thousands of dollars. No one is exempt by virtue of age, sex, religion, or previous jobs held. I've seen thieves who were altar boys, teachers, sailors, Boy Scouts — you name it.

Spell out your policies regarding employee theft in your employee handbook. In your employment package, you'll have a signed statement from the employee indicating that he has read this handbook. After that, once you terminate an employee for theft, you are fairly well-protected against claims of unemployment insurance or litigation from that employee. As with all such things, check your state's Department of Labor for details.

BURGLARY AND ROBBERY

Robbers target small businesses for the cash they carry in the cash register. Most robbers are unlikely to rob you for your Magic singles. Even if they knew what they were, they probably do not know where to sell them quickly.

Most robberies occur on Friday night, followed in frequency by Saturday night. These are the nights when you are most likely to stay open later as well. Most robberies take place after 11:00 PM, so closing before then reduces your chance of an unwanted violent encounter.

Keeping your windows free of clutter is a good way to reduce your attractiveness to robbers. If passersby can see inside, robbers have less chance of robbing you without being seen from outside. Clear windows also allow you to see potential robbers that might be watching your business, trying to identify traffic patterns, watching your cash drawer practices, identifying how many employees you have, etc.

The largest deterrent to robberies is keeping cash out of the store. If you have clean and clear windows, a high-tech video camera surveillance system, alert employees, panic buttons, and all of the security gadgets and procedures you can imagine, robbers will still target your store if you have accessible cash inside. Keep money out of your store, advertise that you have no money in your store, and stay safe.

Removing the money from the store means skimming your cash drawer and making regular deposits.

Skimming your cash drawer involves removing more than a certain dollar amount to a safe location, like a time-delay safe. Floor drop safes are available starting around $200, with time-delay models starting around $500. You might not want to consider any low-end models that the robbers can steal intact! Invest in something sturdy that will resist their efforts for long enough that they give up and leave empty-handed.

You should make deposits at least once per day. Morning deposits are safer, but that means leaving the money in the store overnight. On the other hand, making night drops carries its own risk. You are susceptible to robbery as you leave your own parking lot and while you are making the drop.

Whether you choose to make your deposit at night or in the morning, do not take the cash in an obvious bank bag. You could carry a bank bag full of rolled pennies as a decoy and carry the deposit in your pocket, in a card box, or something innocuous like a Sabol Army Transport case.

If your sales exceed $1,000 per day in cash, take an additional deposit during the afternoon to remove some of that money. If you are not comfortable carrying that much money, you might consider lowering your threshold to a smaller number and making more frequent drops.

If you do find yourself the victim of a robbery, keep calm and remember that the statistics favor your survival if you follow some rules. Comply with the robber's demands and tell him right away that you intend to do what he says. Do not fight. Do not use a weapon — statistically, you are more likely to get hurt if you do. Remember that most robberies are over in less than a minute.

If you have a time-delay safe, the robber might wait for you to open it, if he even knows it's there. About 75% of the time, he will not wait the delay out. If he does wait it out, his chances of being caught by the police triple.

During the robbery, try to get a good look at any descriptive details you can for the police: height, weight, age, clothing, identifying marks, weapon, etc. Do not be too obvious, because that makes the robber nervous, and nervous robbers shoot people. Note where he put his hands so that the police can check for fingerprints.

Afterward, call the police. If anyone needs medical assistance, ask for an ambulance and render what first aid you can. Secure the building in case the robber returns. Write down details of the event so you will have a record of it before the police arrive. If other witnesses are present, have them do the same and ask everybody not to collaborate with each other. Talking to each other taints the testimony for the police and reduces the likelihood of catching and convicting the right person.

Other Theft

Till-tapping involves reaching into the cash drawer, yanking out a fistful of bills and running. The thief usually attempts to distract you and might have accomplices to help with that part of the job. While most common in malls, be aware of the scam and prevent potential problems by keeping a light drawer and staying in close proximity to the cash drawer whenever you have it open.

Scams

Once you have a business license and a listed telephone number, you become the target of a large number of scams. Protecting yourself from these scams does not require a great deal of time, but it does require constant attention. A small amount of preparation and foreknowledge goes a long way toward reducing the chance of falling victim to one of these scams.

Point out to your employees that they are not authorized to place supply orders or handle phone or e-mail transactions over a certain dollar amount. Scammers often count on pressuring uncertain people into making a purchase commitment. Once an employee places an order — even without your knowledge or approval — your obligation to pay for that order is hard to contest.

People might e-mail you or place orders on your website for large orders of random product delivered to a foreign country. Signs of potential fraud include usually large orders, rush orders, deliveries to P.O. boxes, or a difference between billing address and shipping address. Asking for a phone number so you can verify the order is one way to reduce theft; make sure to call it back, too. Another method is confirming the order, but with a minor difference from the actual request. Thieves often won't catch it, but real customers almost always notice the change.

A frequent scam attempt involves callers purporting to be from a service provider you use and offering to sell you goods or services. Credit card supplies, phone book ads, price gun labels, and other universal small business needs are all likely candidates. Ask for the service provider's name. Better yet, don't place an order when somebody else initiates the phone call. Tell them that you'll be happy to call them back tomorrow. Tomorrow, of course, you'll refer to your records to look up your service provider's phone number instead of calling one that some stranger on a phone gave you.

Convention Sales

Some retailers feel that conventions are a waste of time. You will hear arguments about the conventions taking all of the customer's money for a weekend, or that customers stop spending for a week or two before a convention. They say that convention sales are not worth the table fees, labor costs, and all the sales lost at the store while the store's entire inventory is at the convention.

These people do not know how to use conventions.

Choosing Conventions

You might know about the conventions local to your area already. If not, an internet search should reveal most of the gaming conventions in your area. The convention promoters, if they're doing their job well, should make a strong effort to recruit you and encourage you to promote their convention, also.

Once you know which conventions are available to choose from, decide which ones are feasible. Small local conventions which are a great distance away do not generate enough sales to justify the travel cost. For a first convention, I suggest that you start with a small local convention to gain experience and fine-tune your procedures. Your risk is less, the stress is less, and you stand the best chance of gaining new long-term customers.

Draw Up Your Plan

Decide which of your staff are going to the convention, who's going to cover the store, how many tables you want, how you will arrange transportation, whether you will do any special promotion, how many people you take, how much product to bring, etc. Set yourself a sales goal and a budget to help you realize that goal.

Sales Goal

Setting a sales goal for the first time can be daunting. You have no reference points by which to gauge. The primary meter for anticipating sales is the number of attendees the convention expects to draw. For a well-organized gaming convention with the right number of vendors, you can expect to generate at least $2/guest, so for a 200-person local convention, you might count on $400 in gross sales. Exceptional vendors might generate much more, but that's a good first goal.

Assign a Budget

Write down the list of equipment you need, labor you need to spend, travel expenses, table fees, etc. Make sure you have the cash-flow for the expenses you can foresee. Allow an additional amount to cover unexpected expenses, like parking, electricity or a phone line at the convention site.

Budget for:
▷ Table fees
▷ Additional fees
▷ Gas/travel expenses
▷ Hotel costs
▷ Labor at the store and additional labor at the convention

Learning Curve

Your first convention or two might not make as much money as you hoped. Plan for that. Take a notepad and take notes on things you will do differently next time. Watch other vendors and see what they're selling. Compare how long customers spend at your table compared to the other tables.

Learn to feel the ebb and flow of activity. Take your meal and restroom breaks in the middle of events, because the vendor room is busiest in between game slots. After the last slot of the night starts, you are not likely to see much activity in any case. If you plan on events like game demos, learn when to best schedule those.

Summary: Convention Equipment List
❀ Tablecloth
❀ Register or cash drawer
❀ Business cards
❀ E-mail signup list
❀ Money or product for table fees
❀ Store sign

Store, Ship, and Sell All In One Box

Whether you use large flat Tupperware boxes or milk crates, you should find a consistent size container in which you store, transport and display your product at the convention. This system reduces your setup time dramatically. It takes up a minimum of space in your storage area, takes the least number of trips from your vehicle to the convention booth, and sets up the quickest.

Make the most use of your space. Set up rows of your containers across the tables, on the floor in the front, and around the sides. If you have a booth instead of a table, set up aisles of product, like your store.

Keeping your cash on your person in a pocketed apron or in a bank bag gives you freedom to move about. It also allows customers to move in and out of your sales area without fear of walking in on a private area — which allows you to fully utilize the space you paid for. With you on your feet, you also remove your need to take up valuable sales space sitting in one place. At a convention like GenCon, that chair you sit in might eat up $100 worth of the space you paid for!

SUMMARY: CON NECESSITIES

- ❀ Cash for till
- ❀ Sign
- ❀ Tablecloth
- ❀ Snacks and drinks for your use

BRING WHAT SELLS

Bring the last week's worth of new products. It's likely that gamers have been in their local retail stores within the past two weeks so and have seen the new items. You might see some sales among the very latest items. Be happy to get those, because they are not where you will make your money. You will make your normal margin and deny other local retailers a sale.

Gamers look to convention vendors for something different. They want the exotic, the unusual, the stuff they do not see at their local store. Sell your clearance items here at aggressive discounts.

Gamers love to dig through bins. Take a bunch of plastic miniatures and toss them in a box instead of carefully arranging them for display. People will paw through them all weekend.

Some things sell consistently at conventions. Dice sell well. Cubes of d6s sell for large Warhammer and Warhammer 40k tournaments, while 7-die sets sell to D&D players. Tape measures also do well for miniatures tournaments. Plush toys generally sell well.

Before boxing up merchandise for the convention, check the game schedule. Scan the list of games being run and add some material for those games. Taking a core book for each of those games is usually a good idea. That way, if a player plays a new game and enjoys it, he can buy a copy of it right away.

Bring Money to Buy

Everybody in the building is a gamer. They all have games. They might have games they don't want. Some of them will want to hock their prize loot. If you sell second-hand merchandise, conventions are a great place to find new product.

Be prepared to buy collections of any size. Local gamers might very well go home and retrieve their collections, hoping to get cash to buy other things — including your product. If they sell it to you and go buy from somebody else there, you are making money by buying inventory you will sell later at a great profit.

Bring Stuff You Don't Own

Once you are running at full speed at your convention sales, you can start to sell manufacturer-provided goods on consignment. Approach a small or mid-tier manufacturer whose products you know you can sell well. Ask for a heap of items to sell on consignment at the convention.

Having a huge mound of product is an attraction all by itself. Gamers come to your table to check out a pile of games visible from across the room. Besides being a sale item that costs you nothing but shipping, you can use the draw to sell other items at your booth.

You can expect a lower margin on these items because of the consignment deal. Despite the lower margin, consignment arrangements like this are a way to leverage your size because they allow you to sell more items than you buy. They have no upfront costs, so your costs depend solely on your success.

Small manufacturers can often be most willing to work with you on consignment deals. They generate customers in a new market, and they might find other retailer partners who saw the item at your booth, observed you selling the product, and want it for themselves. Furthermore, those new customers expect follow-up products — either directly from the manufacturer, or by purchase through their local retailer.

Convention Promotions

Use some kind of activity to bring gamers to your booth. You can host a raffle, demo games at your table, or offer freebies of some kind to convention guests. Gimmicks include free donuts, running raffles, hosting games, and showing manufacturer-provided demo DVDs on a TV or monitor.

CHAPTER 7:
INVENTORY MANAGEMENT

Inventory is your largest controllable cost. Your inventory management skills make the difference between your store being profitable and failing. Of your initial funds, probably half go into inventory. Over half of the rest of your expenditures throughout your career will be inventory. Over-ordering by a couple of items each week could mean thousands of dollars worth of capital tied up in product and unusable for other things by the end of the year.

Developing this skill will be painful, difficult, and hindered by distribution in this industry. Hot items that you could sell quickly are often out of stock. If an item becomes too popular, the manufacturer drops the discount through distribution. You pre-order heavily for something, and by the time it releases 7 months late, your customers are no longer interested, sticking you with 6 months' worth of product instead of the 30 days' worth you expected.

Using a few guidelines and gaining the inevitable experience of placing regular orders eases the learning curve and helps to minimize your mistakes in the frequency with which you make them and the dollars you spend on your inventory education. You cannot be so afraid to over-order that you leave yourself with no product to sell.

You often hear manufacturers moan that if a retail store ordered one of everything and replaced what sold, they'd be sure to catch all of the winners. What's often happening in that case is that a manufacturer received disappointing pre-orders for a product, printed heavily anyway, and now he's sitting on a pile of dusty games.

To carry all of the role-playing, CCG and miniatures products on the market, you would have to have a store the size of a grocery store. You would have aisles of miniatures. You would have meat refrigerators full of dice. The floral arrangement island would be full of plushies and other promos. Most importantly, you would be broke.

Here is a truth in as a game retailer: you will not have enough product to make all of your customers happy. At some point, no matter how much you carry, a customer will complain that you do not stock this game or that miniature line. Once you accept that fact, you can get on with your ordering with profitability in mind instead of an unachievable goal of total customer contentment.

When you place an order, you have two basic and sometimes opposed needs. You must restock items that sell. Selling once is an indicator that something will sell again. Items that you keep restocking over and over for a seemingly indefinite period of time are called evergreen products. The other need, to maintain cash flow, requires that at some point you stop restocking old products.

SUMMARY: SAMPLE EVERGREEN PRODUCTS

- Card sleeves
- D&D core rulebooks
- Dice
- Vinyl battlemats
- Axis & Allies

BUYING MERCHANDISE

Familiarity with your supply chain is important for any business. The gaming industry uses a well-established distribution tier that consolidates the products of hundreds of different manufacturers. Some of these manufacturers produce a single item. Some produce thousands. Placing orders with each of them directly would be impossible.

GAMING DISTRIBUTORS

Your distributors are the service providers you will come to associate with the most often. Indeed, while you probably will not speak with your sales rep for your credit card account twice in 10 years, you will speak with your primary distributor at least once a week for restocks, maybe once a week to go over preorders, and once or twice a week with general questions.

Their importance is due to being your source for the products you sell. The distributors are your key pipeline for that product flow, and they will frustrate you to no end in this capacity. As you try to manage your largest controllable cost, you often feel that control is out of your hands entirely. Distributors have their issues, too, and they will often be out of stock of something you desperately need. How can you sell it if you cannot buy it?

As nice as it would be to use a single distributor and only sell products that they carry, that luxury is not feasible. If you make your initial inventory decisions based off of the Alliance inventory, you will find frequent outages on several products as you go through their list.

The lack is not their fault. In the same effort to be profitable that you go through, distributors keep their inventory level as thin as they can afford. If demand causes a sales spike in something, distributors run out. They also have to deal with re-order issues. Manufacturers might have high minimum orders policies, requiring a longer period between restocks. Communication errors happen, and sometimes purchase orders get lost. Snowstorms and power outages affect distributors, too. Whatever the cause, unless you carry a very narrow product selection, you cannot get the product you want from any single distributor.

You want to use a second, and third, and sometimes fourth distributor. You want one primary distributor. Give him your pre-orders, go to him first for restocks, and get your news and information from him when possible. Build this relationship.

Then find a secondary distributor, preferably one with product overlap, so you can rely on him when your primary is out of stock, but also some products that fill a gap in your primary's product selection. Occasionally, you will reverse this order when sales or special orders demand that you restock certain items.

Remember that you do not need to hide this double-dealing. Distributors talk to each other. When you apply with one distributor, they ask each other if anyone has had any problems with you. As long as you are up front and do not try to use the presence of other accounts as a hammer (as in "give me a better discount or I'll drop you"), multiple accounts are not a problem. Your distributors know a retailer's needs and they understand why you bounce around from place to place.

Terms

Most distributors want you to pay COD at first. After you've established a history with them, they allow you to go on terms. "Terms" includes at least two numbers: your percentage discount from retail, and the due date on the payment. A distributor that offers 46% net 30 gives you a 46% discount and expects payment in 30 days. Typically, there might be a third number that defines an additional discount for early pay — normally 10 days.

Paying on terms is generally preferred because it helps you manage that all-important cash flow (see page pp). If you place on order on Day 1, receive it on Day 3 and pay for it on Day 30, you have 27 days to sell that order. Switching from COD to net 30 at the same discount rate improves your company's cash flow.

What a Distributor Can Do For You

Ideally, a distributor is one your one-stop shop for information on the products they carry. They consolidate the manufacturer's information so that you can find what you need to make your ordering decisions. They all generally have this information.

A main differentiating point is how they deliver this information to you. If they rely on their sales reps, you might spend all day trying to reach one on the phone. If they cram random sell sheets in with their boxes, they're not doing all they can to give you what you need.

A good distributor provides a website where you can bring this information up at the click of a button in an environment where you are not bombarded by advertisements for "Dave's Discount Gaming 60% off!" When you are looking up the answer to a customer's question about a release date or price, you do not want him to see alternate places where he can go to buy the product for cheaper than he can get it from you.

You also need this information when placing your orders, so you want as much of it there on demand as you can get. Sales reps might have to look something up, ask the guy at the next desk, or might not know. If you can hunt for the information at your own pace, sometimes it's faster.

You can also access the internet at any time, day or night. If your distributor features online ordering, you can do your research or place your orders after the distributor's sales office closes or before they open. You can start, set it aside, and come back later, as you work around your customer volume and other chores around the business. That's awkward to do on a telephone, and those long orders can tie up your phone for long periods of time.

Be advised that not all game store owners are in agreement over the benefit of paying on terms. A small fraction of store owners prefer the iron discipline you must develop if you pay for each delivery as you receive it. In my opinion, these owners fail to utilize a perfectly valid and valuable tool to help them improve their business's profitability.

Distributor Contact Information

United States Distributors
ACD Distribution
2841 Index Rd., Suite 150
Madison WI 53713
(800) SOS-GAME [(800) 767-4263]
New accounts contact Darrell Wyatt, ext. 209

Aladdin Distributors Inc.
1420 Cliff Rd.
Burnsville, MN 55337
(672) 890-8700

By far the largest distributorship in the industry, Alliance has four warehouses, a large and informative website, the most diverse product offering, and Alliance probably maintains the deepest inventory levels, which means fewer stockouts for you to gnash your teeth over.

Alliance Game Distributors — East

1101 Greenwood Road
Baltimore, MD 21208
(800) 669-4263
Fax (410) 602-8140

Alliance Game Distributors — Midwest
3102 Brooklyn Ave., Suite B
Fort Wayne, IN 46809
(800) 444-3552
Fax (260) 747-4940

Alliance Game Distributors — Southwest
9204 Brown Lane, #160
Austin, TX 78754
(800) 424-3773
Fax (512) 834-0447

Alliance Game Distributors — West (Visalia)
7411 West Sunnyview
Visalia, CA 93291
(888) 366-5456
Fax (559) 651-3985

Alliance Game Distributors — West (El Cerrito)
11100 San Pablo Ave, Suite 200B
El Cerrito, CA 94530
(800) 424-4263
Fax (510) 215-0960

Brookhurst Hobbies
12188 Brookhurst Street
Garden Grove, CA 92840-2817
(714) 636-3580
Fax (714) 636-9150
www.brookhursthobbies.com

Diamond Comic Distributors, Inc.
1966 Greenspring Drive, Suite 300
Timonium, MD 21093
Phone: (800) 45-COMIC
Outside the U.S.and Canada: (410) 560-7100
    Although known mostly for comics, Diamond carries col-

lectibles, anime, and a wide variety of other products as well.

GTS Distribution
A merger of GAMUS and Talkin' Sports
GAMUS Atlanta
4300 D Highlands Parkway
Smyrna, GA 30082
(888) 333-9500

GAMUS Orlando
317 S. Northlake Blvd. #1008
Altamonte Springs, FL 32701
(888) 767-5411

GAMUS Lauderdale
5771 West Sunrise Blvd.
Plantation, FL 33313
(877) 485-8581, (888) 333-9500
newaccounts@gamus.com

Hobbies Hawaii
4420 Lawehana St. #3
Honolulu, HI 96818
(808) 423-0265

Old Glory Miniatures
Box 20, Route 981
Calumet, PA 15621
(724) 423-3580
Fax (724) 423-6898

On Military Matters
55 Taylar Terrace
Hopewell, NJ 08525
(609) 466-2329
Fax (609) 466-4174

Peachstate Hobby
995 W. Kennedy Blvd.
Orlando, FL 32810
(877) 743-4263

Peachstate Hobby
4E Easy St.
Bound Brook, NJ 08805
(732) 537-1004
Fax (732) 537-1187

Peachstate Hobby
10221 Corkwood Road
Dallas, TX 75238
(972) 993-4263

Southern Hobby — Nashville
211 Ellery Court Nashville, TN 37214
Toll Free (800) 473-2804
Local (615) 366-5858
Fax Fax (615) 360-9776

Southern Hobby — St. Louis
1208 Ambassador Blvd St. Louis, MO 63132
Toll Free (800) 558-7060
Local (314) 993-3319
Fax (314) 993-8914

Southern Hobby — Chicago
905 Sivert Drive Wood Dale, IL 60191
Toll Free (800) 463-1133
Local (630) 496-9476
Fax (630) 496-9487

Southern Hobby — New York
1930 New Highway Farmingdale, NY 11735
Toll Free (855) 584-6229
Local (631) 414-7860
Fax (631) 414-7867

Wargames Inc.
Box 278, Route 40 East
Tridelphia, WV 26059-0278
(304) 547-0000
Fax (304) 845-7215
wargames@stratuswave.net

Wizards of the Coast
Attn: Merchant Relations
P.O. Box 707
Renton, WA 98057
(800) 821-8028
Fax (425) 204-5916
retailhelp@wizards.com

While not a full-line distributor, WotC offers direct sales through their Premier Store program. The requirements for joining the program are strict: they insist that you have game space, they want photographs of your store, and they want you to run events. Because Wizards' products are likely to provide a substantial part of your income, having an account with them opens up more ordering options.

Wright One Enterprises
909 SE Everett Mall Way, Suite B-200
Everett, WA 98208
(425) 355-5005
sharpwrightone@aol.com

Canada Distributors

Lion Rampart Imports
529 Concession Street, Unit R
Hamilton, Ontario, L8V IA7
Canada
(904) 572-6446
Lion@lionramparts.com

Mindsports
Bay 23, 3610 — 50th Avenue, SE
Calgary, AB, T2B 3N9
Canada
(800) 338-3009
(403) 241-9225
Fax (403) 241-1063
www.mindsports.ca
mindsports@nucleus.com

New Century Distributors
102 – 7889 132 Street
Surrey, BC, V3W 4Nw
Canada
(604) 596-4320
info@newcenturydistributors.com

Universal Distribution
2441 Guenette
Montreal, PQ, H4R 2E9
Canada
(514) 335-9000
Fax (514) 335-9111
angelo@universaldist.com

United Kingdom Distributors
Esdevium Games
Unit 2 Riverwey Industrial Park
Newman Lane, Alton GU34 2QL
United Kingdom
+44(0) 1420 89900
sales@esdeviumgames.com

France Distributors
Millennium
93, rue Dominique Clos
31300 Toulouse
FRANCE
+33-534-364-050
Fax +33-534-365-111

Germany Distributors
Pegasus Spiele
Straßheimer Str. 2
61169 Friedburg
GERMANY
+49 (6031) 7217-0
Fax: +49 (6031) 7217-17

Australia Distributors
Alternate Worlds
P.O. Box 1278
Windsor, Victoria 3181
AUSTRALIA
011-613-95292255
Fax: 011-613-95292040
jitaliano@labyrinth.net.au
http://www.alternateworlds.com.au

Jedko
134 Cochranes Road
Moorabbin Victoria 3189
AUSTRALIA
011-61-39-5551022
Fax: 011-61-39-55-33-339
peter@milsims.com.au

Ventura
Unit 5, 32 Lilian Fowler Place
Marrickville, NSW 2204
AUSTRALIA
011-612-951-72288
Fax: 011-612-955-73026
farago@bigpond.com

Walrus & Carpenter
P.O Box 2450
Smithfield, NSW 2164
AUSTRALIA
011-61-2-9632-7755
Fax: 011-61-2-9632-7181
Walrus@iinet.net.au

Pre-Orders

Pre-orders are a hot topic in the gaming industry. A pre-order is an order you place with your distributor in advance of a product's release date. Your distributor then tells the manufacturer how many they would like after collecting this information from all of their customers. The manufacturer prints enough copies to cover that, and then everybody has enough to go around without the manufacturer losing his shirt because he printed too many copies. So goes the theory.

In reality, pre-orders are often turned in after the manufacturer has had to go to print to make his release date. In these cases, the manufacturer has to use other guidelines for his print numbers. He uses prior sales history of similar items, modifies by the expected relative success of this item to others, and takes a guess.

If the print is too small, distributors might not have enough product to go around — sometimes not enough to cover pre-orders, which is extraordinarily frustrating for retailers. The manufacturer has to go to press again, which might take weeks. In the meantime, all of his customers are getting excited about the next big thing and not as interested in this product when it finally becomes available again.

If the print run is too large, the manufacturer does not make back his initial investment. Unlike you, the manufacturer cuts his check for his product about four months before he gets paid for those same sales. When that happens too often, the manufacturer goes out of business.

Manufacturer problems aside, it is in your best interest to pre-order as accurately as possible. Also, give your pre-orders to a single distributor. By default, that makes that distributor your primary source for product. You will be ordering from that distributor at least once a week. If you have a good relationship with this distributor, then when a game comes out late or is otherwise undesirable, and you have to reduce or cancel your pre-order, your distributor will not begrudge you the change.

Note that technically, you are liable to some degree for pre-orders. That is, you are legally obligated to buy them once you place the order. However, the distributors do not want you to go out of business, either. When it comes down to it, ask your distributor if refusing a pre-order is a problem. Most of the time, they have other customers interested in the same product and they will not mind. If they hesitate or waffle at all, you might want to buy the product to maintain that good relationship.

This guarantee of business has value to a distributor. Because pre-orders represent a commitment to buy, distributors want to be your pre-order source. They are willing to make concessions to you to keep that business. If you are trying to decide where to take your primary business because two distributors offer similar terms, ask what your distributor can do for you. While they might not be willing to offer a greater discount, they might be willing to offer extended dating or reduced order minimums or waive COD fees.

ORDERING DIRECT

Ordering directly from the manufacturer for every vendor you carry is not possible, much less feasible. If you spent 15 minutes ordering from each manufacturer represented in your store, you might spend 100 hours per week. While inventory control is an important part of your job, those manufacturers who are too small or new to sell through distribution are usually not going to make or break your store. You could run your store for years without ever placing an order with a manufacturer.

That said, ordering direct from select manufacturers is sometimes a good idea. You might want the manufacturer's products because you think that it has great sales potential. It might be a great add-on for another product you sell. Sometimes, manufacturers choose not to sell through distribution for their own reasons, and ordering directly is the only way to get those products. Or, you might choose to order directly to save money.

Sometimes you come across a company whose product is both very good and underpriced. If you are the only local store that carries it, you can set your price above their SRP and raise your profit margins considerably. Of course, you can't be the only store with the product if the product is available through distribution. Once your competition hears that you have it on the shelf, they can add a sample or the entire product line the next time they place an order.

SUMMARY: BENEFITS OF ORDERING DIRECT
- Greater profit
- Exclusive products provide a competitive edge
- Merchandising materials

Most manufacturers do not want to sell to stores. Their infrastructure is designed around making games, not selling them a handful at a time directly to hundreds or thousands of stores. They prefer to sell to a half-dozen or so distributors. Selling through distribution requires less manual labor, less paperwork, and less sales staff.

However, selling to stores is often necessary, and so manufacturers often accept direct orders from stores. Terms are simple, and setting up an account is easy. Orders usually have a minimum amount — $100 is common — and have a decimal discount: 50% or 40% off retail. The retailer might pay actual shipping costs, or the manufacturer might pay shipping if the order is large enough.

Suppose your normal discount from your distributors is 46%. Ordering directly from a manufacturer who sells for 50% saves you 4%. That's $4 for each $100 you sell. If you place a large enough initial order, like $1,500 when you're bringing in a new line, that number adds up.

Restocks are an issue to consider closely. High minimums will be harder to meet, forcing you to make a decision: do you order more than you need to keep the product full on the shelf, or do you wait until you can meet the minimum order, leaving yourself exposed to stockouts? That $100 minimum that wasn't a barrier for an initial $400 order, but if you sell only $10 a week, the decision on when and how much to restock becomes difficult.

You could place the initial order with the manufacturer and go to the distributor for restocks, of course, if the manufacturer sells through distribution.

In two areas, manufacturers usually excel over distribution: merchandising assistance and product information. When you place an order, you can often receive flyers, catalogs, signage, sell sheets for your sales staff, and any current or upcoming promotional information. While this information is usually shared through distribution, its delivery through to the retail level is inconsistent.

One side effect of the lack of infrastructure is shipping time. Your turn-around time through distribution is reliable. Ninety-five percent of the time, you know within an hour or so how soon you receive any given order you place, because you know the day it will arrive, and you know what time the UPS or FedEx carrier arrives at your store. Furthermore, that delivery time is usually no more than a couple of days. With direct sales, the variation in delivery time can be great. Some manufacturers might take no longer than your distributor, while some might take two weeks or more to deliver your product.

Another issue of concern with direct ordering is the impact on your distributor relationship. Sales volume is important. Your discount overall might be based on your sales volume, as with

Alliance. Saving $60 by placing a large direct order might lower your sales volume below a discount threshold, costing you hundreds of dollars in lost discount with that distributor. Also, sales volume matters for other reasons. If you receive less of an allocated product because your purchasing decreased during recent months, that savings of $60 might look pretty insignificant.

SUMMARY: CONCERNS OF ORDERING DIRECT
- Time spent
- Shipping costs
- Variable shipping time
- High order minimums
- Smaller distributor volume

MAKE IT YOURSELF

Assuming that you want to be a retailer and not a publisher, you probably don't have the discretionary funds or skills set necessary to become a manufacturer. You might be able to write a role-playing game supplement that will sell a few copies in your store, but you probably won't risk $1,000,000 on a CCG or $100,000 on a miniatures line.

On the other hand, some low-risk premium items that you can commission for your store might pull double duty as both revenue-generating sales items and marketing tools. T-shirts bearing your logo are a prime example. Other promotional items are covered on pages 249-250.

YOUR CUSTOMERS

You buy most of your secondary market products right on your own counter. Customers bring them in from their own collections. Because this flow of product is irregular and unpredictable, you should set aside some funds from your order budget to accommodate it. Place a sign in the store or on your window to encourage them to bring you these items.

Similarly, if you intend to make convention sales a part of your sales strategy, you can buy games at conventions as well. A sign on your table informs customers that you will buy from them as well as sell to them. You could include a reminder when you ring up a sale: "How will you pay for this? Cash, credit card, or trade-in?"

Local Designers

You might be fortunate enough to have local publishers, artists or game designers in your area. If these people are not yet established through distribution, you might want to consider buying directly from them. If they are nearby, they might be willing to come in and promote their own game directly. Games signed by the designer have an automatic sales feature built in to them. Games signed by the designer after he runs a demo of the game are even better. Here's a secret: a player who beats a designer at his own game will talk about that experience for the rest of his life.

Sometimes it can be helpful to carry these products even if they aren't something you would buy blind. A small buy-in could be a low cost to build a good relationship with somebody you know will visit other stores and talk to other gamers. If all else fails, think about it as paying that person not to talk badly about you!

Do not keep your mind fixed on traditional game products in this regard. At one store, the contractor who made the store's game tables was a gamer. He made a wooden painting station that far exceeded the production values of the Games Workshop painting station and sold very well at the same price — and at a higher margin. The product was heavy and handmade, so shipping costs would have made its sales anywhere else impossible.

Consignment Sales

In earlier discussions, you've seen the risk of unproductive inventory. Consignment sales might seem like an easy solution. If you do not feel the product will move, call the owner and have him pick it up. Replace it with other product.

That would indeed be a simple solution if that were the only consideration. Let's look closer.

In a consignment arrangement, you typically agree to sell a product for an individual for a small percentage of the final price. A typical charge for this practice is as low as 10%.

Ten percent is not a great deal of money. You pay for the display space, you pay the labor that goes into answering questions about the product, you paid for the signage and other advertisement that brought the customer in. You handle the money, and you are responsible for that cash until you can deliver it to the customer.

Often, the consignor sets his price too high for the item to sell, or too low to fully realize the product's potential. Prices that are too low do not make you any money and might compete with other products in your store. Prices that are comparable with your prices for similar products are questionable. Why would you want to make 10% gross profit on something that belongs to a gamer when you could make 80% on something you paid for with store credit?

You also have to deal with liability. Suppose a glass display breaks and the consignment product is damaged. As long as it is in your store, the product is your responsibility. What about an employee who fails to record a sale properly, thus losing track of what you owe and to whom? With consignment sales, you carry the risk, you do the work, you make the sale, and you receive a fraction of the price you would get if you sold other items.

You can make consignment sales work if you plan out your policies ahead of time, addressing each issue in turn.

With the electronic forms of payment like PayPal available, holding onto money is not the issue it used to be. You could pay people the day a product sells without having to hope they answer the phone or get their message or wander into the store on their own. You can promote this additional service as part of the reason for your higher-than-expected margin.

A POS system makes this concept easier. Part of the information on the item's bar code could include the seller and the consignment terms. In this fashion, you can retrieve full information concerning regular sellers, including balance owed and sales history.

To make it work, however, you have to be very proactive. You set the terms, including the percentage the seller receives and the retail price. You can choose to remove the product and box it up if it is unproductive. Spell out every item of your terms clearly, preferably on paper, to protect yourself from loss and stay on good terms with your consignors.

Order From A Budget

The trend in the industry is to place orders for new products, then look to your budget for your restocks. If things are going well and you are allowing some items to simply go away when their time is done, then your budget should cover these restocks. How do you set that budget?

The simple version is this: take last week's sales and multiply by .6. That 60% figure represents a typical inventory goal. If you do $4,000 a week in sales, you can spend no more than $2,400 on inventory. After you buy new products, spend what's left on your budget on restocks.

Obviously, this system requires a bit of prioritizing on your restocks. If your restock list is higher than your budget, look to items that should be discontinued. Are any of those items being replaced by a new version anytime soon? Are any of them being overshadowed by new competition? Cut those.

If all else fails, look to their turn rate. When trimming your restock list for budgetary reasons, leave off the item with the lowest turn rate first. You stand the least chance of a customer walking in and looking for the item with the lowest turn rate while it's temporarily out of stock.

Ordering New Releases

It's important that you get this number as close to perfect as possible. The majority of a product's sales often come within the first 30 days of its release. Exceptions include product lines that are currently rising in popularity and those that become evergreen.

If you order too few copies of an initial release, you miss out on potential sales, and you limit a game's maximum growth. You can't have 10 game groups using this product if you only sell 4 copies. If something else new comes out by the time your restock comes in, then suddenly those customers that missed out have to choose between the thing they missed last time and the new thing they also want. Your re-order sales will be lighter as some customers inevitably choose the newer product.

If you order too few copies of a new product, you also lose customers. People who were interested in the game go to another local store, go online, or spend their money on another form of entertainment. Customers who miss out on products repeatedly become regular customers of somebody else. If your customer service is excellent and you have established procedures for handling special orders, you might be able to retain that sale, but do not rely on special orders to make up for ordering mistakes.

Ordering Restocks

Keeping track of restocks is easy. The method varies with whether or not you have a computerized POS system.

With a good POS, you can create a report of items sold. Restock those.

It gets more complicated when you factor in theft. You might be out of some items — due to shoplifting or employee pilferage — but fail to show them on your list of items sold because they did not pass through your register. See page 299 for tips on loss prevention.

Without a POS tracking sales takes more work. You have to manually add up sales over time and compare the two numbers without the visual aid of a graph. You might make an error in addition or an oversight that causes you to omit a sale or an entire page of sales in your hand-written notes. You might have had a new employee forget to record a sale and thus your projections will be off.

One such system that works for books is to create a "reorder card". The reorder card is a note card with the product name and stock number on it. When the customer brings the product up to the shelf, the clerk removes the card and adds it to the stack of items sold. Naturally, reorder cards work best for books, where you can insert them between the pages.

For miniatures, you can use place-holder cards. You can use a manufacturer-supplied placeholder card when available. Reaper and Games Workshop both offer these. You could also use a note card with a hole punched in it. Better yet, custom-created placeholder cards enhance your image and help build your brand. You can get black and white ones for about $5 per 100 from your local copier.

The placeholder card lists the product name and stock number and goes on the peg behind the mini. When the item is sold, you see the placeholder card. You can walk down the aisle with a sheet of paper and scribble down the missing items quickly. Another system involves a notepad and a pen by the counter. When the clerk rings an item up, he records the product name or manufacturer and stock number. It's easy, if a little tedious.

Watch That Creep

Ordering too many copies has a less visible impact than ordering too few, but a potentially deadly one nonetheless. Let us say you order 6 copies of a new $35 board game. You intended to order four that you thought you could sell, and then mentally added in one because you think you would like to open a display copy and then counted another to have on the shelf after you sold those four you were counting on.

You open one and sell two, not four. Maybe the rules were an incomprehensible translation of a foreign language. Maybe they omitted a major element of play. Maybe the final components were dissimilar to those advertised. For whatever reason, you did not achieve the sales you expected. You find that you have spent $111.30 on product (53% cost x 6 copies x $35), but you have only received $70.00. You have $41.30 negative cash flow (that is, forty bucks less in the bank than when you started this transaction) but according to the IRS, your profits have increased by $125.65 (the value of your 3 copies still in stock, plus the cash you received).

Multiply this single error by the number of orders you place in a year (400 or more for a healthy store) and you can see the scale of the threat. Your bank account is down $16,000, while your taxable profit is up by over $50,000! Ordering more than you sell leads to a concept known as inventory creep. Inventory creep represents a crushing negative cash flow.

An alert here before we continue with inventory discussion: customers like to see inventory on the shelves. They will notice, however, if you have the same inventory week after week. Stale product does not impress them.

You cannot look simply at either restocking procedures or initial orders. You must combine the two. Typically, the procedure works like this: the distributorship's sales rep calls you sometime in the day after their warehouse has entered data about the new items they received. The sales reps go over new material with you, asking you item by item what you want and how many. Then you spout out a list of restocks. Easy enough.

Do not wait on these lists for new products. Once the distributors receive their inventory and have it in the system, they also post this information on their website. Some of them e-mail it to you. It'll save time for you and your sales rep if you review these lists and have your order ready by the time they call.

Naturally, at times you want more information than your distributors provide. You might want information about trade dress, price, author, page count, binding, cover art, dimensions and all the other things you need to know to decide how many to stock. It's sometimes easier to ask your sales rep these questions. Sometimes they don't know, but it's their job to help you make your decisions. The good ones will find out for you.

Save your phone time for placing new product orders when

possible, and your distributor's sales rep will appreciate you. You do not need a great deal of information to place your restock orders. You got that information when the item was new. You need to know whether or not the supplier has any copies in stock.

Send restock information by online form, e-mail or fax when possible. That avenue reduces the number of errors that creep into your order by a human element from the process. Mistakes cost you sales. Take steps to reduce them.

When Creep is Good

Sometimes you want to increase your inventory. Suppose you started your role-playing section with *Dungeons & Dragons*. It's the best-selling role-playing game and appeals to a diverse market. You could argue that because you already have the best-selling fantasy role-playing game, you do not need a second one. Its sales would simply take away from D&D sales.

That's not quite accurate. Some potential D&D players might stop playing that game and play *Ars Magica* if you offer them that choice. A more likely scenario is that some players will switch from D&D to *Ars Magica*, some new players will start with *Ars Magica*, and your *Ars Magica* selection might draw in new customers, all in combination. Some customers play and buy both. Your RPG category sales might look like this:

1st Quarter sales, D&D only:	$2,400
2nd Quarter sales, D&D:	$2,200
2nd Quarter sales, Ars Magica:	$350
2nd Quarter combined RPG sales:	$2,550

In this case, some things happen to your numbers. Your inventory amount increases. Your average turn rate decreases, because the turn rate on the new, lower-volume product line is lower than the established, higher-velocity product line. Your accessories sales increase.

As your sales for a product line grow, you need to make this decision across the board. After your RPG sales increase, for example, you probably want to increase your dice inventory. Because of the overwhelming choices of dice out there, their high rate of sales and their low price per piece, ordering dice could very well be the worst chore you ever have. A large dice restock can take tedious hours. Nevertheless, dice sales add up quickly, and adding some complication to your order can increase sales along the line.

Once you discover that more selection equals more sales, your natural reaction might be to run with that idea. If you do $20,000 per year with D&D, and you add 20 other full lines of RPGs, your sales will go through the roof. You might do $80,000 or $100,000 a year in RPGs!

If only it were so easy.

Doubling your inventory does not double your sales. Depending on the product line, how you display it, and customer demand, doubling your inventory might increase sales by 5%, by 20%, or by 50%. You need to take into consideration the cost of the inventory, the overall turn rate, and the sales increase you see after the increase in inventory.

Let's return to dice. Let's say that you have a few sets. In fact, you have a lot of sets because your sales have been good and the line has been growing for some time. In fact, you pull up some numbers and find that for the first quarter of this year, you sold $425 worth of dice (at cost) with an average inventory amount of $300. During the third quarter of this year, you sold $640 worth of dice on an average inventory amount of $600. Your turn rate went from 1.4 to 1.1. That additional $300 you invested in your dice inventory has increased your annual sales rate from $3,200 per year to $4,800 per year.

But your goal for dice sales is $6,000 per year. You want another 25% increase in your dice sales. Given that dice come at your normal discount and you price them at SRP, you stand to make about $565 in profit per year from that $1,200 increase in sales. Before you set your budget to make it happen, check your cash flow. Are you comfortable with taking up to two years to see a return? One year? Six months?

In this case, let's assume that you see weak short-term growth for RPGs after looking at the release schedules for the next three months and decide that six months is the longest you are willing to wait for a return. Six months' worth of profit on the sales increase is $282. You decide to spend $250 increasing your inventory and spend the remainder on a small sign and a contest designed to generate the most interest. In this case, your contest involves a scale and bragging rights for "largest dice collection in the state."

The lesson is that not all inventory increase is a bad thing. A low inventory sometimes means a high turn rate, but you don't put a turn rate in the bank. You put profit dollars in the bank. If your inventory runs too low, you might be missing out on potential sales because of stockouts.

The important point is to control this inventory growth. Control it by carefully liquidating the inventory you do not want. Support the product lines that support you. Set yourself goals that you are willing to live with, and count your inventory frequently to make sure you are on track to hit that goal. Above all, check your order budget against your sales to make sure your cash flow is staying in a range you can afford.

OPENING INVENTORY

Your opening inventory sets your tone for your store. It lets all of those people walking in the door know what you sell. Your goal with your opening inventory is to give your customers a taste of the industry. Once they bite on something, you can provide them with more.

WIDE, NOT DEEP

Products do not have a uniform popularity across the country. Some oddball stores do not sell *Magic*. Some sell three times as much *Rifts* as they sell D&D. Because you do not know which products will be popular in your location, you want to provide your customers with the option to try just about anything.

Order one copy of several RPG core rulebooks. Rely on your distributor's sales rep for specific titles for lines you are not personally familiar with. For large product lines, order some key supplements, but no more than four different titles and only one copy of each title.

For CCGs, order 3-4 individual starters for each game you plan to carry if your distributor allows you to break up a case. Order no more than one booster display. Order enough different colors of card sleeves to be representative. Pick up a handful of glass counters.

Follow this mentality throughout your selection. If you intend to carry board games, order *Axis & Allies*, but not the Pacific or Atlantic expansions. Order *Settlers of Catan*, but none of that game's expansions.

Initially replace each sale. You do not yet know if that sale indicates a trend or a single curious buyer. You could have sold that starter to somebody who likes to look at the art but will not bring his friends into the hobby. A knee-jerk reaction to a single sale that causes you to spend $300 expanding a product line is a mistake.

If your customers indicate otherwise, feel free to allow the inventory to grow. For example, if a man comes in and says that he's been looking for a place to play a *Warhammer 40,000: Rogue Trader* game, you might want to add a couple of titles for that system on speculation.

At this stage, pay close attention to your special orders. A person ordering the latest supplement for a game probably already has the core book and several other titles in that product line. Find out where he got them, how many players are in his group, and whether or not he runs the game. You might make a note to order the next supplement for that game, expecting that he will be interested in it, too.

Special Orders

Some stores do not take special orders. You will not be one of those stores. You will outlast those stores.

These store owners argue that some customers do not pay for their orders. To compensate for a small percentage of deadbeats, these stores refuse their customers a powerful loyalty-building service. By handling special orders carefully, you can minimize that small actual loss and increase the value that special ordering provides the customer.

Special orders give you the ability to sell more inventory than you carry. At times, customers want an item you don't stock. If you deny them the sale, you might give up that one item to another company. If you deny them enough sales, you could lose the customer. Special orders are a chance for you to gain a competitive advantage against big-box markets and sell more inventory than you carry in the store, increasing your turn rate and your overall profitability.

If you get more than one request for the same item, it's time to consider adding it to your regular mix. Few customers go to the trouble of asking for something they do not see, and for every person asking for it, there might be a half dozen who would buy it off the shelf — yet another reason to make special orders a key part of your business.

Design a standard request form to kick off your special request program. You should be able have a local print shop make copies for about a nickel a page. Memo pads, for example, are available in batches of 10 with 50 copies per pad. The form should have a space for product name, customer name, customer contact info, date and your notes recording your efforts to order the product.

Instead of a paper copy, your point of sale system should allow you to handle special requests or backorders. Check your POS literature or ask your customer service rep how to handle it. If you have a website without a shopping cart, provide an e-mail link or a web form so that customers can send requests directly to you.

Let your customers know about the service. Mention the service in paper newsletters or in e-mails. Put up a sign in your game room or on your bulletin board. Don't just mention that you offer special orders: identify why a customer would want to special order. Customers don't want to waste a trip to your store in search for something that isn't on the shelf. Point out how easy special requests are to place. Let them know that you don't require a deposit and that you'll call them and let them know the product is in stock. Bag-stuff with the form so that everybody has one.

If you use a lot of catalogs, include a form between the pages of each catalog. If the customer takes a catalog home and finds something he likes, he can bring in the request form with his next visit. Fantasy Flight Games, Mongoose, Reaper Miniatures, Rio Grande and Kenzer & Company all provide excellent product catalogs.

You can use the same form for pre-orders for a new product that hasn't been released yet. Fill out the product's name & price and leave a stack of forms on the counter or in your game room. Your initial product order is important to get right. If you under-order, you lose customers to other sales avenues. If you order too many copies of a title, you might never recover your initial investment money.

Special orders represent a perfect opportunity to upsell a customer. He has already indicated that he wants one thing you do not have in stock. Perhaps he wants more. If he asks for *Nuclear War*, offer to order *Nuclear Expansion* while you are at it.

Follow up with your special orders. Call customers after you place your weekly order so that they know whether or not to expect the item. If it doesn't come in, call and let them know so they don't waste a trip. You can use the opportunity to ask if they want anything else next time you try to place the order, too.

To minimize the loss, record any deadbeats on your POS system or keep notes concerning unpurchased special orders to share with your employees. A customer abusing the system loses his privilege to special order further products. Implementing a standard policy for cutting off a customer's right to place special orders prevents the abuse and keeps your risk as low as possible.

MERCHANDISING: THE POWER OF POSITION

Merchandising is how your physical store sells your product. It includes product placement, highlight lighting, product displays, signage, and all the other physical factors that combine to draw a customer's eye to the product and encourage him to pick it up and handle it.

While it might not seem like much, proper merchandising can be enormously effective. Something as simple as moving a product line from one place to another can double or triple your sales. Do not underestimate its importance.

GENERAL PLAN

In general, you want to encourage traffic flow so that customers move freely throughout your entire store. Avoid dead ends. Areas of high interest should have browsing space around them to avoid creating traffic jams. Place your fixtures to create natural avenues that direct customers throughout your entire store. A circle or racetrack pattern is best for this, depending on the shape of your store.

Place items by game type and genre, not by manufacturer. In other words, your CCGs go together, with all of your anime-based games in the same display section. Your role-playing games all belong on the same shelves, with fantasy next to fantasy and superhero next to superhero. Ideally, buy or make display methods that best serve the item in question. A wire bin works fine for plush toys, but it's terrible for books. Bookshelves work well for books, but large board games might fall off of shelves that are too short or too thin.

NEW RELEASE RACK

When new products come in, they go in a specific area or to a

218

specific shelf. A brightly-colored visible sign should proclaim this area loudly to all customers. With a large percentage of a product's sales coming within the first 30 days of its release, this area should be prominent and convenient and should be flanked by high-margin impulse items.

Make sure this area has browsing room for multiple customers. Lighting should be bright, and if you use highlight lighting anywhere in the store, this display is a good candidate for it. Another good idea is laying stick-on footprints on the floor that make a path leading from the front door.

EMPLOYEE FAVORITES

The gaming industry is well-suited to use this method of promotion. Employees often voice their favorites anyway, and displaying them all in one place is a great way to strike a bond with customers. People who like one of the games on the display feel predisposed to like the others.

Keep these racks small to minimize duplication of product. Definitely do not move your only copy of a game from its normal place on the rack to the Employee Favorite shelf. You might miss out on the customer searching for the game from a word-of-mouth reference or who came in because he found you on the manufacturer's retailer locator or who is already familiar with the game but new in town.

Plan a rotation cycle for the Employee Favorite shelf. The period should be no less frequently than once a month, but no more than once a week. Depending on your volume and the number of new releases you bring in, once every two weeks is probably best. Between two and four weeks is also the time period between your average customer's visits. Change the display too frequently, and some people miss it entirely. Change it too rarely and it becomes stale.

IMPULSE ITEMS

Retail stores typically glob all of their impulse buys near the cash-wrap. It's a natural reaction once you understand the concept of impulse buys and know that they frequently occur at the cash-wrap while people are in line.

Long lines are not something you often see at a game store. Checkout times tend to be quick, while volume is relatively low. While the cash-wrap has a strong influence on impulse sales, it's not the only place in the store that you can effectively place them.

Maybe you have a dice display near the counter, where nearly all game stores keep them. Including some tubes of dice near the core D&D books can increase sales. In fact, have everything a new player or GM needs within arm's reach. Keep a clear plastic tube with Chessex or Crystal Caste battlemats there. Make sure character sheets are visible — face out, because they're practically invisible when placed spine out. A brief sign helping the new player identify what he needs is useful for increasing sales and reminding customers that you provide a service. You do not merely stock games, you support them.

The goal of such a sign should be to encourage sales slightly above your historical average, which you determine by comparing your sales records. Keep it under 25 words, if possible. Reinforce the sign with a verbal reminder at the point of sale. "What color sleeves do you want for your deck?" is a perfect example.

Display Management

Creating a display is a form of in-store advertising. It brings attention to a product that you want to promote. A well-designed display earns back the additional square footage is occupies by increasing sales of the product displayed.

An effective display shows the highlights of a game. It should not try to teach game play. Show components, graphics, and the box art prominently. Do not worry about rules, creating realistic "hands" of cards for the display, or anything contradictory. If the item is used with another game, show how by using components or pieces from the game it's supposed to accompany.

Signs accompany the display when appropriate. You might need to indicate the price, point out similar games or products, or explain what it's for. As with all in-store signage, it should be professionally drawn or computer-generated. Hand-printed signs are unprofessional and present a poor image. Remember to include the game's name so that interested customers can ask for it.

Once the components of a shrink-wrapped game have been used for a display, you cannot sell the game as new. You can leave it behind the counter as a store copy, sell it on your second-hand game shelf or use one of your other liquidation techniques. You might give it to a prominent game player in exchange for running a few demo games.

Displays might have another cost, too: additional inventory. If you make a D&D display that highlights the key components of that game, you might include dice with your D&D core books.

Count this small amount of duplication, monitor it, but do not remove a display because you fear reducing a turn rate or raising your inventory. Change a display when it's no longer effective overall or after your normal display rotation.

Window Displays

Window displays attract the interest of people walking by the store front. They also offer a first impression to people already approaching your store. Place something attractive, colorful and not too weird there. Plush Cthulhu toys are right on the edge of comfortable (it's plush) but exotic (nothing is more "exotic" than Cthulhu).

Too much clutter in your windows invites robbers. Robbers love the thought that nobody will see them hold you up. Make the displays visible, but keep them at low height or on the edge of the windows to maintain maximum visibility through the window.

Cross-Mix Displays

Cross-mix displays are those that show diversity of product rather than uniformity of product. They showcase your whole range of products for people not familiar with what you carry. They do not promote any one game; they promote the idea of games.

One such display might feature a Player's Handbook, a Warhammer 40k tank and a couple of miniatures, a handful of dice, some cards from different CCGs, and a couple of hexes and road pieces from Settlers of Catan. Images like this might be good for TV ads, window displays and for off-site sales such as trade shows.

Lighting

Good lighting generates sales. Be careful of moving into a place with poor lighting, because you can spend hundreds or thousands of dollars bringing it up to your standards. If you are negotiating to move into a place, make sure the lighting is up to par. Ask the landlord if he intends to replace all of the lighting or if he wishes to make allowance for you to replace it. Most of the time, the landlord will try to wave off lighting, as if it's a negligible expense. If it's so negligible, point out that it should not be a burden for him to pay for it.

Asking a local expert for a lighting analysis can pay off in improved sales and in reduced costs. If your building is old, replacing light fixtures with newer, more energy-efficient fixtures can save on monthly bills.

Consider adding accent lighting for popular displays, such as D&D, *Magic*, or Games Workshop. A 5% increase in sales for a product line that sees $30,000 a year in annual sales brings in an additional $1,500. Spending $200 to install a track of lighting could pay for itself repeatedly, despite the increase in utility and replacement bulb cost.

THE CARE AND FEEDING OF PLANOGRAMS

Planograms are an important inventory control tool that you can use to maximize your stocking efficiency. Essentially, a planogram is a map of your shelf that indicates where your stock goes. If the shelf were to dump over, you could use the planogram to replace the inventory where you had it before.

If you do not use a POS system, having a planogram is more important. Restocking your store becomes a question of simply printing out your planogram, comparing it to the inventory on the shelf and circling what you need to restock. Bang, it's that easy.

Planograms help your employees in restocking the shelf, too. Once they receive product, they refer to the planogram when they place the restocks. Because you already know what's coming in, you should have new product figured into the planogram in advance.

Restocking from a systematic method like this has several purposes. First, it reminds you of each and every product. No more forgetting to order a title because you do not have the entire product line memorized. Second, it keeps things consistent for the customers. If they see a title they mean to pick up next time they come in, they will look for it in the same place when they come back. If they do not see it, they might forget about it. Next, it makes sure that your staff is stocking items where you want them placed for maximum sales. Placement is important to sales, and you spend a great deal of thought in exactly where you want items placed in your store. That thought is reflected in your planogram.

Sample RPG Product Line Planogram

Core Book	GM's Guide	Adventure 1
Character Sheet	GM Screen	Adventure 2
Supplement 1	Sourcebook 1	Adventure 3
Supplement 2	Sourcebook 2	Adventure 4

Build-Tos

Notice that we've described two ways of counting up your re-stock orders manually. One identifies items that you have sold, and another identifies items that you have in stock. The difference is minor, but for items for which you want to keep multiple copies in stock, paying attention to your in-stock goal is important.

Plainly speaking, these items are those that have an average turn rate less than your restock time. You sell more than one *Magic* booster, for example, per day. Hopefully, dozens per day. Obviously you do not want to keep one of those in stock.

You would never run out if you kept 10 cases in stock, right?

True, but you would also be making poor use of your money.

You need to find the magic number that lets you keep product in stock as much as possible while allowing you to spend money elsewhere. For the cost of those 10 cases of *Magic*, you could experiment with a dozen other CCGs, or get a quick-pay discount from a distributor or run another week's worth of off-prime time cable TV ads.

Keep a number in stock such that you do not run out of product and have enough extra for an occasional exceptional sale. If somebody comes in with an income tax return check and wants to spend it all on one thing, you don't want to lose the sale because you did not have enough product in stock.

To arrive at this number, you need to know how fast you sell the item and how long it takes to get a restock.

Say you sell 30 copies of a product per week on average. You got this number by either checking the notepad by your register or by printing a report from your POS system. That's 4.3 copies per day. You check your inventory Monday morning while you are prepping your order. You have 18 in stock. Order 12? If your restock order arrives on Thursday (a three-day ship from your distributor) you'll sell an average of 13 before you get your order. That means when your restock arrives, you would add 12 to the five you have left, giving you 17 to last until next week. That's not enough merchandise for a game that sells 30 copies in a week.

You need to order enough to cover the period until the re-stock arrives. In this case, you need 43 to cover those 10 days. Subtract the 18 you have in stock, and order 25.

Now that you know you need 43 copies of that product to cover that 10-day period, record this number as your build-to. Now any employee capable of doing elementary-school math can prep your restock order. Next week, your clerk can count 9 copies of that same product in stock, subtract that from 43 and order 34.

Sample Partial D&D Build-To

Item	Build-to (-)	In stock =	Order
Player's Handbook	5	3	2
Dungeon Master's Guide	4	2	2
Monster Manual	3	3	0
Character Sheets	4	3	1
DM Screen	2	0	2

Unproductive Merchandise

Unless sales demonstrate incredible growth because every item you bring in is a big hit, you eventually need to drop some items. Part of this rotation is the nature of the items. Collectible card games constantly rotate out old product. Collectible miniature games are the same. Roleplaying games and some board games undergo revisions, rendering some of your inventory obsolete.

Improving Performance

Checking a game's performance record is the first comparison. For example, if GURPS seems slow from your point of view, check your POS or your notepad sales record. If you are using a notepad, you need to separate out some numbers. Track sales of each product in the line by month.

The trend will reveal one of several choices.

The line is steadily decreasing. A knee-jerk reaction is to cut off a line right away. While that's probably the best choice, check for resurgence. Visit the company website. Do they have new products coming out? Is there a revision coming? If nothing is changing, this line probably needs to go. Before you abandon it, try to gather some feedback about the product nationally.

If the product seems stable at other stores, consider a promotion. You might do a bundle sale, make a display, or reconsider where you have it displayed (maybe GURPS should not go with your science fiction lines but next to the Hero System, another generic RPG system). Give it an effort that corresponds to its potential reward based on past sales history. You probably wouldn't run TV ads for GURPS, but you could bag stuff flyers for a month or hand out a couple of hundred GURPS buttons at a local convention.

Core book sales are consistent, but supplement sales are decreasing. Supplements do sell less than core books, so be careful about what you are seeing. Steady sales of the core books usually means that you will see steady supplement sales soon. Contact the manufacturer or a customer that knows the line and find out what supplements are considered essential. Make sure you have those in stock.

Supplement sales are steady, core sales are weak. The most typical incidence here is that your core books are out of stock. Double-check your inventory to make sure you have the books on the shelf. If you order from a POS record of items sold and the book has been misplaced or stolen, of course your core book sales are off.

If the core books have been out of print for a while that could spell trouble for the line. At best, it means that you have a few veteran players who are filling in their collection but no new customers buying into the line. Consider offering the veterans a benefit of some sort if they bring in some new blood.

Core book sales are up, supplement sales are weak. This line is growing, but your customers might not be aware of the product. Maybe your selection is not as strong as it could be. Consider making a display promoting the products that new customers are most likely to need or checking the manufacturer's list of available products (either directly or through your distributor) and adding products you hadn't carried before. If you don't have catalogs, ask the manufacturer for some. If they do not have any, make up a flyer or small product listing and stick it inside each core book.

GURPS is an atypical choice for this example, because they maintain an excellent list of titles with their availability (out of print, limited supply available, going to reprint, etc.). The direct link for the list is *http://www.warehouse23.com/pstatus.html.*

Moving It
Moving product from one part of the store to another is a cheap way to give it a second chance. Bring it closer to high-turning product lines, or turn the display to face a higher traffic walkway. You might be surprised at how effective this trick can be.

Repackaging
Repackaging a product is an excellent way to convince people to buy it. One of my favorite presentation anecdotes came from

a restaurant owner who offered a crab side dish for $4.50. Sales were sluggish and waste was high because the product failed to sell through before it exceeded its shelf life. When the restaurant owner priced the same dish at $13 and called it an appetizer, sales went through the roof. A product's presentation has an enormous impact on its sales.

WizKids at one point offered metal miniatures for its first game, *Mage Knight*. These figures were unpainted and the packaging was awkward. Well, the whole attraction of *Mage Knight* was that it offered pre-painted plastic miniatures for a good price, and higher-priced miniatures that you had to paint were not what the audience wanted. The price soon dropped, and the stores that carried Mage Knight were soon stuck with 30 to 100 unproductive miniatures. Some distributors offered them for a penny each within an alarmingly short time of their release.

Stripping these miniatures out of their packaging allowed them to be sold at $1 or so each as singles. While $1 each was a huge loss compared to the original retail price, it was an excellent margin on purchases of a penny per figure and offered an excellent sell-through rate for clearance product.

Similarly, one store viewed Double-Sided Tokens as a potential upsell opportunity for *Magic* players. Token cards had been popular in the *Unglued* set, selling for as much as $6 each on the secondary market, and a pack of eight of them would be a great value at $3 or $4 (this was well before Wizards of the Coast started including token cards in booster packs).

As it turned out, the art on the cards did not match the quality of the art on the official tokens, the variety was limited, and the tokens' fixed format meant low sales. After an initial half-dozen sold, interest fell off. Eventually, opening the packs and repacking them in bundles of 10 improved sell-through, but at a slight loss.

Bundled Deals

A bundled deal combines two or more products at a single price. Bundled deals encourage customers to spend more than they would normally. You might bundle a low-cost adventure with a *Dungeons Master's Guide*, dice with a *Player's Handbook*, or the D&D *Monster Manual* and low-selling third-party monster book.

A shrink-wrap machine is an excellent aid for bundling offers. Include your offer as a sticker on the outside or on a tag inside the bundle but visible thru the shrink. This sticker should identify exactly what's in the bundle. Place it carefully to cover up as little of the manufacturer's art and sales features as possible.

For best effect, target the bundled price at slightly above your average sale for the appropriate product line. If your average RPG sale is $40, set a bundle price at $45-$50. Compare this with the price of a *Magic: the Gathering* fat pack. Wizards of the Coast set the target price at a little bit above the average sale to increase how much the customer spends.

Try to bundle a high-margin item in with a normal or low-margin item to soften the real cost of the discount. If you include a $13.99 sprue cutter with every $50 *Warhammer 40,000* tank purchase, bundle the two together for $55. The sprue cutter normally costs you $5.30, and the tank costs $27.50 through Games Workshop. The customer thinks he's getting a 15% discount, but you are making an acceptable 40% profit margin on a larger-than-normal ticket price.

You can also use bundled promotions to advertise a new product line or a new manufacturer. You can use this technique to encourage accessory sales. You could use this promotion to lead customers away from one line toward another, more profitable line.

Call It Used

If you offer second-hand sales, moving the product from the new to the used section is an easy way to clear up that space. Change the price tag, amend your inventory records to show the change, and let it go. A customer that refused to touch the game new might be eager to buy it at 70% of the cover price if he finds a "like new" condition game in the used section.

The advantages to this method are simplicity and greater margin than some methods of elimination. The disadvantage is time: the product still might not sell.

LIQUIDATION

At some point, you must remove unproductive merchandise. Product that doesn't sell costs you money by its presence. It ties up a valuable resources — your space — that could be used to sell other products.

Many game store owners insist on holding on to this product. Maybe they are fond of the game and have difficulty with the decision to remove it. Maybe they hate the idea of receiving less for something than they paid for it.

Remember that your square footage is a resource, like your employees, your cash, and your time. Do you pay your employees to sit around and do nothing? Would you leave cash sitting in an unused bank account? Do you sit in a chair facing the wall?

Well, you might, but these examples are perhaps clearer indications of underused resources. Few would disagree that employees are more valuable when they work than when they do not work. Your cash serves you better in your primary bank account. Your time is better spent in managing your business than doing an impression of Auguste Rodin's *The Thinker*.

Your space, too, is better used in the display of sellable products.

It helps to keep in mind that the lack of sales is not a cipher. You pay rent for that space. Count up your square footage given to that display area. If your rent plus CAM and taxes comes to $14.50 psf and those unsold products take up 5 sf of space, you spend over $70 a year storing those products don't sell.

Clearance Sale

A notice that you are clearing out a line spurs those people who were interested but not interested enough to buy it at full price. Because your potential profit on these sales is very low, keep the advertising cost to a minimum. You might place a sign near the product, and send out an e-mail notice. You probably wouldn't spend $200 on a mailout except in the case of a very large line.

For a clearance sale to generate excitement, the numbers must usually be very high. A 60% discount might not attract much notice. If the game was popular at one point, you can start with lower numbers, because some players might want to add one or two more items to their collection. If it never had much of a following, you might need to offer it at 70% or 80% off to get attention.

Each week or two, step up the discount until the product is gone.

Batch Deals

If the product line is representative — one of each title, for example — offer it all at a discount. You only need to make one sale to clear up a large section of the shelf, you have the potential to make a very nice ticket on a single sale, and the discount

228

is often very acceptable for clearance items. A 40% reduction might be enough incentive to move product in this manner.

Ideally, price these batches at an impulse price. Instead of being a purchase unto themselves, you can add them onto another ticket.

Convention Inventory

Product that doesn't move for you might be the best-seller at a store 40 miles away. You can move this product to your convention inventory and it might sell in another market when you work a convention there. If you track your convention inventory separately, this method might involve a small amount of paperwork. Otherwise, move it into storage and make better use of the space.

eBay

Using eBay or other online auction sites virtually guarantees you a sale within seven days. If you set a high minimum, you see less activity and might not get any bids at all. A lower minimum with a reserve discourages bidders, also. Setting a low minimum and no reserve offers the best price, though it allows for the occasional sale to go for far less than you intended.

Remember that eBay has costs associated with it, too. You spend time or pay labor for the listing, responding to questions, sending a statement, processing the payment, shipping the product, and recording the transaction. You pay fees for the listing, the prominence of the listing and the final price of the auction. You sometimes have issues with non-paying bidders, forcing you to double your cost in time by re-listing the item.

On the other hand, you have a nearly-guaranteed sale within a week's time. The astonishing turn rate might make up for low revenues if you can make good use of those revenues once you receive them.

Trash

As the math shows, product sitting in a usable space bears a cost. While you want to receive cash for it if you can, if the product still won't sell at an aggressive discount, throw it away. Ignore your instincts telling you that it's wrong. Trust the math.

Chapter 8:
Financials

G etting hard numbers can be the hardest part of planning a game store. Some people aren't willing to help. Many people are willing but don't know enough to help. Others fear that giving you their numbers will cause you blame them if your business fails.

The formula with which you'll apply these numbers is fairly simple. Compared to game publishing or distribution, the math part is graciously uncomplicated. You need a few guidelines and you'll be ready to fill out your own forms.

Calculating Startup Funds

The amount of money you need is composed of two elements: your opening expenses, which you'll spend before you open, and your capital reserve.

Opening Expenses

This figure is the simple sum of a long list of items. This book includes a sample checklist to aid you in your planning, and you can find a more complete spreadsheet online at *http://d-infinity.net/GRG*. Note that your specific business plan might not call for all of these items. In fact, no store uses all of them — it includes line items for both rent and mortgage, for example.

Administrative and Operating Expenses

These costs apply regardless of the type of business you start. A movie production studio, a casino, a tractor-renting business — they all need a name, a place to work out of, a bank account, and a business structure.

Sample costs include:
▷ Incorporation
▷ Accountant fees
▷ Attorney fees
▷ Utility deposits
▷ Rent deposit
▷ Bank fees and costs

How do you get these figures? By calling people who offer these products or services and asking how much they cost. For others, you might want to ask other businesses in your neighborhood how much they spend (trying to get a projected bill out of your electric company will probably drive you nuts, but they might be willing to give you a billing history of the suite you're leasing). You'll make dozens or hundreds of phone calls before you open. You'll want to keep extensive notes for your comparisons.

Sample Store: Sample store incorporates personally, saving attorney fees but still paying state fees. Sample store has no bargaining position with deposits and so pays the full $4,800 in rents and utility deposits. Total for this category: $5,500.

FFE: Furniture, Fixtures, and Equipment

These items are the material tools you need to conduct retail sales. They include shelves, computer hardware and software, and miscellaneous items.

Sample costs include:

▷ Tables
▷ Chairs
▷ Counters
▷ Wall fixtures
▷ Shelving
▷ Computers
▷ Receipt printer
▷ Printer
▷ Fax
▷ Telephone(s)
▷ Bulletin board
▷ Miscellaneous office supplies
▷ Shrink-wrap machine
▷ Cleaning supplies

Sample Store: Sample store has been buying fixtures for a year from liquidation sales and the owner is willing to build additional fixtures. However, the owner doesn't want the store to all look second-hand, so he's willing to spend $500 on a few slatwall fixtures, planning to upgrade the rest of the store in two to three years. Adding up the supply cost, the cost of a cash-wrap, POS system, and miscellaneous equipment he hasn't obtained yet, the FFE comes to $4,000.

Build-Out

The build-out turns a vacant commercial suite into a welcoming place to buy games. It covers everything in the space, from lighting to flooring.

Sample costs include:
- Materials
- Paint
- Tools
- Flooring
- Lights
- Miscellaneous repairs
- Signage
- Contracted work

Sample Store: The owner is willing to do the work himself, except for the electrical work, for which he has neither the tools nor the training. Also, he knows that commercial suites have a history of building up stop-gap wiring above the drop ceiling, and he wants a pro to minimize the fire hazard . He plans on $1,500 for the electrician (who also replaces the ballast in all the light fixtures, something the owner learns is easy to do and does himself from then on), $2,000 for flooring and $500 for miscellaneous tools and repairs.

Inventory

Your inventory expense is probably the largest single category on your list of opening expenses. It's also the greatest variable between stores. There's no easy answer here.

Here's a rule of thumb to help until you sit on the phone with a distributor for an hour or so and work out an initial order: figure on spending $20 for every square foot in your store devoted to retail. That is, take your square footage, deduct for your game space, bathrooms, office, and wasted space, and multiply by 20. If you use 1,200 square feet out of a 2,000-sf location, figure on spending $24,000. If you only have 700 square feet and you're going to be using all of it for retail, figure on $14,000.

That's a rule of thumb, which means it'll be wrong for most stores. However, it'll be close enough for planning at this stage.

Sample Store: Our sample is a large-ish 2,000 square foot store. The owner knows it's a bit of an indulgence for an opening location, especially with no local competition, but he plans an aggressive event schedule and wants room for multiple tournaments or demos in the game room, which will take up 1,200 square feet. Also, he has to sign a 4-year lease to get the rate he wants, so he's going to be here for a while. That leaves about 750 square feet for inventory, which means roughly $15,000 in merchandise.

As a general rule, I wouldn't spend that much before opening. I'd spend less initially and hold back some of my inventory dollars to spend after gauging customer interest. If miniatures are hot for you to the exclusion of other game categories, you can buy more inventory in that category and maybe add a second line of paints. If you had instead spent ¼ of that hold-back money on minis, ¼ on cards, ¼ on RPGs, etc. most of it would be tied up in slow-moving inventory and you'd be missing sales opportunities in your best category. Despite that distinction, you're going to be spending this money in the first year, and it messes up the math if we count it under your capital reserve, so we include it here.

Sample Store: We're up to $28,500 in pre-opening expenses.

Capital Reserve

Before you can calculate your capital reserve, you must determine your burn rate. Your burn rate is the rate at which you spend money before you start to break even. It's a combination of your fixed expenses like rent and utilities and variable expenses.

While technically labor is considered a variable expense, I include it under the fixed expenses category. Initially, your need for double coverage will be slight. Your primary concern with scheduling is making sure every shift is covered. You might need two employees only during Friday night and Saturday afternoon. This schedule scales very high. It works for a store doing $100,000 per year, and it works for a store doing $200,000 a year.

That leaves for your variable expenses only the cost of replacing the inventory you sell on a daily basis and credit card fees. Our calculations assume that your inventory level remains constant (which it won't), but we've already accounted for your first year's inventory gain in the calculation above, so we're okay there.

234

Finding Your Break-Even — How Much

Add up the total of all of your monthly expenses. These include but are not limited to:

▷ Rent (including CAM or triple net)
▷ Utilities (electricity, water, phone, Internet)
▷ Labor (including tax and payroll service fees)
▷ Trash Removal
▷ Pest Control
▷ Alarm Monitoring
▷ Bank Fees
▷ Insurance
▷ Repair and Maintenance
▷ Advertising

Include a salary for yourself. A healthy business pays its manager, whether the manager is the owner or a hired employee.

One tricky amount to include is your loan repayment. You don't know the amount of the payment because you don't know the amount of the loan yet. Leave it out at this stage and then revise the break-even afterward to include the loan repayment.

For the items that you don't spend every month, like your business license renewal, food permit, memberships, CAM adjustment, etc, add up your annual expenses and divide that number by 12 to find a prorated figure.

You should also include a "fudge factor." You might forget to include a line item, something might cost far more than you anticipated, or prices might increase between your estimate and the date you make the purchase. There are two methods for including it. The first is to add a small amount to each line item. Personally, I prefer the other method: add an additional line item to your fixed costs. Call this category "fudge factor." Make it 5-10% of your other costs. For $4,000 in fixed costs, add $400 for your fudge factor.

The total of all of these line items is the amount you spend each month. For your convenience, I have a break-even analysis that I'm willing to share on the website supporting this book at *http://d-infinity.net*. Fill in the numbers specific to your store as you gather your figures.

Sample Store: Without going into detail, let's say monthly expenses total $5,000, requiring $12,500 in sales to pay the bills.

Finding Your Break-Even — How Long

You're not likely to do reach your break-even your first month. The trick becomes to calculate how many months you'll operate at negative cash flow before you start to break even. For the record, the majority of the plans I've seen or store sales records I've seen reach their break-even between months 9 and 14.

Sample Store: With a break-even of $12,500/month, it'll take 13 months to reach break-even. Partial months round up.

Thirteen months at $5,000 a month is $65,000 in capital reserve.

Using an online loan calculator like the one at *http://www.bankrate.com/brm/popcalc2.asp*, your loan payment is $1,700 a month. Let's add that to our monthly expenses and get $6,700 per month, or a total capital reserve needed of $87,100. Round that up to $90,000.

Sample Store: Opening expenses of $28,500 and capital reserve of $90,000 means this store needs $118,500 to open.

As you can see, if this store owner has $30,000 available, he could afford everything he needs to open his doors. He'd have $1,500 left in his bank account. One month later, he might do decent sales, but he'd owe $5,000 in expenses before he thought about restocking the merchandise that sold. He's bankrupt already.

Believe it or not, some variation of this scenario is the single largest cause of business failure. The big variable is how long the owner can survive by racking up credit card debt, cannibalizing inventory, not taking a paycheck, etc., before he runs out of money. If you've learned the lesson here, you've increased your likelihood of success tremendously.

PRE-OPENING SALES PROJECTION

Projecting the sales for your business plan or for a major modification to your business plan is the trickiest part of the job. When you calculate costs you can get price sheets from distributors, rate cards from advertising media, and rent figures from commercial leasing agents. You don't have similar tools when calculating income.

What do you have?

Matrix Projections

If you had access to the sales figures for other game stores like yours, you could compare the size and scope of your store to

236

theirs and estimate your sales based on the comparison. If, for example, a nearby store does $400,000 a year in sales and you plan to carry similar product lines and have similar space, you might be able to count on anywhere from $250,000 to $450,000 in sales, depending on the comparison.

This method faces two major difficulties. First, unless your store is identical in every way to the comparison stores, the comparison will be invalid. You have to adjust your comparison up or down based on the areas in which you are strong or weak. If the stores in your state are doing $200,000 a year, you'd need an exceptional reason for projecting $350,000 annually. With experience and a personal visit or two you can look at a store, gauge its foot traffic, gauge its inventory levels, and estimate its annual sales. Unless you have industry experience, you're not likely to be able to do that.

Secondly, and more importantly, you aren't likely to know how much other game stores do in sales. Most people don't share that information, and some of those are less likely to share it with a potential competitor. Even on industry-only message boards, discussions of sales are usually relative rather than absolute: "I had a good week", or "Is anybody else way down from last year?"

Inventory Levels and Turn Rates

Add up the value of the product lines you intend to carry. You have your inventory costs from your expenses sheet, so you know about how much you'll spend on your goods. Multiply by a reasonable turn rate (for simple math, I'm using annual sales divided by an average inventory at cost). What is a "reasonable turn rate"?

It depends.

Different products turn at different rates. Collectible card games turn quickly; role-playing games sell more slowly. If you plan to earn most of your dollars from the card-floppers, your overall average turn ate will be higher than that of a store selling principally historical miniatures.

Comparative Rates

CCGs: 6x to 20x
RPGs: 1x to 6x
Minis: 2x to 8x
Board games: 1x to 4x

Stores with a narrow focus — those that see more than half of their sales from a single category — can report higher turn rates than these.

Obviously, these rates vary tremendously. How do you know whether you could use 6x or 12x for your CCG sales? Look at the marketing section of your business plan. To whom are you advertising? CCG players are younger than RPG players or minis players, and they're more likely to be male. Minis players, especially Games Workshop customers, come from higher income groups. If your focus is broad, you'll bring in more board game players than the other groups. How about game tables, if any? If you have enough space to support competitive events, CCG and minis sales go up (RPGs do increase, but not as much). If your tables are the skinny conference tables, they're more comfortable for cards. If they're chest-high and covered with felt, you'll attract miniatures players.

Another factor in calculating an expected turn rate is your inventory level. If your inventory level is too low, your turn rate will be comparatively high but total sales will be small because you're missing out on a number of sales. A 25x turn rate on $1,000 worth of Magic yields only $25,000 a year. That's a great turn rate, but you're not putting much in the bank. You'd be better off if you add a second game for a total category turn rate of 18x on $2,000 in inventory, or even 14x on $3,000 by carrying a couple of more games.

On the other hand, having too much inventory gives you greater total sales but a lower turn rate. If you carried $15,000 in CCGs (which would be tough), you're not likely to keep a double-digit turn rate at all.

Things to suggest a higher turn rate:

▷ Good product knowledge
▷ A well-rounded advertising plan
▷ Game space
▷ Good image
▷ Multiple product lines
▷ Frequent activities
▷ A younger population base
▷ Good merchandising skills
▷ A marketing plan that emphasizes competitive prices
▷ Face-out book displays
▷ A focus on high-turn products like CCGs

Things to suggest a lower turn rate:

▷ Low visibility
▷ Low traffic count
▷ Unfamiliarity with the products you carry
▷ High competition
▷ An older population base
▷ Carrying used products
▷ A marketing plan that emphasizes product selection
▷ Spine out book displays
▷ A focus on low-turn products like RPGs

All of this brings us back to "How do I calculate my store's turn rate?" Look at your business plan. Multiply your planned categories by one of the turn rates given within each range. Use a figure closer to the top of the range if you check off items on the "high turn rate" list and a figure closer to the bottom if item of the "low turn rate" list apply to you. Project your sales for each category and add up the totals.

That's a good figure for your second year.

Your first year will be one of growth, culminating in figures near those. You might want to work backward, counting at month 12 and scaling back a little bit until you get to starting figures half or lower than your final figures. Your first three months should include fairly brisk growth. Monthly growth should slow for a few months and then slow even further near the end of the year. Sales growth of 10-20% a year for the next couple of years is normal.

The Wrong Way

Calculate your sales projection based on a realistic expectation of what your business model and resources can generate. If your plan does not work off that level, rewrite your plan to grow sales or reduce costs. Don't keep raising your sales projection to meet your needed capital. That's a recipe for failure.

OBTAINING FINANCING

The largest obstacle to most would-be business owners is obtaining the financing. Sometimes it seems impossible to convince a bank or potential lender to part with the very funds that they have set aside for investing. Convincing a potential lender to loan you capital requires two things: a good business plan and credit rating.

If the facts are solid, support your estimates, and allow for repayment of a loan, you have a strong advantage. If your presentation shows the right mix of optimism and caution, the lender's confidence grows. If both elements are strong enough, you will meet the lender's criteria for a safe investment.

Your Money

One obvious source of money is your own. While you might not have $70,000 in cash sitting in the bank, you might own equity in your home that you can borrow against. You might have long-term investments from which to draw some funds. You should be prepared to invest some of your own funds, however little. If you aren't willing to take a risk, nobody else will, either.

A large amount of cash up front has another benefit concerning lending as well. You are providing equity, while lenders are providing debt. A business begun with $35,000 in cash and $15,000 in borrowed money is stronger and more likely to attract the attention of further investors than one with $3,000 in cash and $47,000 in debt, even though they both have the same number of dollars in the bank.

I often recommend that, while you're planning, you take on a second job, preferably in the retail sector. If you don't have any prior sales experience, the time you spend learning the skill is a direct investment in your business. If you do, it's a chance to adjust to the long work-hours of a small business owner. If you can't handle the schedule, it's much easier to quit a part-time job than it is to exit your store without owing a hundred thousand dollars or more on a loan and a lease.

The biggest benefit, though, is the cash. With a decent part-time job, you might be able to save up $5,000 or $10,000 while you're working on opening your store. That extra cash creates a huge savings. You subtract your cash on hand from any start-up capital you might borrow, which can save you thousands in interest and reduce your store's monthly break-even by a couple of hundred dollars.

Family Money

Borrowing money from your family can be tricky. If you decide to pursue this option, be prepared to offer a full presentation like you would a bank or an outside investor. Have the full panoply of information available for inspection.

Having someone in the family that is interested in supporting the business can have two benefits. The obvious benefit is that you have more capital. The second benefit is that you have convinced one lender to invest in your business. That investor's support might encourage others.

If you choose to go this route, insist on a written contract. You will reassure the lender with your professionalism and the agreement could resolve a bitter dispute later.

PRIVATE INVESTORS

Whether you meet them through your current job or through a newspaper ad, or seek out angel investors online, investors expect to see many of the same things a bank sees. Usually, they'll look at the viability of your plan more closely than they will your personal financials.

You might find a single investor willing to finance the whole business. Most likely, you'll have to seek out more than one, each contributing a certain amount in exchange for partial ownership. You can set up these "shares" for investments of $5,000 or $10,000, or some other amount. You certainly want to include buy-out options for your investors so that you don't have to pay them indefinitely.

You might wish to involve a different kind of investor, one who brings talent and labor in addition to cash. This investor would be an active partner in the business. When you consider a partner, you have to consider more than how much cash he brings with him. You'll want to compare skill sets. You want someone whose knowledge and experience complement yours. If he knows the Warhammer 40k line and you know collectible card games, you're a good match. If you wish to have a partner, you need a clear delineation of duties, expectations, percentage of ownership and rewards.

If you involve investors, the relationship might dictate your business structure. Business format is a huge decision and one size does not fit all. Talk to your lawyer about exactly which structure best fits your needs.

A BANK'S MONEY

In its infant stages, a small business is a slight extension of a single person. In many ways, you are the business. Nowhere is that concept more apparent than when you apply for a loan.

Before you apply for a bank loan, obtain a copy of your credit report by contacting the three main reporting companies, Equifax (*Equifax.com*), Experian (experian.com), and Trans Union (transunion.com). If it has any errors, correct them. If the report shows legitimate strikes against you, you might want to wait for six months or a year before you approach a bank.

The bank considers your personal credit risk over any business plan. A business plan isn't a promise; it's an idea. Your credit report is history. They bet on history every time.

You must know how you want to structure your financing. If you rely on bank financing, try to acquire your pre-opening expenses as a term loan. A term loan puts a certain amount of money in your banking account right away, and payments come due monthly, starting from the day you take out the loan. The benefit is that you have all of your money to work with. The drawback is that you pay interest on the full amount.

Ask for your capital reserve in the form of a line of credit or credit card. The advantage of this method is enormous. Because you're only paying interest on the amount you withdraw, your monthly payments are a fraction of your term loan, even if the interest rate on the LOC is higher than the loan's rate. Fourteen percent of $5,000 is a lower dollar amount than 10% of $50,000. Structuring your start-up capital in this way can you save hundreds of dollars each month.

Another way to save cash is to ask for a balloon payment for your start-up capital. The balloon is a big lump-sum payment at the end of your term. The advantage is that your monthly payments are much smaller. Again, you reduce your monthly payment (and thus your break-even amount) considerably. When the balloon comes due, if you've made your payments on time and your credit history is sound, you can refinance the balloon. Thus, you never write a check for that huge lump sum. In a best-case scenario, you've built up enough cash to pay the balloon.

Lastly, the bank expects that if they provide you with the majority of your working capital, you will make them your primary financial institution.

SBA Loans

You might have heard recommendations that you go to the Small Business Association for a loan. You might be surprised to learn that they don't make loans.

The SBA *guarantees* a fraction of a loan to a lending institution through its 7(a) program. If you meet the SBA's requirements, their guarantee makes banks feel more secure about lending you money. If you default on an SBA loan, the bank stands to recover a significant portion of its investment. The bank knows that the SBA has its own requirements and guidelines. Conversely, if you don't qualify for the SBA-backed loan, why should the bank take a risk on you?

SBA loans are not for everyone. For one thing, they charge a guaranty fee for loans between $150,000 to $700,000. If your loan falls within this range, the additional 2.5 percent interest on the loan rate costs thousands over the life of the loan.

Success costs, too. Prepayment too fast earns a subsidy recoupment fee. That comes on top of an annual service fee. The totality of these fees can make an SBA loan unattractive to you.

If you wish to apply for a 7(a) loan, be aware of certain facts. The SBA insists that the business be able to repay the loan from cash flow. Make sure your cash flow projection shows that ability. They also look at the applicant's character, specifically, past willingness to repay loans. They evaluate the value of your collateral and your ability to manage the business. If you have no retail experience, your game store plan won't qualify for the 7(a) loan. They also require all owners of 20% or more to sign as personal guarantors.

One curious fact about the 7(a) program: game retailers are considered "small businesses" if their annual sales is less than $6,500,000. I think that's all of us.

VENTURE CAPITAL

Venture capitalists are not interested in you. They are typically interested in medium-term investments that promise a very high rate of return. If your only financing option is a 25% APR loan that you have to pay back over 5 years, go back and revise your business plan until it works under different circumstances.

UNCONVENTIONAL FINANCING

Textbooks talk about bank financing as a primary method of starting a business. Banks aren't the only sources of money.

BUILDING ASSETS

Building assets is your best method of financial positioning. If you abort your plans late in the planning stages, you can use these assets for other purposes.

IndieGoGo

Kickstarter has led the charge of a new and exciting way to finance a venture — crowdfunding. Appealing to a large number of people to make small contributions in exchange for a benefit of some kind can enable a venture of any kind to succeed if you can just reach enough people.

Kickstarter 's mandate claims that it's for creators. They're not likely to approve a project that is purely a commercial venture with no creation involved. Even if they do, there's no guarantee that they'd allow the project to finish once they discovered your deceit. You're better off not trying.

At *www.IndieGoGo.com* there is no such restriction. You can raise funds for a vacation, medical bills, a charity, or a business. They don't care. They also allow an option where you keep any funds raised, unlike Kickstarter, in which you only get your funds if the project is successful. The downside to IGG is that it does not have nearly the infrastructure for sharing your project as Kickstarter. You won't get much more traffic than what you drive there through your own methods.

Here's the short version: make a video describing your goals. Offer incentives for people who make contributions. In the case of a game store, offer games. Advertise it through social media. If you like, add traditional media like business cards or flyers. For thirty days, shout it from the rooftops. At the end of your campaign, collect your funds and deliver on your promises.

Other crowdfunding sites, albeit with orders of magnitude fewer resources to help you, include:

▷ *www.Fundable.com*
▷ *FundRazr.com*
▷ *www.GoFundMe.com*
▷ *GoGetFunding.com*
▷ *www.RocketHub.com*
▷ *www.Upstart.com*

Home Equity

Despite the current housing market, many people have considerable equity in their homes. In fact, home equity loans and lines of credit are a primary financing source for many first-time business owners. If you're beginning your planning, you might consider making modest upgrades to your home to increase its value.

Retirement Funds

You might be able to borrow against a 401 (k) plan, choosing the interest rate of your loan to yourself. In any case, having a retirement plan improves your net worth, which helps when you apply for a conventional loan. If you're still in the planning stages, adding to your retirement plan now can pay off later.

I'm mostly including a mention of retirement funds for completeness. Due to the risk involved, I like the idea of borrowing from a retirement fund less than I like leveraging home equity. It shouldn't be a primary source of your financing. Its primary use should be in establishing a healthy picture for your banker, so that you can invest his money instead.

Stocks & Bonds

You might not have an investment portfolio, but if your current job offers stocks, it's time to evaluate what you have or start buying in while you're still planning your store. Depending on how you plan to finance your store, you might want to keep the stocks or liquidate your holdings. If you do cash out, watch your timing and try to wait as long as possible.

Trade Magazines

Virtually every industry has its own trade magazines, and these trades pay good money for articles. If you can explain something in simple terms, stick to a topic, and follow a publisher's guidelines, you might be able to crank out an article or two. With some trades paying up to $2 a word, a single article might net $500 to $6,000. You don't have to be a professional writer. The most important skill is knowledge of your topic.

Multiple Bank Accounts

It's easy to rack up multiple bank accounts. You have your main account for your family. Then you have the old one you used when you were single. You might have a cash reserve in an investment account. There's that account with the expensive bank that you only opened to collect the $25 sign-up bonus. You have some money in PayPal. Corral all of these stray dollars into one place and you might be surprised at how much it is.

Yard Sale

Turn a bunch of junk into cash. A successful yard sale might net up to $1,000. It might also clear up space in your garage where you can stockpile fixtures until you're ready to move into your storefront.

Your Test-Market
Earlier I recommended testing your local market by running a convention space, hitting trade shows, or helping an existing retailer. I've seen game retailers run flea market tables. This method works best with second-hand merchandise that you can buy cheaply and sell quickly, often starting with a personal collection. Start with $200 or so in inventory and build up from there, reinvesting your sales into more merchandise. If you're lucky, you might start with $2,000 to $5,000 in second-hand goods that you won't have to buy when you open your store.

Demo Materials
If you took another bit of advice to become a demo volunteer, you might have a collection of materials to start with. If you ran with it and become a volunteer for multiple companies, you could have more materials than some stores use. Between promo material and any unopened compensation they sent you in the form of product, you could have a few hundred dollars in assets.

Start a Fixture Collection
Retailers often end up becoming fixture junkies. You can't help but look around any given store, not just to see what they have, but how they display it. You'll ask yourself "Can I use something like that?" surprisingly often. Start your neurosis early by acquiring cheap and free fixtures while you're still in the planning stage, months before you sign a lease. Picking up a usable piece each month might save hundreds or thousands off of your start-up costs by the time you open.

You can find cheap fixtures in auctions and going-out-of-business sales around town. You might make an offer to a landlord who's stuck with the property of a vanished tenant. You can find free fixtures occasionally when stores of any size — convenience to big-box — remodel. If you're in the right place at the right time, or put yourself in the right place at the right time, you can snag very expensive fixtures that would otherwise be thrown out.

Manufacturer Charity
The manufacturers whose products you'll sell have a vested

interest in seeing you succeed. The attitude of manufacturers toward retailers runs the gamut from heavy favor to outright disdain, but asking for promotional materials and products can yield some much-needed inventory. As always, don't ask for things you don't need and don't get greedy. Asking for a bonus on top of an order is better than asking for a freebie outright, for example.

Also, many manufacturers have standard offers for fixtures with a purchase over a certain threshold.

Buy Debt

While many people avoid debt, the right use of your company's credit and your personal credit is a tool for you to use. Carpenters don't refuse to use nails out of some crazy sense of elitism or personal acumen. Neither should you be afraid to indebt your company if it's the best thing for your company's overall health.

Assume the Seller's Debt

If you plan to start by buying an existing business, then you can reduce your purchase price by acquiring debt at the same time. Suppose, for example, that a store owner wants $25,000 for his store. When you ask about his current debts, he tells you that he owes his distributors $4,000 in current and late bills. Tell him you'd be willing to take over that debt if he'll reduce his asking price by $4,000. If he has any intention at all of paying that bill, there's little reason to reject your offer. You can then negotiate repayment terms with the distributors to whom he owes money. Offering to repay $200 on top of each weekly order defers that final payment by 5 months.

Continue that exercise with each of the seller's individual outstanding debts (rent, utilities, other service providers, etc.) and you might save yourself $15,000 in upfront cash. You'll pay off most or all of it eventually, but you'll reduce the start-up funds needed by a substantial amount.

Credit Cards

No sane person would tell you to put all of your start-up expenses on a credit card, but it can make sense to finance your capital reserve on personal credit of one kind or another. Notice the careful and deliberate use of the word "can." That doesn't mean it always makes sense. Some factors in favor of this plan include a) a low burn amount needed, b) low interest rates on the credit cards , c) a strong incentive plan with your credit card company, or d) high local commercial loans rates.

Bring On Investors

Someone investing a few thousand dollars can put you over a benchmark and turn on the light green for you to continue forward. These investments need not be large. An investment of $500 up front could be worth far more than its face value in its reduction of your primary loan repayment, depending on how you word your investor agreements (hint: defer any repayment for six months to a year after opening). Such low-dollar investments are much easier to get than a $20,000 lump sum.

Chapter 9:
Advanced Lessons

N ow that you've grown to the point where you are able to maintain positive cash flow, you've established a powerful brand, and have an established customer base, it is time to look at what you can do to create a competitive advantage. The keys that got you to this point were tight inventory management, excellent customer service, and cost-effective advertising. Sales have reached a plateau where increasing your customer count might b1e difficult due to the size of your local market. Your sales staff is already upselling your customer by the price of a small car. Your customers return three times per week. Where is there more money to be made?

Increase your market share by offering products nobody else has. Reduce costs on everything.

Premium Items

Premium items are small, cheap items whose real purpose is not to directly generate sales but to advertise your store and promote your brand. The important thing is that they feature your store name and either address, phone number or website. Here are some items that work well:

T-shirts. One of the best promotional items you can find. You can get tees for as low as $5 each if you buy in quantity. Sell them for a dollar over cost and watch your customers display their store loyalty everywhere they go. They take them to work, to the movie theater, to the beach, to conventions — even to other game stores.

Try to get a season-neutral color such as gray or khaki or go with the gamer-favorite black. Oddball colors sit on the shelf. For a size break-down, order extra of the large sizes. XXXL gamers are common, and people like the oversized shirts.

Buttons. Gamers love sarcastic or humorous expressions. You can find a button-maker with supplies for about $80, or a cheaper version for about $40. The procedure is simple and provides employees with hours of productive down-time. Make one of each button for a display and store the overstock in a handy box so they don't take up much space.

Caps/Hats. While not as popular as t-shirts, you can wear a hat every day, which is not recommended for a single t-shirt. They're available for as low as about $5 with simple designs and bulk purchases.

String bags. These nylon drawstring backpacks are good for carrying books or other gaming gear. Alex Shvartsman of Kings Games says "Those string bags are really popular with the kids." Alex earned a hefty profit margin at a very fast-moving $6 price. You can find them for under $3 — how far under depends on the exact quantity ordered.

Tape measures. Miniatures players always need these, and they always lose them. You can sell the same forgetful player a dozen tape measures. Make sure every miniatures player for miles uses your store's tape measure at every tournament and game he goes to. Buy them in bulk for less than $1 including customization and sell them for $2-3. If you bring tape measures to a convention featuring a miniatures tournament, you will be the hero of the day. Tape measures display well on one or more pegs with your hobby supplies.

Pens and pencils. Role-players will buy them at your store, and all they need for display is a coffee mug. Role-players buy both pens and pencils on a regular basis. If role-playing makes up more than 10% of your sales, these items will move.

Laser pointers. You can find these popular toys for $3 or less. While annoying in the hands of kids, miniatures players love them for determining a model's line-of-sight. Display them at your counter and with your hobby supplies so they will be visible to both walk-ins and your regular customers.

SUMMARY: PREMIUM ITEMS
- T-shirts
- Buttons
- Caps/hats
- String Bags
- Tape Measures
- Pens & Pencils
- Laser Pointers

Reduce Costs

For every dollar you increase sales, you increase net profit by a nickel or a dime. For every dollar you cut costs, you increase profit by $1.00.

Increasing your profit margin per item is the luxury of the already-successful. To free up your time to do this, you need to make the transition from chief clerk to full-time supervisor. Having skilled employees who are capable of doing skilled tasks as well as cleaning up and running the cash register is essential to this kind of growth. If your staff is not up to speed, improving their performance should take top priority.

Bulk Buys

Whether ordering direct or through distribution, ask what kind of terms you can get for a very large supply of product. Count out a year's worth or more and see what they offer. You might be able to find a price that's worth a large cash investment.

Bulk buys work in several situations. Christmas season is one. While game stores don't see the 5-times or 10-times sales increases that big-box stores see, they sometimes see a significant increase in sales. If your store is one of those, it might be worthwhile to stock up heavily, both to ensure that you don't run out of product and to promote the item in-store.

Second, you might be coming into a product late. Your competitors beat you to the punch on a hot new product, and you want to join in. You might make a bulk buy, hoping for a discount that you can pass on to your customers. You can then run an advertised sale on those products, hoping to capture or re-capture those existing customers.

Renegotiate Distributor Terms

If you have maintained a good relationship with your distributors in the form of timely payment and committing to pre-orders, you might be able to negotiate more favorable terms with them once you reach a certain volume. Perhaps two distributors offer very similar terms. You like the one with the better website, but the distributor without the website offers 2% better discounts. Offer to transfer the weekly orders you place with discount-distributor over to website-distributor if he matches the discount.

Distributors work on a tight margin, and you might not be able to convince them to change what they're offering. On the other hand, discounts are only a part of the terms. You might ask for your payment terms to be extended from 30 to 45 days. You might ask them to waive shipping at a lower minimum.

Increase Direct Orders

At the cost of increased work, you could increase the orders you place directly with manufacturers. On page [pp] we discussed the risks involved with direct orders: switching to direct orders from distribution might harm your relationship with your distributor.

If you're already at the maximum discount your distributor offers (or you've tried to negotiate better terms and failed), you have less to lose by switching to direct orders if the overall terms are more profitable. Remember to consider shipping costs, although shipping costs are a tax-deductible expense, so an order for $230 plus $20 shipping is better than spending $250 on product alone, as long as you sell the product for the same price.

REVIEW PROGRESS

By this time, you've been concentrating on making sales for a long time. You've been thinking about your displays, running events to keep customers coming back, and concentrating on ways to increase your volume. It's time to step back and make sure you are not wasting anything or open to any more liability than is necessary.

Managing Credit

A common theme in this book is the concept of managing your assets. While credit typically means that you owe somebody money, your credit rating is an asset. You can use it to strengthen your business. At least once per year, get a copy of your credit report. Review it for errors and contact the reporting agency if you find any inaccuracies.

Improved credit might mean you can refinance the balance of your initial funding loan. You might wish to obtain a short-term loan to buy out a competitor, move the store, or meet emergency needs. Whenever possible, of course, you want to be able to meet those needs out of your cash reserves, but in certain circumstances, you might want to take out the loan now and use your cash reserves for another purpose. Having the financial strength to be able to make these decisions provides your business with a great deal of flexibility.

Review Insurance

Fish out the old insurance policy. If you've added anything expensive like a LAN or other expensive equipment, make sure the policy covers it all. It might be a good time to check with your agent again and see if they have changed any discounts. Maybe you can get a discount if you install fire extinguishers, for example.

Review Distributor List

If you have not used a distributor in over a year, it might be a good idea to consider officially closing that account. Each vendor account is an open line of credit, just like a credit card. When you apply for a loan, each of those unused accounts is a potential liability that could count against you. Even if you are not planning on borrowing any money in the immediate future, you should at least give the distributor a call. He might be willing to offer an increased discount or free shipping to earn your business again. His policies or discount structure might have changed without your notice, and you could be missing out on a good source of products.

Review Inventory

By now, constant managing of your inventory should have kept it from growing beyond your control. It might happen, however, that a review shows that you are acquiring too much of one category or a little too much in each of a dozen different categories.

The excess might not be a problem. It could contribute to an image of a well-stocked store. On the other hand, dusty products with faded covers could portray an image of poor inventory that doesn't sell. It might be worthwhile to move that product or review your liquidation procedures in general.

On the other hand, your inventory level might be too low. If you carry a broad spectrum of product offerings and have only $19,000 in inventory, you might need to check to see what areas need to be strengthened. Spend a few hours with your sales records and look for decreases over time among product lines. Compare those notes with current inventory levels of those products. Did low sales cause you to cut back on restocks, or did frequent stockouts cause you to miss sales? Perhaps your customer base already has all of the current products and they want you to fill in some backlist products.

The Store Is Your Staff, Not You

As your store ages, your role should change. Initially, you should be a main face behind the counter, if not the main face behind the counter. You must either develop strong sales skills or exercise existing strong sales skills to grow your store.

As sales grow, you will be able to afford the labor to step back and more carefully manage your growth. Instead of handing somebody a key and letting him stand behind the counter for a couple of hours, you must make time to train that person in the way that you wanted to from the beginning. Otherwise, you'll find that he is doing a poor job and you are still unable to manage your store's direction.

The difference between a single store and a store that can survive beyond the owner is procedure. With standard procedures in place, any employee can be taught how to generate the same success you achieve — or so the theory goes. If you want to leave the register in good hands, you have to teach someone how to do things the way you do them.

OPERATIONS MANUAL

An operations manual is a good place to start. You do not need a fully-interactive hyperlinked document with video for this manual. A notebook is fine to start out with. You use this manual to make sure that everybody learns to do things the same way — your way. The right way.

The operations manual might contain these elements:

Introduction
    Company identification and history
    Mission statement

Store Description
    Description of products
    House of operation

Cash Register Procedures
    Money handling procedures & standards
    Customer service expectations
    Paperwork/reporting procedures
    Daily operating procedures
    Specific equipment operation: the LAN, shrink-wrap,
        or credit card machine

Cleaning and maintenance procedures and standards

Event Management Procedures
    Event scheduling procedures
    Event supervision procedures
    Event reporting procedures

Inventory Procedures
    Ordering procedures
    Receiving procedures
    Merchandising procedures
    Inventory control procedures

Human Resources
    Hiring procedures
    Training procedures
    Attendance and timeliness policies
    Job descriptions and duties
    New hire paperwork procedures

Loss prevention policies
    Safety and security
    Emergency procedures

Employee information and emergency contact numbers

Your Operations Manual is your business model on paper. It can be an excellent tool, but many people fear writing down their business model. In reality, the fear of another person stealing your operations manual and opening his own business is overrated. Yes, it could happen. However, that manual-stealer still needs to come up with a large amount of cash, and not many people overcome that hurdle. Furthermore, he must be able to adopt policies to fit specific needs and a changing market. If he can't do that on his own, he'll fail even with the manual.

You can take simple precautions to protect yourself from this kind of issue. If you print a copy, include a text watermark that identifies the book as "Confidential." Your introduction page should identify it as your property. If you suspect an employee has stolen a physical copy of the book, it should be a simple matter to report the theft to the police and show them exactly what they're looking for.

Diversification

Adding related product lines accomplishes two goals. First, it provides more revenue potential. A customer might be able to justify $50 a month on gaming, but if you have fantasy art prints, too, maybe he can consider a self-indulgent purchase of $100. The addition of that new product line turned a $600-a-year customer into a $700-a-year customer. New revenue also comes from increasing the size of your customer base. The woman who works at the bank further down the shopping center might see your prints when she comes in for her daily soft drink and buy one for her sister.

Secondly, new product lines provide a leveling base for seasonal or industry sales variations. When role-playing games are slow, your replica weapons sales might continue unabated. This consistency of sales helps maintain your cash flow and reduces your reliance on a single product line in case of a disastrous manufacturer closing or industry downturn.

Financial Impact

Adding a new product line takes its toll on your checking account. You must advertise the new products to existing customers and to new customers whom you hope to bring into your store. People cannot buy it if they do not know it exists.

One way to bring more people into the store is to add a new yellow pages listing. If you have only one listing, you might be able to add a second at no charge, depending on local policies. Adding further listings in the same phone book incurs a low fee.

Your initial order for the product line is likely to be your largest order. In the case of Games Workshop, your initial order could be as high as $10,000. Consider a worst-case scenario: nothing sells. Count how much you think you could recoup if you liquidated the product through conventions or eBay. Are you comfortable risking the difference?

Beyond the initial order, you have to restock the product as it sells. Depending on how aggressive the line's release schedule is, you might have to scramble to keep up with new releases as well. Can you afford a period of slow sales while you spend further dollars keeping the line fresh?

Finally, the product has an indirect cost, as well. An opportunity cost is the difference between your return and return you could have gotten elsewhere. Could you see a better return on your investment by increasing your current Games Workshop inventory levels than you would by adding historical miniatures? If the answer is 'yes', then bringing in historicals has an opportunity cost associated with it.

TRAINING

Before you start ordering, you should attempt to learn all you can about the product line you want to bring in. Who are the customers, and what are their buying patterns? Will this new product line cannibalize your existing sales? If so, to what extent? How do other retailers display this product? Who else are you competing with?

After you learn about all of these specifics, you have to teach your staff. The education might be as simple as a 10-minute meeting before a shift starts, or it might be a series of demonstration events. You might have to teach new register procedures, sales techniques, or product background. You might know all about fantasy art, but if your sales staff doesn't know the difference between Boris Vallejo and Erol Otus, sales will suffer in your absence.

SPACE

Besides the impact on your checkbook and your sales staff, you have to consider the space the product line requires. Decide how much space you want to devote to the product line and consider your store's available space. What do you have to give up bringing in the new product line?

ATTENDING THE GAMA TRADE SHOW

The GAMA Trade Show, held annually in Las Vegas, is the industry's trade show. Important: it's a trade show, not a convention. Leave your dice at home. Manufacturers make every effort to attend and speak directly with store owners. Without the general public allowed, you stand a much better chance of being able to hear what manufacturers are releasing, how they will help you sell it, and why you want to have their product on your shelves.

Take a reference sheet that describes your store. On a single page, identify your store, who the manufacturer should contact, what method of contact works best, what products you carry, your store's physical size and sales volume, which distributors you use, your customer demographics, and what products sell best for you right now. When you meet a manufacturer, you can hand this sheet to him. It serves as a snapshot of your store that helps him understand your store and your customer base.

Take notepads for the seminars. Seminars are volunteer-delivered and usually targeted specifically toward retailers. The seminar selection is usually good, but you might find that two or more conflict. If you are traveling with a spouse or partner, you might want to split up to cover the overlapping seminars. With the current schedule, seminars are also delivered during the daytime — exactly the time the exhibit hall is open. So GTS currently offers two events happening that you want to attend and then closes down for the remainder of the day.

If they do not change that practice, you can still make use of your evenings. A lot of retailers hit the casinos while they're in Vegas. You can certainly do that. I recommend maximizing your limited time by trying to schedule a one-on-one meeting with the manufacturers whose products interest you. If a manufacturer does not initiate this kind of contact, do it yourself. Ask for 15 minutes of private discussion sometime after the exhibit hall closes. You might also offer to meet with him in a small group, say 4 or 5 other retailers with similar interest. That way, the manufacturer can schedule fewer meetings. You benefit because another store owner might ask a question you hadn't thought to ask.

Several times during the trade show, you will have an opportunity to attend a meal provided by a manufacturer. The trade-off is that you are a captive audience to listen to their spiel about their latest game. Because it's usually only the largest manufacturers that do this, you will probably want to hear what they have to say. These meals are also a great opportunity to talk to other game store owners, because you are seated with several others at a table. Introduce yourself and compare notes. Find out how they address problems you are having, find out what's selling at their stores, ask what's not working for them. Be willing to share some information, too. People are more willing to share information if you are free with your own.

CAPITALIZING ON FAILING COMPETITORS

Sometimes game stores fail. No, I'm not talking about you this time. I'm talking about your competitors. You might think this is the time to pop a bottle of champagne. Your sales doubled! All of their customers are going to come to you now, right?

Wrong.

Anecdotal evidence consistently supports the industry consensus that 10-15% of the closing store's customers will gravitate toward other nearby game stores. Some of the rest will buy their gaming products online. Most of their customers, sadly, leave the hobby.

It's mind-boggling that people who seem so dedicated to what they do will stop playing *Dungeons & Dragons* or *Warhammer 40,000* simply because the closest game store went out of business. Why are not they willing to drive a few minutes more, or drive south instead of north? Don't try to understand it. Just be prepared for it when it happens.

If you are in a position to expand, you might consider buying the store. If you are not, don't try to force it. It's a natural option to think about, but consider that they've already failed there. It might not be a location you want. A full discussion on the option to buy another store comes up shortly.

Talk to the owner of the closing business. Offer your condolences on the situation. Tip: do not refer to the closing as a "failure"; plenty of businesses close for legitimate and unavoidable reasons. Ask plainly what you can do to help. If you've spent the last few years building good relations with the stores around you, that goodwill can pay off. Most of the time, they won't mind at all. They want to find a way to keep their customers happy.

The store might offer you a deal on inventory, fixtures, or both. Consider the reason for the store closing before you buy inventory. If the store's cash flow has been hemorrhaging for a while, their valuable inventory value might be close to zero. They might have plenty of *Forge* in stock but no D&D left. *Harry Potter CCG*, 12 cases, *Magic* zero? The value won't be much.

As a recommendation, assign a value to the store's inventory based on how long it would take you to sell it. High-velocity items might be worth 45% of retail. Lower-turn items that still sell might be worth 30%. Count slow items as 10-15% of retail and "dead" items worth nothing. You should not pay the same thing you would you are your distributor because you are not getting the items of your choice, you are probably responsible for arranging your own transportation, and you cannot return any of it.

You might also offer 10% of the retail value for everything in the store. It's easy to calculate and quick to negotiate from.

Fixtures could be worth considering. If their fixtures are better than yours, you might take the opportunity to upgrade. If you plan to expand into a larger location or an additional store, consider buying the fixtures in anticipation. Remember that you might be storing the fixtures for several months, and if you have to pay for the storage space, then buying them now might not be a net savings.

At the very least, try to buy the store's customer lists. If you can gain that entire 15% that stays in the hobby, you might have gained an additional 45 or 50 customers. If the store is closing for other reasons, the list could be a full 600 customers or more. A full list could easily be worth $10,000 or more in annual sales to you. Offer $50 and see if the owner blinks. He might not have thought that his customer list has any value at all. He might think you are doing him a favor by throwing money at him. If he's shrewd enough to know how much it means to you, ask for his offer. If the list is up-to-date and contains enough names, it could easily be worth $2-3,000.

If your relationship is very good, ask if you can post a sign or flyers in his store. Offer his customers something special for coming to check out your store, such as a one-time discount. If his customer base is concentrated on one area, such as CCGs, offer a specific deal: a free booster pack with any purchase over $5, or free sleeves for any deck purchase.

Whatever you do, preserve his dignity. Don't be a ghoul. Stores close for a variety of reasons. Rampant employee pilferage or a personal injury could mean that you are the guy closing up shop next time around. Treat him like you would want to be treated.

MAXIMIZING CAPITAL USE

By now, positive cash-flow should be a casual thing. You have learned to manage your inventory such that you have no qualms about putting dying inventory to rest and your inventory level grows or shrinks at your command. Your losses from waste or theft are minimal, the bills are being paid, and you are seeing a steady growth in your bank account.

In fact, the bank account is growing to the point where you are pretty certain that you don't want to leave that money in a checking account. It would be more useful elsewhere, but you don't yet know where.

BANK FOR EMERGENCIES

Decide how much you think you might need for an emergency and let your bank account reach that amount. Three months' worth of fixed expenses is a good benchmark. You might assign a dollar amount, such as $10,000. Leave that amount available in case you need it.

SPEND IT

You could spend your surplus. Ask your accountant about the procedures. Go have fun. Make sure the store is staffed and go take a well-earned vacation.

Similarly, you could give yourself a regular pay raise. You could raise your standard of living or start a college fund for your children. You might buy a new car, or look for a larger home. Discuss it with your family, compare goals, and make yourselves happy.

PAY DOWN DEBT

At this point, you might still have debt from your opening, either money you took out of savings, a loan you incurred, or investors who are expecting repayment. Pay down the smallest debts first. This move allows you to improve cash flow sooner rather than later, and cash pushed forward makes for a healthier company. Reducing your long-term debt will saves you money on interest payments in the long run and frees up available credit for later growth.

If any of this debt is available as a line of credit, you might not wish to pay it in full and close the account. You might wish to keep that line open for other uses. In that case, pay it down to a minimum and expect to spend a small amount in monthly interest. Keeping the account open could save you from having to reapply for a loan later.

Repair, Upgrade, Improve

If you are comfortable with your salary, have cash reserves for emergencies, and show no debt, now is the time to consider investments. At this point, it's assumed that you don't plan to open additional locations. If you did, you would have a pretty clear idea of where to spend your cash.

Give your store fixtures a critical look at this point. If you started with pegboard and intended to upgrade to slatwall, do it. If it is time to repaint, you might do that. If your game room furnishings need an upgrade, consider that option.

Write a list of everything you could do to improve your store's image. Prioritize these things and address them one at a time. Keep an eye on your cash-flow and bank account while you make these improvements and make sure you are still happy with those numbers. Steady, measured improvements are better than a big burst of changes.

One major upgrade is the purchase of your own building. Read the comparison between buying and leasing on page [pp] and consider if buying property is right for you. By this time, your store has seen most of its growth, and it should not need much more room.

Increase Volume

This cash surplus could be put to good use in advertising. If your average ticket prices are strong, you are already selling large amounts to existing customers. If customers are visiting the store frequently, you are already excelling at the goal of increasing the rate of customer visits. The only way left to increase your sales volume is to gain new customers.

An increase in your marketing budget could pay for itself far more quickly than improving your store image could — but only if your image is very strong to begin with. If you spend money to bring people into your store, and those people are unimpressed with your image, they might not return. Make sure you are comfortable with your store's appearance before you ask strangers to come in.

Don't grab the phone and order twice the number of cable TV spots. Analyze your marketing plan, count the numbers, and budget the growth.

Carrying a deeper inventory can also add volume. Reducing stockouts to a minimum by adding depth and adding new lines for greater breadth of product both generate more sales. If adding slow-turn items wasn't in your best interest when your cash had higher priorities, that lower turn rate might be acceptable now. Customers notice inventory increases, too, which means your perception of success rises, and your brand strengthens.

Continue Your Education

Taking one or two business courses each semester could pay off immediately in the store without requiring you to totally abdicate your store management ability. Accounting, marketing or business law might apply right away. With tuition in a community college costing relatively little, this knowledge could reimburse you in sales or profitability within a short period of time. Better yet, gaining a degree can increase your personal marketability should the business fail.

Invest

Talk to your financial adviser about investing your discretionary cash into a mutual fund or a diversified stock portfolio. Statistically, your money off is safer there than invested in your own store. A healthy and diverse investment might provide some security in case of market fluctuations or local conditions that hurt sales volume in the store. Your portfolio can help you build wealth that you can use to leverage your store's growth.

266

Chapter 10:
Growth or Exit

I f you are smart and lucky, cash will come in faster than you spend it. Sales will grow at a steady pace. The store operates independently of your direct attention, creates new customers based on the policies you set in motion, and makes a premium off of each of those customers. Your staff might think they do not need you by now because you no longer need to take a direct hand in every activity. They know to how to promote the new game coming out and start the demos and promotions with little motivation from you.

Then what? What options open up to you once you've created an operationally strong retail store? Aside from ordering more stuff and spending more on advertising, how do you increase sales?

Second and Subsequent Stores

One natural desire after you've become successful in your store is the desire to expand into additional stores. That's certainly possible. Before you assume that it's the only option for growth, compare the benefits and threats and decide where your personal skills and goals match up with the reality of owning more than one store.

Benefits of Owning Multiple Stores

Owning multiple stores within the same market offers several advantages. Because game popularity varies even on the local level, if product does not sell at one location, you can try moving it to the other before you attempt to clear it out.

The same concept applies to employees. You do not necessarily need to hire new clerks if your existing clerks want more hours. It would cost less to offer a small raise to encourage clerks to work a full week instead of 20 hours per week and split their shifts between two stores.

Your second store is cheaper to open than the first. You have the experience, and you've done the research already. You get a chance to fix the mistakes you made last time around. You do not have to duplicate certain costs, mostly administrative, such as a new bank account. You do not need to double most of your advertising costs, because the same ads list both locations.

You also gain a sense of accomplishment from opening a second store. If your personal measure of success is based on total sales, opening additional stores puts you closer to your goal. You will find that your success translates into superior bargaining power with others in the industry.

If your goal is prestige within the industry or from your customer base, you have a powerful reason for expanding into multiple locations. A second store is a visible sign of your success. Having your name on two store fronts is twice as good as having it on one. Having it on seven is even better.

Once you reach beyond the "danger zone" of two to three stores, having multiple locations gives you a margin of safety against failure. If one store's sales begin to decline precipitously, you might have cash reserves to pour back into it. If the store can't be saved, you can move it, or at least salvage the fixtures and inventory for use in other stores. You will also be the retailer best prepared to recover any of the lost customers, as those that did stay with you until the end are more likely to visit your other stores than they are to turn to a competitor.

If your distributor discount is based on the amount you purchase with them, additional sales volume will give you a greater margin across the board. Another 1% gross margin on $400,000 annual sales is a nice pay raise for you. Even if the distributor does not offer a sliding discount, he might be willing to negotiate a special rate for your initial inventory if you agreed to buy it all from him.

One of the most attractive benefits of additional locations is the potential for increased income. A business with $1,000,000 in annual sales should provide you with a higher salary than does a business with $200,000 in annual sales. Taken as a percentage of costs, you can draw a higher salary while still making your stores more profitable on paper.

DANGERS OF OWNING MULTIPLE STORES

Opening additional locations brings risk. In addition to the new store failing, you could lose your original location if you overextend your resources. Being obligated to paying a 5-year lease could soak up all of your cash.

Sales at the original location decrease if you open an additional location in the same market. If 10% of your original customer base decides to move to the new location then sales at the original store decrease 10% right away.

The new store will require a great deal of your time. You can't be in both stores on Friday night, for example, to work the sales floor. The store that doesn't have your full attention will suffer from inefficiencies and greater labor costs.

Studies show that expanding small businesses are most likely to fail at two to three locations. At fewer than four or five locations, your company revenues do not support another tier of management. You will find that you are trying to act as both direct store manager and multi-unit supervisor. That's too much work for one person to do thoroughly. The skills required are different. You lose focus, and the business suffers as a result.

You might find that this administrative job is not to your liking. If you truly enjoy managing your store during the day-time and working the sales floor at night, you might be disap-pointed with your new duties. You have to work with managers who are inherently less motivated than you. If they fail, they lose a job. When you did that job, you risked losing a significant investment in time, money, and pride.

Worst of all, you risk total loss of your business. With ten stores, you have ten times the opportunity for a lawsuit brought on by a slip-and-fall or a similar incident. The damages involved in a liability lawsuit could potentially exceed your insurance policy's coverage, leaving you vulnerable. Similarly, an unsu-pervised manager allowed to order product could obligate your company to a huge debt. While you might be able to spread the inventory around to other stores to minimize the loss, you could find yourself owing a distributor a large amount of money — large enough to cause cash flow problems or cut off further pur-chases from the vendor.

OPEN OR PURCHASE

Once you decide to grow into more than one location, you must decide whether you prefer to open additional locations or to purchase existing businesses that have attractive features like a good location or an extensive customer list. Both methods offer opportunities.

For most of the comparison, you'll want to re-read the ear-lier chapters. Keep in mind that, in many cases, your business is in a stronger position now than when you first started. Prop-erty managers who barely acknowledged you as human are eager for your money now. They might not casually wave off deposits, but you might find that the amount of a deposit they demand drops during negotiation.

Opening new stores typically requires less cash up front than buying a store, although it might require more spending over a longer period as it builds to a self-sustaining level of sales. Purchasing a distressed business might cost more, but a desperate owner might sell out for enough to cover his debts, handing over existing inventory, fixtures, and other assets for virtually nothing. At the right price, it can be worthwhile to buy out a competitor and close the location just to increase your market share or to gain access to customer lists.

FRANCHISING

Once your store is successful, you might be tempted to franchise your business. After all, if it worked for you, it can surely work for somebody else. Right?

Not necessarily.

A small business is very much an extension of the owner. To your creditors, you and the business are virtually inseparable. If you are injured in an accident or hospitalized for a long period of time, your business is likely to fail. Your customers might not make the same connections with the hourly clerks that they do with you. Frequency of customer visits deteriorates in your absence, as does your average ticket price. Growth slows.

If you know this idea to be false because you have outstanding training skills and your employees are capable of continuing in your absence, then franchising becomes a viable growth option. The success of a chain of stores or a franchised business depends on the company's policies and procedures, not the individual talent of any one person in the company.

How to Do It

At its core, a franchise operation is a simple trade. The franchisee pays a franchise fee up front and periodic royalties for the right to use the company's trade name, corporate identity, and procedures. The franchisor benefits from the regular influx of cash and the expansion of the company's recognition, and the ability to leverage strength. The franchisee wins because he gains a proven method of operating a business without having to go through a costly trial-and-error period himself. The franchisee also finds that lending institutions look more favorably on franchises than upon independents, allowing the prospective business owner access to more initial capital.

The full details of starting and operating a franchise are beyond the scope of this guide. However, keeping some things in mind from the start can make this transition easier should you choose to pursue this possibility.

Selling franchises requires you to have a strong brand and strong operational procedures because these are two of the main benefits you offer to franchisees. Typically, but not always, claiming a strong brand requires the operation of multiple corporate stores. In the case of a single-location company, a history of high market share in the local market can establish a strong brand.

The second criterion, that of strong operations, requires a written guideline. As a general rule, the more of your procedures you have written down, the better your preparation for a franchise. Having written job descriptions is a good start. If you have an operations manual, you're a step ahead.

In one respect, franchising is like adding yet another business to your company's interests. You must market the franchise to potential buyers. You have to spend time with potential customers, answering their questions and making sure they meet your criteria. You have to create legal documents, which must be done right, or your franchisees might sue you. Underestimating how much work franchising requires on the part of the franchisor can cause you to waste thousands of dollars before you abort the whole plan.

Why It Hasn't Been Done Yet

Hobbytown USA is a franchised business with that includes a game section, "Game Town" as one of 13 elements of its business of 160 locations. In that respect, a gaming-related franchise has worked.

However, a national or even large-scale regional franchise that produces the majority or entirety of its sales from gaming-related products doesn't exist. One reason is simple: nobody has yet thrown enough money at it to make it work.

The Federal Trade Commission regulates the sales of franchises nationally, and most states place additional restrictions on their sale as well. One of these key requirements is the Franchise Disclosure Document. Updating an FDD is an expensive proposition. Its drafting and annual maintenance can cost thousands of dollars in legal fees. Yet it's a key document to your franchise success. You can't sell franchise rights without it.

Promoting the franchises, screening franchisees, and training franchisees is a full-time proposition. If you do it, it will be tough or impossible to manage your business. If you pay somebody to do it, it costs you an additional employee's salary, an employee in a position that needs high-demand skills.

Advertising your franchise offering on the local level probably does not reach enough interested parties that meet your qualifications. Franchise advertising achieves better results among a larger pool, usually requiring expensive regional or national advertising. Marketing something with such a limited pool of buyers costs far more than what you spend on a few flyers for the newest CCG.

The expense to offer franchises, let alone sell any, could exceed $50,000 a year.

PLANNING YOUR EXIT

At some point in the future, you might want to sell your business. Maybe you like the challenge of creating and building the business, but you don't want to continue with the same job for 40 years. Maybe you want to try another segment of the game industry, such as publishing or distribution. Maybe you've made a bundle and want to retire.

For whatever reason, at some point you decide to part ways with your company. You are ready to leave or believe you will be ready to leave in the near future. Planning for the exit takes almost as much care and attention as planning the entry.

SELLING

For some people, selling the store might be the entire point of the exercise. Maybe you saw game retail as a means to an end. Maybe you want to move to another part of the country and start a new company with a different business model. Whatever the reason, you might want to sell your business after you have built it.

Preparing for a Sale

Have your paperwork in order before you make the announcement. Prepare a P&L statement, a cash-flow sheet, and a balance sheet, accurate to the date or for the previous quarter. Dig out your tax returns for the previous three years. Do a complete inventory and mark the date. Hint: if longer history shows strong growth, offer earlier tax returns, too.

Create an overview that details everything included in the sale. Besides the obvious inventory and fixtures, include any procedural documents, such as your business plan, employee handbook, or operations manual. Include intellectual properties such as trademarks or logos, and list your current staff, vendor accounts, and customer lists.

Create a non-disclosure agreement that requires potential buyers not to share any proprietary information you discuss with outside sources. You might wish to have your attorney review the document. For maximum protection, have your attorney draft an original non-disclosure agreement.

Assuming you are leasing a commercial property, review your lease and make sure you have the right to assign the lease. If so, create a lease assignment outline that you will finish after you identify a buyer. Again, have your attorney review or draft the document for you.

If your business is incorporated, contact your registered agent and make sure your minutes and corporate books are current. Expect to pay for this service.

Create a sales contract. Once again, after you think you are done, hand it to your attorney to review.

Make copies of everything so you are prepared to hand them over when asked. Keep them in a safe place.

Placing the Company on the Market

Announcing the sale of your business is a tricky situation that requires tact and timing. You need to announce the sale or you won't be able to find a buyer. Yet news of a sale harms customer confidence and costs you sales in the meantime — which drives down the value of your business.

You can keep this period of doubt short by going directly to the people who have the most interest in keeping the business alive: employees and competitors. If neither of them is interested, then you can advertise on the open market.

You could go straight to a business broker and go right to the open market, bypassing your employees and competitors. Your employees will feel slighted. Your competitors will not mind, but by going to them first, you help maintain good-will for the buyer. If you are uncomfortable with them seeing your "insides", skip making the offer. It is not that important.

To Employees

Selling your business to an employee offers several advantages. The employees have already indicated an interest in the industry by their employment there. They have knowledge of the industry overall and your store's policies and operations. This type of transition is very easy for customers to accept.

Employees might also have an emotional attachment to the store that makes them very eager buyers. In fact, more than one employee might even be interested in purchasing this store. In this case, create a priority list, preferably by seniority or position within the store, so that the sale does not descend into a bitter bidding war between the crew.

To the Competition

Other independent game retailers will almost always consider buying out a competitor. They might have greater resources than newcomers, including a long relationship with their bank. If you have built a solid relationship with these other business owners, you might be able to cash in on that goodwill.

Outside the Industry

Hiring a business broker to sell your business to a national base of prospective investors is the standard course of action. The business broker has access to a wide range of prospective buyers that you could not reach without extensive advertise expense. The broker's experience can also help you avoid costly mistakes during the process. Even if you already have a prospective buyer coming to you, hiring the broker can help you avoid potential litigation arising from gaps in the information you provide to the seller. The broker's fee is usually written as a percentage, usually in the 10-12% range.

CLOSING

You might wish to close your business. Perhaps you can't find a buyer. You might not want to take the time to sell because you have another business opportunity that requires immediate action. Perhaps your lease is expiring and you can't afford to stay and can't find a suitable location.

Contact your distributors and let them know your intentions. Tell them how long you plan to continue ordering, and at what rate. Ask them about accepting returns in exchange for credit toward your final statements.

A main issue during closing is timing: you want the process as short as possible, and you want to generate as much income as possible with which to pay off your debts. If you can keep the news secret from your customers for the last 30 days, do so. Releasing the information to your customer base earlier costs you sales as customers begin to look for a new source for their gaming purchases.

Don't be surprised if you post record sales during this final 30 days. Closing sales often generate very large numbers — large enough to make you wonder if you shouldn't stay open after all. Understand that you won't be able to maintain sales at that level, and don't let the temporary volume deceive you.

Try to time your closing with the end of your lease — you're still responsible for paying that lease, even if the business is not there. If you were able to include an exit clause in your lease negotiations, good for you. Invoke that clause.

List your fixtures and equipment for sale in the local paper, sell them on eBay, or work out a deal with a local used fixture store to buy them after you close.

If you lease any equipment, check your leases for termination clauses. Be prepared to have a vendor come pick the equipment up or arrange for delivery back to them, as your lease stipulates.

Inform all government agencies and service providers you do business with about the closing: pest control, alarm monitoring, insurance, utilities, etc. If you need time to move equipment or fixtures out after your official closing date, make sure you maintain electrical service during that time. Contact the manufacturers whose retailer locator lists you're on about amending their lists. If you participate in any co-op advertising plans, end those.

You still owe federal income taxes for the last year that you were in business, so keep your financial records. You are responsible for any taxes that you paid while the store was open, including payroll taxes, state sales taxes, etc. Make sure you submit all final payments due on those taxes.

If you're dissolving a corporation at the same time as you close the storefront, you need to file certain paperwork: a form 966 Corporate Dissolution or Liquidation, an 1120S, 8594 Asset Acquisition Statement or 4797 Sale of Business Property. Your accountant or attorney should be able to help finalize the paperwork.

You might also need to close business banking accounts, including credit cards, credit card processing contracts, and other business accounts.

GLOSSARY

Abatement: A reduction in rent, detailed in amount and time, usually offered as a concession to the tenant as an inducement to lease.

ADA: The Americans with Disabilities Act of 1990. It essentially states that your business must be accessible to disabled people (not just Americans) and includes a long, detailed list of specific requirements. Its website is http://www.usdoj.gov/crt/ada/adahom1.htm.

Allocation: If a supplier doesn't have enough product to meet demand, he allocates product; that is, the supplier sells a fraction of the requested amount based on the quantity he has on hand. Your store might receive a larger share based on previous orders rather than on current order size.

Anchor: In a mall or a strip mall, an anchor is a large store that takes up the central or dominating position. Usually a large department store like Sears or Target, the absence of an anchor is a sign of death for a strip mall.

Backlist: Older titles that still sell.

Build out: Improvements or construction made to a property.

Buy-in: The minimum amount required to carry a product line. For a CCG, the buy-in is at least a starter display and a booster display, so the buy-in might be $150.

CAM: Common-Area-Maintenance. This number includes lawn maintenance, shopping center security, parking lot maintenance, and all other factors that apply to the entire shopping center.

Capital: Monies invested in a business. If you spend money on new product, you are investing capital.

Cash wrap: The area around your cash register where customers check out.

COGS: An acronym for Cost of Goods Sold. This is your price for the product you sell.

Competitive edge: A reason for customers to shop with you instead of a competitor.

Conversion rate: The number of customers who buy something divided by the total number of people that walk into the store. If 50 people enter your store per day and you sell products to 30 of them, you have a 60% conversion rate.

CPI: Consumer Price Index. You sometimes see it mentioned in a commercial lease as a reference for your rent increases. It's an

277

aggregate figure that describes the local cost of goods compared to the national average. A CPI of 120 means that goods in your local market sell for 20% more than the average.

CPM: Cost Per Thousand, the cost for an advertising medium to reach 1,000 of your target customers.

CPP: A radio advertising term that stands for Cost Per (ratings) Point, or the cost to reach 1% of your target market.

DBA: Doing Business As. A DBA is your trade name, as opposed to your legal business name.

Decompression zone: The area inside your store entrance. The customer has not yet adjusted to his entry. He ignores any signage or product placed here. The size of this area varies, but it's about 10 feet into your store.

Depreciation: A non-cash loss on your P&L that represents the lessening value of equipment over time. It's supposed to represent the estimated lifespan of the equipment, such that when the depreciation period is over, it's time to buy new equipment.

EBIDT: Earnings Before Interest, Depreciation, and Taxes.

Escalation rate: The rate at which your rent increases. It might be described as a dollar amount or as a percentage of a previous rate.

Evergreen: A product with a long lifespan of regular sales is evergreen.

FEIN/FIN: Federal Employer Identification Number. For a proprietor, this number is the same as your Social Security Number.

FFE or FF&E: Furnishings, fixtures and equipment.

Footprint: The square footage of your store that a product or display takes up. Thus, a 2' by 2' spinner rack has a 4 square foot footprint.

Frontlist: New products.

GAMA: The Game Manufacturer's Association. Despite its name, it has members among the retail and distributor tiers also.

Gross Profit: Sales minus COGS.

GW: Games Workshop, the manufacturers of Warhammer 40,000 and Warhammer Fantasy Battles miniatures games and other, finite-term games.

HVAC: Heating, ventilation and air-conditioning unit.

IC Code: Industry Classification code. For game stores, your code is 451120. It's determined by the North American Industry Classification System.

In-kind: Payment in product instead of cash. For tax purposes, it's the same as cash. That means if you trade a starter deck for lunch, you might be required to turn over the sales tax for that deck to your state as if you had sold it. Check with the Department of Revenue guidelines for your state.

Just-in-time (JIT): An inventory system in which the retailer keeps a minimum of product on hand and relies on quick reorder ability to meet demand.

Keystone: To set your price so that your markup is 100%. If you buy dice at .40 and sell them for .80, you are keystoning your dice.

Lien: A claim against your property as a defense against default on your part. Everybody wants a lien on your property. Banks typically only count inventory as worth 30-60% of your cost. So if you go to a bank for a loan to open a second store, your $25,000 in inventory might only serve as collateral for $7,500 in loans.

Markup: Your gross profit divided by your cost. If you sell at product at $10 and it cost you $6, your gross profit is $4. Your markup is therefore 67%.

Merchandise: The stuff you sell. It's counted separately from your FF&E.

Merchant Association: An association of tenants and (usually) landlord formed for cooperative marketing to increase traffic to the shopping center.

Net Price: Most of the items in this industry are sold to distribution and then on to you at a percentage of retail price. A net price product is sold for a flat price.

Net Profit: Money left over after all expenses have been paid.

NGW: National Games Week.

P&L: Profit and loss statement.

Personal Guarantor: When you guarantee that you will pay a debt if your business fails, you are signing as a personal guarantor. As a small business owner, especially a new small business owner, you will be required to sign just about everything as personal guarantor.

POP: Point of purchase.

Premium Items: Small, often inexpensive items that you sell or give away as promotional items rather than as primarily profit-making ventures. They carry your store name or logo and serve as an advertising tool.

Primary Draw: This radius around your business from which 50% or more of your customers come. In the gaming industry, your primary draw in a city is about 4 miles. Rural draws are larger.

PO: Purchase order.

Profit Margin: Your gross profit dollar divided by the retail price. If you sell at product at $10 and it cost you $6, you made a 40% margin.

Release Date: The date a manufacturer allows distributors to ship a product. Customers often see a release date and expect the product to be on store shelves on that date.

ROI: Return on investment.

ROS: Run of Station, a radio advertising term that means that your ads will air at any time during the day. While often less expensive, ROS ads are potentially unproductive.

Sales Velocity: The rate at which a product sells.

Shrink: Loss through shoplifting and employee pilferage.

SKU: Stock Keeping Unit. It's an item in your inventory.

Stockout: Running out of an item in your inventory.

Street Date: The date a product is allowed to go on sale. Theoretically, a street date allows for all sales channels to have a level playing field, but some sellers break the street date by selling early.

Strike zone: Follows the decompression zone. Prices here should be attractive, not shocking.

Swag: Jargon for free promotional items given out, usually referring to the GAMA Trade Show.

Trade Name: The name your business is known as to the public. Your company name might be Joe Blow, Inc., but your store sign says "Frank's Friendly Games."

Triple Net: A lease in which the tenant pays all expenses of maintaining the property in addition to rent, plus utilities, insurance, taxes, and other costs.

Turn Rate: The number of times you sell an item per year.

Undercapitalization: Failure to maintain enough capital to continue operations.

Vanilla Shell: Also known as a vanilla box or a white box, vanilla shell refers to an empty commercial suite with plain white walls.

282

APPENDIX I:
MARKET STUDY

Adventure Game Industry Market Research Summary
Version: (RPGs) V1.0
Release Date: February 07, 2000
Summary prepared by:
Ryan S. Dancey
Vice President, Wizards of the Coast
Brand Manager, Dungeons & Dragons

* * * * *

Permissions: This file is Copyright 2000, Wizards of the Coast. This file may be freely redistributed or quoted in whole or part, provided that this attribution remains intact.

* * * * *

Methodology: Wizards of the Coast regularly surveys various aspects of the adventure gaming channel; distributors, retailers and consumers to better understand their preferences, concerns, and needs. That data is regularly reviewed and distributed internally to senior management. The contents of this file are excerpts from those sources; the source materials themselves are confidential internal documents and are not available to the public. You have my assurances that to the best of my ability, the information presented in this document represents a fair and accurate representation of the data.

Sources: The primary source is a market segmentation study conducted in the summer of 1999. No confidential information provided by non-Wizards companies was used in the preparation of this report.

Exclusions: The internal information gathered by Wizards is considered an important competitive advantage. Therefore, not all the information available to Wizards is incorporated in this document, and there may be areas where substantial, significant information is purposefully not included. An effort has been made to ensure that the absence of any portion of this confidential information would not render the material provided herein inaccurate or invalid.

Pokemon Effect: As this study was conducted just as the Pokemon TCG phenomenon was gathering speed. For this, and several internal reasons, I have elected not to present information on the TCG component of the industry at this time.

Updates: From time to time, I intend to revise and update this file to reflect our ongoing efforts to understand the industry. When an update occurs, the version number of the document will be changed, as will the 'release date'. Interested parties can write to me at *ryand@frpg.com* to request an up to date copy of this document.

* * * * *

Section 1: The Segmentation Study

Because so much of this data is derived from the '99 Segmentation Study, it is important that the reader understand how this data was gathered.

For the purpose of the 1999 study, the following methodology was employed: A two phase approach was used to determine information about trading card games (TCGs), role playing games (RPGs) and miniatures wargames (MWG) in the general US population between the ages of 12 and 35. For the rest of this document, this group is referred to as "the marketplace," or "the market," or "the consumers."

This age bracket was arbitrarily chosen on the basis of internal analysis regarding the probable target customers for the company's products. We know for certain that there are lots of gamers older than 35, especially for games like *Dungeons & Dragons*; however, we wanted to keep the study to a manageable size and profile. Perhaps in a few years a more detailed study will be done of the entire population.

Information from more than 65,000 people was gathered from a questionnaire sent to more than 20,000 households via a post card survey. This survey was used as a "screener" to create a general profile of the game playing population in the target age range, for the purposes of extrapolating trends to the general population.

This "screener" accurately represents the US population as a whole; it is a snapshot of the entire nation and is used to extrapolate trends from more focused surveys to the larger market.

A follow up survey was completed by about a thousand respondents from the 'screener'. The follow up survey is an extensive document with more than 100 questions. The particular individuals chosen to participate in this expanded survey represent the population, as determined by the screener. In other words, the small detailed survey group can be reasonably extrapolated to the larger screener group, and the larger screener group can be logically extrapolated to the public in general. This is a common, standard, and accepted methodology within the market research field.

The data from the detailed survey was collated and prepared by the Wizards market Research Department, in conjunction with an external consulting firm. We believe that the data is a fair and accurate representation of the hobby game consumer profile and that it does statistically correlate with the population as a whole in the US for the target age bracket.

* * * * *

Section 2: Basic Terms

As a part of the detailed survey, the following terms and examples were provided to the respondents:

Term	Example
(*)Paper RPGs	Dungeons & Dragons
Card Games	Bridge, Solitaire, Uno, Poker
Trading Card Games	Magic, Pokemon
Word/ knowledge	Scrabble, Trivial Pursuit
Puzzle computer games	Tetris
Non-competitive	
problem solving	Sim City, Myst
Puzzle table games	Jenga, Dominoes
Class board games	Chess, Monopoly, Go
Action/Shooter/Arcade	Doom, Mortal Kombat
Miniatures table-top	
fantasy/sci-fi	Warhammer
Games that use miniatures	Battletech
War games	Historical
Simulations	Flight/car Simulators
Strategy games	Risk, Civilization
Social/party games	Charades, Pictionary
Strategic sport simulations	Madden, MLB
Other non-sport games	N/A

Specific questions were also designed to separate users of "computer Role Playing Games" vs. "paper Role Playing Games."

(*) For my own purposes, I choose to use the term "Tabletop RPGs" in this document; the term "paper RPGs" was used in the study. The terms are synonyms; my choice is simply personal. I believe that in the fairly near future "paper" RPGs will hybridize with computer assistance - not becoming 'computer RPGs' as that term is commonly understood, but not being games played simply with paper anymore either. Consider this a "forward looking" terminology.

The term "D&D" is used herein to describe all flavors and types of D&D play; from old "white box" players up to people playtesting 3rd Edition.

* * * * *

Section 3: Basic Demographics
The study provides the following information about the basic demographics of the tabletop RPG marketplace:

Size:
6% play or have played TRPGs (~ 5.5 million people)
3% play monthly (~ 2.25 million people)

Gender:
19% are female (monthly players)

Crossover:
17% of the total play MWGs monthly
46% of the total play computer RPGs monthly
26% of the total play TCGs monthly
The study provides the following information about the basic demographics of the computer RPG marketplace:

Size:
8% play or have played CRPGs (~7.3 million people)
5% play monthly (~4.5 million people)

Gender:
21% are female
286

Crossover:
33% of the total play tabletop RPGs monthly
21% of the total play TCGs monthly
13% of the total play MWGs monthly
The study provides the following information about the basic demographics of the MWG marketplace:

Size:
4% play or have played MWGs (~3.7 million people)
2% play monthly (~1.8 million people)

Gender:
21% are female

Crossover:
37% play tabletop RPGs
40% play computer RPGs
29% play TCGs

The age breakdown of players within the marketplace is:

Age	TRPG	MWG	CRPG	All Gamers(*)
12-15	23%	27%	23%	11%
16-18	18%	17%	16%	7%
19-24	25%	24%	23%	13%
25-35	34%	32%	37%	29%

(*) "All Gamers" means people in the study population who reported playing any of the game types monthly, not just TCGs, RPGs, MWGs, or CRPGs.

Conclusions:
1. Few "General Gamers":
The first, most notable conclusion we can draw from this information is that the mythical "hobby gamer" who plays TRPGs, CRPGs, MWGs, and TCGs comprises a very, very small portion of the total market. A minority of gamers play more than one category of hobby game; very few play all three. The largest overlap, though still a minority, is with CRPGs and TRPGs.

This is an exciting conclusion, because it indicates that a company can successfully create brand in one of the three hobby categories, and extend that brand into the other two without significantly cannibalizing sales. In other words, the people who buy the RPG are not likely to be the ones buying the MWG or the TCG.

2. There are "Women in Gaming"
Second, it is clear that female gamers constitute a significant portion of the hobby gaming audience; essentially a fifth of the total market. This represents a total population of several million active female hobby gamers. However, females, as a group, spend less than males on the hobby.

3. Adventure Gaming is an adult hobby
More than half the market for hobby games is older than 19. There is a substantial "dip" in incidence of play from 16-18. This lends credence to the theory that most people are introduced to hobby gaming before high-school and play quite a bit, then leave the hobby until they reach college, and during college they return to the hobby in significant numbers. It may also indicate that the existing group of players is aging and not being refreshed by younger players at the same rate as in previous years.

Section 4: The Role of Computers
There is an intense, ongoing discussion between publishers and customers about the use of computers and the interaction between computer game play and adventure game play. The market research study presented some revealing insights into this ongoing debate.

Internet Gaming: 51% of the TRPG players report that they have ever played a game on the internet. 28% report that they play an internet game monthly.
% Who want to buy software to help manage game and speed up combat: 52%
% Who want to play D&D over the internet with others: 50%
% Who read newsgroups, mailing lists and web sites: 37%
% Who currently play with computer assistance: 42%

What computer do gamers use?
Wintel Platform: 63%
Macintosh Platform: 9%
(The question was essentially "What platform have you used in the last month," and "none" was an option, probably accounting for the missing percentage.)

What's sitting at home?
Wintel Platform: 54%
Macintosh Platform: 7%
Three quarters of the sample use the Internet at least once a week, but only two thirds have access from home.

"Who plays electronic games?"

	Computer	Console/Handheld	Both
Average Age:	26	23	20

Education

	Computer	Console/Handheld	Both
% 6th-8th:	5	20	27
% 9th-12th:	23	52	37
% College:	53	26	31
% Post Grad:	20	2	5

Marital Status

	Computer	Console/Handheld	Both
% Single:	52	65	76
% Partnered:	46	29	22

Games electronic gamers play monthly:

	Computer	Console/Handheld	Both
% TRPGs:	72	54	57
% CRPGs:	44	21	50
% Puzzle Comp:	39	41	49
% Classic Board:	39	48	44
% Action/Shooter:	32	55	61
% Simulations:	25	36	40
% Strategy Games:	26	26	32

One conclusion we draw from this data is that people who play electronic games still find time to play TRPGs; it appears that these two pursuits are "complementary" or "noncompetitive" outside the scope of the macroeconomic "disposable income" competition.

* * * * *

Section 5: Tabletop RPG Business

We asked questions of people who play TRPGs to get a better and more detailed picture of that category. This section explores some of that data.

The market research study provides some useful information on the games TRPG players play when they're not role playing:
51% play a non-TCG card game monthly
43% play a puzzle computer game monthly
43% play a classic board game monthly
58% play an "action/shooter" computer game monthly
41% play a "simulation" computer game monthly

The *least* played game types were:
26% play a TCG monthly
24% play a puzzle table game monthly
17% play a MWG monthly
17% play a social/party game monthly

When asked how likely a person was to be the DM/GM, the responses were:
2+ Sessions as DM/GM: 47%
Don't DM/GM: 41%

When asked to describe a variety of past game experiences, the market provided the following data:
Used detailed tables & charts: 76%
Included Miniatures: 56%
Used "rules light" system: 58%
Diceless: 33%
Combat Oriented: 86% (*)
Live Action: 49%
House Rules: 80%
(*) Looked at in reverse, this interesting answer tells us that 14% of the gamers who play an RPG *have never played* a combat oriented RPG.

Of the people who reported playing a TRPG, we further screened for people who played D&D and asked those individuals some more detailed questions. This data comes from people who have played D&D, not necessarily those who play monthly.

Age:	<12	12-15	16-18	19-24	25
Learned D&D:	23%	41%	15%	12%	9%

* * * * *

One conclusion we drew from the data was that if a player had played longer than one year, the chances they would play another year were greater than if they had not yet been playing for a full year. In fact, the longer a person plays, the higher the chance they will stay in the game; in other words, players are less likely to quit playing D&D the longer they play, not more likely.

	<1 Year	1-5 Years	>5 Years
Expect another Year:	40%	75%	88%

We asked what the frequency of play was:

	Total D&D	<1 Year	1-5 Years	>5 Years
Monthly:	7.2	4.9	13.2	5.9

So we see that the longer a player is in the game, the fewer times per month they play after the 5th year. Once the "acquisition" period (1st year) has passed, frequency of play accelerates tremendously, then drops. One explanation for this fact may be that since acquisition happens most often at age 15 or less, "new players" may have a lot of time available for gaming, but as they age, they have less time per month to play.

We looked at a few other questions based on how long a person had been playing the game:

	Typical Session 5+ Hours	4 or More Gamers In Group	Average Sessions before Restart (New Characters)
Total	28%	62%	15.4
<1 Year	10%	48%	8.8
1-5 Years	14%	60%	12.9
(*) >5 Years	42%	71%	19.6

(*) Remember that frequency of play is down sharply for these gamers.

This data tells us that the longer a person plays the game, the longer the game sessions get, the more people play in the game, and the longer the game progresses before a character restart. In fact, if you look at the >5 year group, you realize that the big jump in long sessions and in average sessions before a restart means that the 5+ year gamers are playing the same characters, on average, vastly longer than anyone else.

One conclusion might be that it takes 5 years for a player to really master the system and really figure out what kind of character that player likes to play.

The following financial figures are for TRPG players in general (D&D information, where available, is provided as well).

This data seems to validate the theory that young gamers, while very active, don't spend a lot of money. (The following data is reported by for RPG expenditures) The big dollars come from adults ...

Total spending by age:
12-17: $297
18-24: $850
25-25: $2,213

And, the longer they stay in the category, the greater their total outlays ...
Play <1 Year: $116
Play 1-5 Years: $562
Play >5 Years: $2,502

And if they can be induced to become a DM/GM, expenditures skyrocket.
Will DM/GM: $2,048
Will not DM/GM: $401

Some breakouts for the D&D population in particular ...

Total D&D spending by age:
12-17: $164
18-24: $443
25-35: $1,642

Monthly D&D spending by age:
12-17: $10
18-24: $12
25-35: $14

Total D&D spending by time in game:
<1 Year: $123
1-5 Years: $338
>5 Years: 1,756

Monthly D&D spending by time in game:
<1 Year: $7
1-5 Years: $22
>5 Years: $16

(Interesting note: Monthly spending in the first five years after adoption of the game is higher than the spending beyond that point — though the older, longer gamer plays the game more, they spend less. This may relate to the frequency of a character/game restart.)

D&D DM willingness effect on expenditures:
Will DM: $1,444 total/$21 monthly
Will not DM: $187 total/$7 monthly
(Interesting note here: Even people who don't DM buy a heck of a lot more than just a PHB ...)

Effect of miniatures addition to RPG mix:
Few miniatures owned/used: $139 total RPG spending
Many minis owned/used: $4,413 total RPG spending

We found that players who were "lapsed" — reported that they had played TRPGs but were not currently doing so; had spent more money than the current players, and had played more different games monthly — but interestingly, they had spent less money, on average, on D&D than players who were "current."
(Current/Lapsed)

Mean RPG Spending: $1,273/$1,667
Mean Total D&D Spending: $895/$599
Number RPGs Played: 2.2/3.3

One conclusion that could be drawn from this data is that gamers who don't like D&D will spend a lot of money and try a lot of systems to find something they do like before they quit. Gamers who like D&D will spend less money and try fewer systems, but will spend more on D&D than those who don't.

When asked why a gamer lapsed, the answers (multiple choices allowed) were:
Got too busy with other things: 79%
Too few people to play with: 63%
Not enough time to play: 55%
Found a game I liked better: 38%
Unhappy with the game and the rules: 38%
Cost too much money: 32%
Burnt out from frequent play: 29%

Getting back to the people still playing the games, when asked what games TRPG players play monthly, the answers (multiple choices allowed) were:
D&D: 66%
Vampire: The Masquerade: 25%
Star Wars: 21%
Palladium: 16%
Werewolf: The Apocalypse: 15%
Shadowrun: 15%
Star Trek: 12%
Call of Cthulu: 8%
Legend of the Five Rings: 8%
Deadlands: 5%
Alternity: 4%
GURPS: 3%

When asked to describe aspects of their games, on a scale from 1 to 5, answers were *(normally/rarely)*:
Create Own Adventures: 42%/11%
Create Own Campaign Material: 29%/17%
Replay Adventures: 18%/35%
Use adventures from magazines: 21%/40%
Follow official D&D Rules: 33%/17%

When we asked RPG purchasers how many had purchased D&D at a particular retail type, the answers were:
(*)Hobby/game shops: 36%
Book Stores: 27%
Comic book stores: 18%
Specialty toy and game: 17%
Large toy store chains: 15%
Conventions: 4%
(In other words, 36% of the respondents indicated they had purchased a D&D product at a Hobby/Game shop.)

294

Appendix II: Forms

This appendix includes some useful documents and samples of legal forms that game store owners may find it convenient to have. They include:

Break-Even Analysis
Cash-flow Projection
Balance Sheet
Employee Handbook Outline
Sample Non-Disclosure Agreement
Sample Lease Assignment
Pre-Opening Timeline
Start-up Expenses Worksheet

Break-Even Analysis

To calculate the break-even sales level, divide the total fixed expenses by your contribution margin. The spreadsheet is available for download at *http://d-infinity.net/GRG*.

	A1	▾	*fx*	Variable Costs	
	A	B		C	D
7					
8	Fixed Costs				
9	Rent				
10	Payroll				
11	Payroll Taxes				
12	Utilities				
13		Phone/internet			
14		Electricity/water			
15		Website			
16		Waste removal			
17	Administrative				
18		General liability insurance			
19		Prorated business license			
20	Marketing & Advertising				
21		Promotional use items			
22		Direct Mail			
23	Repair & Maintenance				
24	Miscellaneous Expenses				
25	Loan Repayment				
26	**Total Fixed Costs**		**sum of above items**		
27					
28	**Monthly break-even**		**Total Fixed Costs/Contribution Margin**		
29					
30					
31					
◄ ◄ ► ►	Break-even_Analysis				

Employee Handbook Outline

Table of Contents

Provide a table of contents if you like. A good word processor
can do it for you.

Introduction

Include your mission statement and brief history of the company and its owners.

Not a Contract

This section should clearly identify what the handbook is and
what it isn't. The handbook is a guide to company standards,
and those standards can change at any time. Disciplinary actions defined in the handbook are example only, and management reserves the right to discipline employees for actions outside those identified in this handbook.

The handbook does not state or imply a contract for employment. State that you recognize the employee's right to re-
sign at any time, and that the company can terminate an
employee's employment at will. As always, check your local
employment laws.

Confidentiality Statement

Reinforce the concept that this document is not for outside use.
The company also does not share sales information, employee
information, or customer information with anybody outside of
the company. That means employees don't talk about sales figures to anybody, don't give out another employee's phone number, and don't give out a customer phone number. Provide as
many examples as you can.

Identify alternate methods of customers reaching each other

to meet for games, such as through your bulletin board or online message board.

Compliance with the Law
State your company's willingness to work within the confines of federal, state and local laws. Include wording to the effect of "If any policy or procedure in this handbook is found to be in violation of any law, contact the manager immediately."

Job Descriptions
Identify each position within the company and its job description. Include all duties you can think of that the person in that position might be called upon to perform. Include the general-purpose "Other duties as assigned" to accommodate the natural growth and change of the job's description as the nature of the company changes over time. Ideally, create bulleted list of duties and list them in order of priority.

In addition to merely describing tasks, specify the standards to which you hold employees. Lastly, provide a list of punishment for failing to perform duties or complete duties to your standards.

Image Standards
Include your standards for what employees are allowed or required to wear, makeup and accessories, behavior, and other factors that affect how customers perceive your company. If you have a uniform, mention it here, and you can mention practices such as docking the employee's first paycheck for replacement shirts or anything else.

Cleaning and Maintenance
Describe what cleaning duties you expect employees to perform, and on what schedule. They might have to sweep at least once per shift, for example, but what replacing about air conditioning vent filters? Or replacing light bulbs and ballast? Identify who must perform all of these duties and when.

Hours of Operation
Give the hours your store is open, including seasonal variation, if any.

Pay and Benefits

You don't need to identify each person's individual wage in a handbook. Give details on when payday is, what time you start handing out checks, when the time period runs, overtime policies, etc. If you deduct any pay for a uniform or other purpose, state it in the manual.

If you offer any benefits like health insurance or profit-sharing, describe when employees become eligible and what they have to do to gain the benefits. Mention employee discounts, free LAN time, after-hours store use, free convention entry, vacation time, bonuses, or anything that you allow employees in addition to hourly wage.

The employee discount usually deserves a section of its own. Identify how much the discount is and which products it applies to, or which products are exempt. Explain that the employee may not ring up his own sales; a manager must ring up all employee sales. Even if you trust the employee, this policy is a good idea. What if you hire a new employee? You can't every well have the first employee ring himself up and the new employee rung up by managers only. Your first employee will also resent the sudden "lack of trust" if you take away his right to ring himself up. Begin with a policy that's safe for you, and make your growth easier on everybody.

Attendance Expectations

Identify when you expect people to show up for work, when you expect them to call if they can't make it, what happens if they don't make it, how many times they can call in before you take action, what actions you take for excessive call-outs, and other concerns related to showing up for work.

This section is a good place to identify your lunch and break policies. Identify what an employee has to do for a lunch break (get permission, notify a manager, clock out, etc.), where the employee is allowed to eat (not on the sales floor!) etc.

Performance Evaluations

If you use them, identify when they will occur, who will be involved and in what capacity, and what impact they have on the employee (if raises are dependent on them, for example).

Loss Prevention

Spell out your cash handling procedures and expectations carefully. A lack of clarity here can cost you hundreds of dollars due to employee apathy. If you can't or don't measure a cash loss or identify your accuracy standards, you can't expect your till to ever be accurate.

If you sell second-hand merchandise, spell out your buying procedures. This statement might be a simple Only the manager is allowed to buy product. Employees should avoid making any absolute or relative statements about the products a customer wishes to sell, such as "Wow, that's some good stuff" or "I don't think he's going to buy that garbage."

Value-laden statements like this interfere with the buying procedure.

If you allow any employees to take the deposit to the bank, describe your deposit procedures. Remember to include the obvious — which bank you use and where it is!

Customer Interaction

Identify how you expect employees to greet customers, and when. Identify how and when the employee should follow up the greeting with conversation designed to draw out information that could lead to a sale. Identify closing and upselling procedures.

If you have a game room, you almost certainly have to deal with behavioral issues with customers as well as employees. If you have policies against foul language, the selling of cards or other products, or other undesirable behavior, state what you expect the employee to do about it, and the employee's rights in case of customer refusal (ask the customer to leave, call the police, etc.).

Emergency Contact Information

Provide information for whom to contact, how to reach that person, and under what circumstances. Wise numbers to include:
▷ Police and fire emergency
▷ Landlord
▷ Owner
▷ Store manager

SAMPLE NON-DISCLOSURE AGREEMENT

This sample document is not intended for actual use. It might contain language making it illegal or inapplicable in your state. As with all legal issues, consult an attorney.

NON-DISCLOSURE AGREEMENT

Your Company Name, Inc. and

_____,

("RECIPIENT") agree:

Your Company Name, Inc. and its designees may from time to time disclose to RECIPIENT certain confidential information or trade secrets generally regarding sales and other financial information regarding Your Trade Name, a trade name associated with Your Company Name, Inc.

RECIPIENT agrees that RECIPIENT shall not disclose the information so conveyed, unless in accordance with this agreement, and shall protect the same from disclosure with reasonable diligence.

As to all information which Your Company Name, Inc claims is confidential, RECIPIENT shall reduce the same to writing prior to disclosure and shall conspicuously mark the same as "confidential," or with other clear indication of its status. RECIPIENT agrees upon reasonable notice to return the confidential tangible material provided by it within 7 days.

The obligation of non-disclosure shall terminate when if any of the following occurs:

(a) The confidential information becomes known to the public without the fault of RECIPIENT, or;

(b) The information is disclosed publicly by Your Company Name, Inc, or;

(c) a period of 36 months passes from the disclosure, or;

(d) the information loses its status as confidential through no fault of RECIPIENT.

In any event, the obligation of non-disclosure shall not apply to information which was known to RECIPIENT prior to the execution of this agreement.

Dated: _____   Dated: _____

_____   _____
Printed Name   Printed Name

Sample Lease Assignment

This sample document is not intended for actual use. It might contain language making it illegal or inapplicable in your state. As with all legal issues, consult an attorney.

ASSIGNMENT OF LEASE

This Assignment of Lease ("Assignment") is started into on this [date], between [Lease signatory, either company or individual]] ("Assignor") and [person taking over, company or individual] ("Assignee").

RECITALS

[Lessor's company], as Landlord, and Assignor, as Tenant, executed a lease dated [date], a copy of which is attached and incorporated by reference as Exhibit A, pursuant to which Landlord leased to Tenant, and Tenant leased from Landlord, that certain property commonly known as [address], and more specifically referenced in the Lease. The Lease was for a term of [duration of lease], commencing on [beginning date] and ending on [ending date], subject to earlier termination as provided in the Lease.

Section 1. Assignment.

In consideration of the mutual promises and covenants set forth herein, Assignor assigns and transfers to Assignee all right, title, and interest in the Lease, and Assignee accepts from Assignor all right, title and interest, subject to the terms and conditions set forth in this Assignment.

Section 2. Assumption of Lease Obligations.

Assignee assumes and agrees to perform and fulfill all the terms, covenants, conditions and obligations required to be performed and fulfilled by Assignor as Lessee under the Lease, including the making of all payments due to or payable on behalf of Lessor under the Lease as they become due and payable.

Section 3. Assignor's Covenants.

Assignor covenants that the copy of the Lease attached as Exhibit A is a true and accurate copy of the Lease as currently in effect and that there exists no other agreement affecting Assignor's tenancy under the Lease.

Section 4. Litigation Costs.

If any litigation between Assignor and Assignee arises out of this Assignment or concerning the meaning or interpretation of this Assignment, the losing party shall pay the prevailing party's costs and expenses of this litigation, including, without limitation, reasonable attorney's fees.

Section 5. Indemnification.

Assignor indemnifies Assignee from and against any loss, cost, or expense, including attorney fees and court costs relating to the failure of Assignor to fulfill Assignor's obligations under the Lease, and accruing with respect to the period on or prior to the date of this Assignment. Assignee indemnifies Assignor from and against any loss, cost, or expense, including attorney fees and court costs relating to the failure of Assignee to fulfill obligations under the Lease, and accruing with respect to the period subsequent to the date of this Assignment.

Section 6. Successors and Assigns.

This Assignment shall be binding on and inure to the benefit of the parties to it, their heirs, executors, administrators, successors in interest, and assigns.

Section 7. Governing Law.

This Assignment shall be governed by and construed in accordance with [your state] law.

Section 8. Authority.

Each person signing hereunder warrants that they have the capacity and the authority to sign this Assignment on behalf of the respective person or entity which is being represented.

The parties have executed this Assignment on the date written above.

[Assignor's name]   [Assignee's name]

_____   _____

Consent of Landlord

The undersigned, as Landlord under the Lease, consents to this Assignment of the Lease to Assignee, provided however that notwithstanding this Assignment and the undersigned's consent to this Assignment, Assignor shall remain primarily obligated as Tenant under the Lease and the undersigned does not waive or relinquish any rights under the Lease against Assignor or Assignee.

[Lessor's company]

_____

Pre-Opening Timeline

Not all businesses follow all of these steps. Also, you do not necessarily need to follow these steps in the exact order. Details vary heavily: if the location you lease is ready to move into, you don't need to allow the 2-3 months implied in this timeline for your build-out. Obviously, it is in your best interest to reduce the time between signing the lease and making use of the space as much as possible. Paying rent for something you're not using is waste of good money.

Start Date	Days to Completion	Task
1	10-180	Research & develop business plan outline
170	1-3	Choose attorney
173	1-3	Choose accountant
180	1	Select name and apply for fictitious name license
181	3-7	Incorporate or form LLC
182	1	Open Bank Account
183	10-21	Apply for & receive EIN
200	1-30	Draft website
210	5-21	Apply for & receive State Sales Tax ID
210	7-21	Apply for & receive Business License
210	1-90+	Obtain Financing
230	1	Register website domain name
240	7-28	Price Fixtures
240	7-30	Scout locations
250	1-7	Website goes live (except for inventory)
263	1-7	Select location
265	1-3	Obtain credit card merchant account
270	5-10	Sign Lease
271	1-5	Contract work for build-out
272	1	Apply for electrical service
272	1	Apply for telephone service
273	1-7	Join manufacturer retailer locator listings
275	1-3	Apply for distributor accounts
305	1-7	Price signs & order final selection
330	3-30	Select & order point-of-sale system
335	1-30	Hire employees
336	1	Apply for internet service
340	1-3	Price and Acquire Insurance
345	1	Order price gun & labels, business cards, etc.
350	1-7	Purchase and Install fixtures
355	1-2	Order inventory
356	2-7	Enter inventory data into POS system
365	1	Opening Day

START-UP EXPENSES WORKSHEET

Not all stores need every item on this list. Some items are mutually exclusive: you either buy your property or you rent it. Instead of feeling that you must have every item on the list, consider its need and price it. Gain your estimates by making phone calls to service providers or by comparing listed prices on company websites.

PRE-OPENING EXPENSE WORKSHEET

Category	Item	Estimate
Utilities		
	Electrical deposit & connection	
	Phone deposit & connection	
	Internet access fees	
	Alarm system installation	

Legal & Professional

Incorporation
Fictitious name registration
Local business license
Accountant fees
Lawyer fees
GAMA membership
Professional business consultation
Chamber of Commerce membership
BBB membership
Local retailer association membership
Food permit
    (if you sell snacks and/or sodas)
Other local business fees

Property

Rent & rent deposits
Mortgage downpayment
Purchase closing costs

Improvements

Light fixtures/bulbs/ballast
Outlets & switch plates
Flooring (tiles, carpet, etc).
Paint
Ceiling tiles
Track lighting

FFE

Sales counter
POS computer
Bar code scanner and rack
Credit card processing machine
Receipt printer
Game tables
Chairs for game room
Telephone
Copier
Fax
Printer
Shrinkwrap machine
CCG Singles binders and 9-pocket pages
Gondolas
Bookshelves
Wire bins
Shopping baskets & rack
Cleaning equipment
Soft drink cooler

Marketing

Storefront sign
Window signage
Signage (departments, shelf talkers, bulletin board)
Neon open sign
Marquis/pole sign
Flyers
Pre-opening radio/tv ads
Radio remote
Employee uniforms
Employee name badge/lanyards
Business cards
Brochures

Insurance

Commercial liability insurance
Health insurance

Technology

Logo development
Website development
POS system
Accounting software
Website hosting fees
Payroll management software
Business plan software

Payroll

Pre-opening payroll
Payroll service fees

Miscellaneous

Travel expenses
Other expenses

Inventory

Board games
Non-collectible card games
RPGs
Used RPGs
RPG Accessories
Collectible card games
CCG singles
Miniatures
Miniatures games
Other

Bibliography

Gerber, Michael E., *The E-Myth Revisited: Why Most Small Businesses Do not Work and What to Do About It*, Harper Business, 1995.

Harper, Stephen C., *The McGraw Hill Guide to Starting Your Own Business: A Step-by-Step Blueprint for the First-Time Entrepreneur*, 2003.

Keup, Erwin J., *Franchise Bible: How to Buy a Franchise or Franchise Your Own Business*, McGraw-Hill/Business & Investing Distributed Product, 2000

Strauss, Steven D., *The Business Start-Up Kit*, 2003.

Sutton, Esq., Garret, *Own Your Own Corporation: Why the Rich Own Their Own Companies and Everyone Else Works for Them*, Warner Business Books, 2001.

Underhill, Paco, *Why We Buy: The Science of Shopping*, Simon & Schuster, 2000.

Wallace, David and Kelli, *A Specialty Retailer's Handbook: Games and Comics*, 1999 *Comics & Games Retailer*, Krause Publications

Dancey, Ryan, *Adventure Game Industry Market Research Summary*

59045107R00170

Made in the USA
Columbia, SC
29 May 2019